# FOOTBALL WITH THE FOE

*By the same author*
Gymnastics and Politics – Niels Bukh and Male Aesthetics, Museum Tusculanum Press, Copenhagen University (book complete with DVD, including 131 film clips and commentary in Danish, English and Japanese).

*This book is dedicated to two people*
ERNST PETERSEN, board member of the Danish sports federation, Dansk Idræts-Forbund (DIF), who was the only representative among the DIF leadership to come out against sport with the occupying forces.

HAROLD PHILIPSON, the British-born cricketer, who played 200 matches in Danish first-division cricket, arranged numerous visits by English cricket teams, and who was responsible for the Gentlemen of Denmark's tour to England in 1926. In 1941, with the launch of the periodical *Fodbold* [Football], he mounted the only journalistic attempt at opposition to "football with the foe".

# FOOTBALL WITH THE FOE

*Danish sport under the swastika*

Hans Bonde

*With the assistance of*

Martin Frei

University Press of Southern Denmark 2008

© The author and University Press of Southern Denmark 2008
Printed by Narayana Press
Cover Design by Anne Charlotte Mouret
EAN 9788776741792

Cover illustration: Football match between Denmark and Germany 17 November 1940.
The later national coach of Germany Helmuth Schön is scoring.

Published with support from:
Danish Agency for Science, Technology and Innovation

University Press of Southern Denmark
Campusvej 55
DK-5230 Odense M
Phone: +45 6615 7999
Fax: +45 6615 8126
Press@forlag.sdu.dk
www.universitypress.dk

Distribution in the United States and Canada:
International Specialized Book Services
5804 NE Hassalo Street
Portland, OR 97213-3644 USA
www.isbs.com

Distribution in the United Kingdom:
Gazelle
White Cross Mills
Hightown
Lancaster LA1 4 XS
U.K.
www.gazellebooks.co.uk

# Contents

| | |
|---|---|
| PREFACE | 11 |
| INTRODUCTION | 13 |
| *Theoretical inspiration* | 15 |
| *Discussion of concepts* | 17 |
| *Previous research* | 19 |
| SPORTING RELATIONS IN THE 1930s | 23 |
| *Fascination* | 23 |
| *The Nazi Olympics* | 26 |
| *From Olympic Games to War* | 39 |
| *War and continuity* | 48 |
| DANISH SPORT UNDER SIEGE, 1940-41 | 53 |
| *Ragnhild Hveger and German propaganda* | 54 |
| *The propaganda of military sports* | 59 |
| *Pressure from the Reich plenipotentiary* | 61 |
| *The hard line begins to bend* | 65 |
| *"Fruit must not be picked until it is ripe"* | 68 |
| *"The Führer would be furious"* | 70 |
| *The ban is raised* | 71 |
| THE STRUGGLE FOR DENMARK'S YOUTH | 75 |
| ENGLISH OPPOSITION TO COLLABORATION | 83 |
| PROFESSIONAL SPORT | 89 |
| *Cycling* | 89 |
| *The boxers* | 92 |

| | |
|---|---:|
| AMATEUR SPORTS | 95 |
| ATHLETICS TAKE THE LEAD | 97 |
| *The first games with the Germans* | 97 |
| *Athletics championships in Germany* | 102 |
| BOXING | 107 |
| *Danish clubs* | 107 |
| *Denmark vs. Germany* | 110 |
| SWIMMING WITH THE TIDE | 113 |
| *Soldiers in swimming trunks* | 113 |
| *Ragnhild Hveger and Jenny Kammersgaard* | 114 |
| OTHER SPORTING DISCIPLINES | 119 |
| *International handball* | 119 |
| *Wrestling* | 119 |
| *Heydrich in international fencing* | 121 |
| FOOTBALL WITH THE FOE | 127 |
| *An international match in Hamburg* | 127 |
| *Austrian Wunder-teams* | 130 |
| *'Heil' salutes from the opponents* | 130 |
| *Trouble on the terraces* | 132 |
| *Renthe-Fink steps in* | 135 |
| *Departure of the Minister of Justice* | 136 |
| *Meeting Hungary* | 139 |
| COLLABORATION WITH NORWAY | 141 |
| *Changing attitudes* | 142 |
| *Athletics games in Norway* | 145 |
| RENEWED GERMAN CONTACT | 151 |
| *Trouble in the boxing ring* | 151 |
| GAMES IN GERMANY | 155 |
| *International football in Dresden* | 155 |
| *The Danish war-time European champion* | 159 |
| *A Jewish and a Communist wrestler* | 163 |

| | |
|---|---:|
| THE LAST COLLABORATION | 167 |
| *Matches against Italy and Hungary* | 167 |
| *Germany backs out* | 168 |
| *Professionals say farewell* | 171 |
| *From international to national sports* | 173 |
| | |
| OTHER CULTURAL COLLABORATION | 175 |
| | |
| SPORT IN 'NEUROPA' | 179 |
| *The new order of European sport* | 179 |
| *The new European Sports Federation* | 181 |
| *The meeting in Berlin* | 183 |
| *Boxing in New Europe* | 185 |
| *A miraculous save* | 187 |
| | |
| TURN OF THE TIDES | 193 |
| *Battles over sports orienteering* | 193 |
| *The situation at club level* | 196 |
| *The loss of Ragnhild Hveger* | 198 |
| *Kammersgaard's comeback* | 202 |
| *August revolt and athletics* | 203 |
| | |
| JEWISH PERSECUTION | 207 |
| *Towards liberation* | 210 |
| | |
| NEW ALLIANCES | 215 |
| *Friend or Foe?* | 215 |
| *Games against the English* | 216 |
| *Norwegian partisans* | 222 |
| | |
| A 'JURIDICAL PURGE'? | 225 |
| | |
| REVOLT FROM BELOW – CONCLUSION | 231 |
| | |
| Endnotes | 249 |
| | |
| LITTERATURE | 265 |
| | |
| ILLUSTRATIONS | 271 |

"Now all the freezing out of sports is over … leaders among Danish sporting circles breathe freely again and active Danish sportsmen start training with fresh courage and renewed desire … It is like when the windows are thrown open at a meeting room where there have been far too many people, or when you stretch your body after a good, healthy sleep and feel the life coming back to you. Everywhere in sporting circles, the sudden change in the situation is being discussed; and those holding the discussions all have smiles on their lips and carefree minds. Now we can get stuck in!" (Denmark's largest sports newspaper *Idrætsbladet*, on the resumption of sporting relations with Germany, August 1940).

# PREFACE

How closely connected is sport and politics? The period up to and during the German occupation of Denmark can throw a surprising light over this question, because the characteristics of a phenomenon are often shown best when it is under pressure. We can gain an insight into sport's potentially explosive force in situations of conflict, when the key question is whether sport should contribute to the improvement of democratic citizenship or instead be tried out embedded in a superiority cult. In those historical periods when Danish sports leaders have been busiest in reassuring that sport is apolitical, it has been perhaps precisely to erase the impression of its enormous political importance, not least during a period of occupation.

Sport is almost absent from Danish historical works on the period of occupation, despite the capacity sport had to forge emotional bonds around people's souls, like no other social phenomena. As this book shows, the top political leaders of the occupying power were entirely aware of sport's ability to create reconciliation and enthusiasm, and they worked energetically to establish sporting relations between Danes and Germans.

The period of occupation is the most well-researched period in Danish history. The same source material has been examined back and forth, and it might easily be imagined that no stone had been left unturned. However, new sources and new perspectives still arise. Sport, too, is a region that fascinates many people. It is therefore surprising that until now these two fields have never been seriously brought together in a publication covering Danish sport during the occupation.

It is my hope that this book will give international readers a rare experience of the dilemmas faced by Danish collaborative policy at grass-roots level, as it were, but also present an existential challenge in the question of whether people now would have acted any differently to the way the Danish sports world did, in deciding to play football with the foe.

Some readers may perhaps wonder why this book does not spell out in detail the careers, lives and accomplishments of particular sporting stars. It is, partly, because much has been written about this elsewhere, and because this book has another theme: namely, the political aspects of sport at a time when Danish sport was exposed to the most extreme form of politicisation ever. Nevertheless, a good deal of work has gone into personal characterisation and into the mental atmosphere of the period, including the often dramatic events at sports matches themselves.

When looking over this book, readers should be aware that interests in sport before and during the occupation were broader than today, where sports that are especially suitable for TV such as cycling, football, basketball and tennis take up much of sport's collective broadcast time. Sports such as wrestling, Danish amateur boxing and not least athletics had a far greater appeal among the sporting public than today.

This work was first published in a more extensive Danish edition (University Press of Southern Denmark, 2006), for which my collaboration with Martin Frei has been essential. Under my direction, Martin Frei wrote a post-graduate dissertation that provides parts of the raw material for this current study, especially the chapters dealing with developments within Denmark's main sporting organisation DIF and its relationship to the occupying forces.

I would like to thank Henrik Lundbak, dr. phil., from the Museum of Danish Resistance, Professor of Sociology of Sport Gertrud Pfister from the University of Copenhagen, Assistant Professor Steen Andersen, PhD, from Copenhagen Business School and Associate Professor Therkel Stræde from the University of Southern Denmark, for constructive comments regarding the text. My thanks to Ulf Kyneb, archivist at the Danish National Archives and to Therese Høeg Jacobsen, librarian at The Royal Library, for assistance with searching for source material. Thanks to Trygve Buch Laub, my student assistant, for valuable support. Thanks to my long-standing translator, Simon Frost PhD, for his extensive ability to convert Danish ways of thinking into English terms. A special thanks is also due to Thomas Kaarsted, managing director of University Press of Southern Denmark, and Martin Lindø Westergaard, editor, for their generous and productive contributions to raising the qualitative level of the manuscript, in which any mistakes and omissions remain the sole responsibility of myself.

*Copenhagen, April 2008*
*Hans Bonde*

# INTRODUCTION

Denmark was occupied on 9 April 1940. The event would prove to have an effect on Danish sport. Both professional sport and many of the associations and unions from the larger Sports Federation of Denmark, DIF, lived and breathed for international sporting relations, which drew in the crowds and – for example with DIF's football and boxing associations – provided their economies with important financial injections. The income from home games, especially, yielded well in the associations' cash boxes.

Usually, international sporting relations only occurred between countries that enjoyed voluntary diplomatic relations, and therefore sporting cooperation was a manifestation of goodwill. In conception, DIF was a non-political organisation, but would not a continuation of sporting collaboration with Germany after 9 April 1940 entail the Danish federation playing football with the enemy, which might well be interpreted as a political decision? On the other hand, to discontinue cooperation would also entail political motivation and, without doubt, would have meant DIF giving up cooperation with neutral Sweden. On 9 April, the DIF leadership stood on the brink of an unprecedented decision.

In the first years of the occupation, Germany seemed to be invincible, and the prospects of a return to old-style European constitutional law seemed remote. For young elite sportsmen and women, being trapped in a sporting vacuum during the few years where their talent could be developed was a bitter pill to swallow. The professional boxers and cyclists lived by competing against international contenders. How should they earn a living when Europe was at war?

The large rural gymnastics associations with their charismatic leading light, Niels Bukh (1880 – 1950), the Danish gymnastics innovator, did not fall directly under the spotlight of the occupying powers, since in the case of gymnastic meetings there was little propaganda benefit to be obtained from an association that traditionally did not take part in competitions with international sportspeople. If rural gymnastics was more-or-less without leverage, the big question then became how to ensure survival in German-dominated Denmark, where sport risked becoming uniformed, and rural gymnastics marginalised. Should you protect yourself from the occupying forces by ensuring the spread of a democratic line of thought among young participants? Conversely, should you gratify the occupying forces by trying to unify and discipline Danish sport so effectively that the Germans would believe their own groundwork had already been prepared? I have treated this dilemma thoroughly in Bonde 2006A, in which there is a multimedia DVD with visual documentation of Danish international gymnastics successes from 1914 to 1952, with 120 film sequences of tours undertaken the world over. The story of Danish rural gymnastics, therefore, will not be retold in this current study.

The same dilemma provides the background for the central question of this study, which is how Danish elite sport dealt with its relations to German Nazi sport.

The book is constructed on four main theses, which are pivotal to the presentation.

1) During the 1930s, a fascination for Third Reich sports policies had developed within Danish sport – so great that a substantial goodwill towards German sport had been built up when Denmark was occupied on 9 April 1940.
2) In the beginning, Danish sport was under intense pressure to resume collaborative sporting relations but, gradually, the Danish sports leadership itself worked actively to enable relations with the occupying forces to function. It was unrest among Danish football fans and a cooling off of interest from the occupying forces and also measures by the Swedish sports leadership that hindered Danish sport from more extensive sporting cooperation with both the Germans and with Norwegian Nazi-dominated sports, and prevented Denmark from joining a German-dominated pan-European sports federation.
3) Danish collaborative sporting relations with the Germans were the most comprehensive form of cultural collaboration during the occupation and the only form that was effective.
4) That 'sport is non-political' was an entirely plastic slogan, which could serve to legitimise actions taken by the Sports Federation of Denmark, DIF, in whatever situation, although these might represent diametrically opposed positions. This led to the most intensive politicisation of Danish sport ever.

Beyond international matches within a number of sports disciplines, the book will also focus on other official matches, on the continuity of Danish-German cooperation in sports from the 1930s and into the occupation, on collaboration with other nations apart from Germany, and on professional sport together with the central role played by sports stars, which has given a far more precise explication of the patterns of collaboration than in the extremely scant research hitherto undertaken. At the work's core is the detailed mapping of official sporting collaboration with Germany and other Axis powers during the occupation.

A temporal division would mark off a period of collaboration and fascination with Nazi sports in Germany from 1933 to 1939, with special focus on the Berlin

Olympics in 1936. Afterwards comes the Danish reaction to the outbreak of World War Two in September 1939, the whole of the occupation period, the aftermath of the occupation in the form of judicial settlements and various purges, together with the attempt by the Danish sporting world to deal with the dilemmas of the occupation period up to today.

The back bone of the source material used for this book is selected from the Danish Sports Federation (DIF), The Danish Football Federation (DBU), the Danish Foreign Ministry, the German Foreign Ministery, the German Legation in Denmark and the Danish press including the illegal press and the sports press.

## Theoretical inspiration

Readers with a sociological and theoretical orientation often wonder at the absence of theory in much historical analysis. It is granted that historical dispositions *can be* theoretically unreflecting, as well as dryly fixated on detail. But often, behind the historical research, lie reflections about the mechanisms of social structure and about the psychology of historical persons. It is just that in the discipline of history, there is a general opinion that circumstantial and repetitive theoretical excursions impede historical understanding rather than promote it. If the overall insights can be expressed in clear prose using simple language, it is considered to have far more scientific precision than if the observations had been clothed in flamboyant theoretical dress. Theory is regarded as a scaffolding that can inspire enquiry and provide interpretative frames, but often the scaffolding is taken away again when the work is done.

Nevertheless, the theoretical premises of the current book will now be briefly presented. They will be named but not as to weigh down the book's main text unnecessarily. Primarily, they will lie in the background as discrete interpretive potentials, as the investigation progresses. The work takes its inspiration from *phenomenological analysis*[1], to express an interest in how the public for sports, as well as sportsmen and women, experienced collaborative sports and more generally in the atmosphere surrounding sport during the occupation.

Impetus derived from Pierre Bourdieu's theory of *habitus*[2] – our direct bodily-based access to the world – has sharpened an awareness of how German and Danish sports competitors could consort with each other, physically through an embrace, and through other signals of sport's emotional ties. It can be seen in several of the photographs in this study, which are open to *pictorial analysis*. However, we should be aware of a certain degree of *stage management* that displays of Danish and German sportspeople in close contact were part of. German propagandists were entirely clear about the value of meetings between bright young Danes and Germans, and they tried constantly to arrange such 'stage-managed spontaneity', and above all to have these scenes photographed.

In the history of sport, pictorial analysis is important since primarily sport is concerned with the fascination of either performing movements ourselves or seeing others perform, which has produced a sizable body of source material. The language of sport is fundamentally non-verbal. Therefore, visual source material must be incorporated to establish an understanding of how symbols and corporal signs are comprehended. The images in the book do not serve simply as illustrations but as visual citations, which not least demonstrate German propaganda.

According to Norbert Elias and Eric Dunning, sport gains its *power of fascination* through an aroused sense of tension in which self-control can be momentarily released, giving passage for an enthusiastic enactment of aggression that can result in a mentally clarified experience of catharsis, especially if there is a chance for victory on behalf of those being so strongly identified with.[3] In the period under analysis, this form of experience appealed especially to men.[4] *Gender studies* have encouraged a focus on the cultivation of masculinity and beauty that was part of the German athletes' world, together with a problematisation of the purely emancipatory sense of progress found in the attitudes of two women pioneers in elite swimming, Jenny Kammersgaard and Ragnhild Hveger, based on their reactions to the great political challenges of their time.

The British sports and social historian J.A. Mangan has listed three circumstances in which sport plays the role of a medium for creating a common sensibility: 1) in the field of national solidarity, 2) during international confrontation and 3) in building international collaboration and *entente*.[5]

As will be seen, Danish sport during the occupation was enacted on all three levels, together with a fourth, which was as the meeting point between occupier and occupied.

The current study, therefore, also touches on relations between sport and Danish *national identity* in that sport during the occupation not only became a central part of the community-singing atmosphere and growing Danish royalism, but also became part of a meeting between what is German and Danish, a place where the Swastika and the Danish flag Dannebrog were often hung in the same space. The peculiarity of sport, compared to other cultural forms such as music or painting, is that sport builds upon feelings of identification, on the excitement of the result and the hope of release, which primarily are experienced in dramatic bodily acts. From around 1900 onwards, sport has become a central arena whereby countries can measure themselves against each other in strongly symbol-laden conflicts, wherein the cultivation of national sentiment is given a ritualised appearance. At large sports events, people rise during the national anthem on behalf of something they feel is bigger than themselves.

During the inter-war period and partially into the period of occupation, gymnastics – especially the internationally renowned Niels Bukh's gymnastics – were the hallmark of the Danish rural populace. The Danish national football team was a phenomenon that was cultivated largely in the cities. Professionalisation was also under way, especially of disciplines such as boxing and cycling. Next to this came the broad appeal of 'the swimming girls', including Ragnhild Hveger, Inge Sørensen, Jenny Kammersgaard and Lilli Andersen, who aroused admiration not only through speed records and medals, but also 'mentally' by binding together the maritime nation of Denmark through cross-channel swimming of Danish straits and sounds.

In politically-oriented, politological sports studies, a division is usually made between two avenues of research called 1) politics *in* sport and 2) politics *and* sport. With politics in sport, the aim is to account for internal contest in sports organisations over the allocation of resources, e.g. as regards age, gender, social group or ethnicity. The leadership of the Sports Federation of Denmark, for example, during the occupation can be said to be entirely male dominated.

Politics *and* sport considers external sports policy, in light of the politicisation that occurs when sports organisations are used politically in relation to other agencies, such as the Danish foreign ministry or the occupying powers. The current book, however, shows the inadequacy of a rigid division between these two avenues of approach, since the interaction with external agencies also led to internal changes in organisation; for example, in German soldiers becoming members of Danish sports associations.

## Discussion of concepts

The grey zone that Denmark found itself in during the occupation has meant that Danish collaborative action has been interpreted in varying ways. Therefore, a short summary will be undertaken of the research traditions concerning Danish collaboration with the occupying powers. At the outbreak of war, on 1 September 1939, the Government of Denmark declared Denmark's neutrality, which was a continuation of the security policy that the country had followed since 1935, where Denmark refrained from taking sides in disagreements between the great powers. With the German occupation of Denmark on 9 April 1940, the German ambassador to Denmark (later the plenipotentiary), Cecil von Renthe-Fink, handed over a memorandum to the Danish Government, in which Germany demanded unconditional surrender and de facto suzerainty, but which at the same time gave reassurances that Denmark could maintain its territorial integrity and political independence. Relations to Germany thereafter were coloured by the Danish Government's attempt to maintain the fiction of neutrality. Collaboration between Denmark and the occupying forces, therefore, would be put into effect through the Danish foreign ministry, as between two sovereign nations. Denmark placed itself into a grey zone between being a neutral country and being an enforced German ally, which led to political and economic collaboration with the occupying forces.[6] The rationale behind this collaboration was the recognition that Denmark did not have the faintest chance of offering military resistance or of defending its territorial borders. A collaboration with the occupying forces, therefore, was regarded as being the only measure by which the Danish Government could retain as much power as possible in Danish hands.

At the 60th anniversary of the liberation of Denmark on 5 May 2005, a turbulent interest in the period of occupation once again sprang up. This more than 60-year-old epoch has become modern, as the central frame of reference that Danes and their politicians use for their own moral self-evaluation. On the one hand, historians can delight in the great thirst for knowledge apparent throughout a wide public. On the other hand, the debate tends to create unproductive oppositions. Opinions are either pigeonholed as cynical narrations of collaborative policy, including industrial contributions to the German war machine with its use of slave labour and the persecution of saboteurs and/or communists; while the opposing tendency is to romantically denounce the policy of collaboration, calling down hellfire onto Danish forefathers so that the denouncer can stand forth morally stain free, 60 years after the fact.

In fact, a position between cynicism and romanticism can be found, between total condemnation and total acceptance of the policy of collaboration. The collaborative policy was realistic and legitimate seen against the background that, up until the occupation, it had proved impossible to create defensive alliances with democratic countries such as Great Britain and Sweden. The policy of collaboration was at best a protection for the Danish people, because it shielded the population against Nazification, terror, hunger, Blitzkrieg against Danish cities, and the immediate hunting down of Danish Jews. We can only try to imagine what a purely Nazi administration of Denmark could have come up with to solve 'the Jewish problem', as it did in the Netherlands. At the same time, there is not much to indicate that the Germans would have gained more from simply plundering Denmark. Furthermore, the dominant tone coming from the British and American Allies was that war was for professionals and not for civilians.

This does not mean, however, that an uninhibited and opportunistic appeasement of German power was called for. That the occupation is a period of such existential importance, also for later generations, is directly related to the way that keeping close company with the occupiers brought with it a long series of trials of civil courage, where it was difficult to draw the line in the right place. The collaborative policy was a grey zone that could quickly turn black, a slippery slope where an initially chilly disposition could develop into an active accommodation of the rulers' wishes, even before the German authorities had formulated them. It was not legitimate to sell military hardware to German representatives and certainly not to develop the assortment of destructive weapons. Nor was it legitimate to send back escaping Jews to Germany. But this was not a direct consequence of Danish collaborative policy but rather the result of a zealous application of a strict rule, which has its origins far back in the traditions of Danish administration.[7] In short, we can remain strongly critical about how the collaboration policy was handled by Danish authorities, organisations and individuals, without denouncing the policy as such.

This is precisely the perspective used by the present study. It was necessary to sell butter to Germany in return for raw materials and thereby avoid Danish economic bankruptcy and starvation for the Danish people. But was it also a necessity to play football with the occupying forces? And if people did, should they then enthusiastically throw themselves at a large historically unique self-service buffet of opportunities within German-Danish sporting relations?

We need to accept that no one formula for correct moral conduct can be found, and that the historic act necessarily will be surveyed differently by the eyes of the historical *acteur* to those of their successors. In the same way, as in our own lives, there is often a difference between what we consider to be right in a given situation and what we believe should have been in retrospect. There is much that historians can agree on but, when existential questions are raised, the forces of human personality come powerfully into play: fortunately, or otherwise historical achievements would amount to nothing but pure bookkeeping. Critical work on source material provides a basis for all historians, but the sources do not answer what the meaning of human life might be – and the choice of source material along with its treatment is coloured by the answer to this question.

The current book builds on a broad concept of resistance, involving not solely the willingness to fight, gun in hand, but also the refutation of the occupying power in daily life, through verbal or physical protests, or in demonstrative anti-German signs such as bearing the English colours, listening to the BBC, or by booing and whistling at German 'heil' salutes. Giving a cold shoulder to the Germans could be the beginnings of a resistance that would later lead to the resistance movement. The idea of a 'mental and spiritual immune system' in the following study attempts to point out a Danish sensibility that rejected involvement with the Germans except by absolute necessity and enforcement.[8]

The book is based on a differentiation between an 'attentistic' position, whereby the goal was to gain time in respect of German demands through an attitude of reticence, and an 'activistic' position, meaning an active collaborative policy towards the Third Reich that aimed through constructive collaboration to establish goodwill with the occupying power.

## Previous research

Danish history books covering the period of occupation have shown little interest in the role of sport. Playing down the role of sport seems by all appearances to relate to the way that studies of the occupation have sprung too greatly from the domestic-policy perception of politics. This national horizon may be a result of the Danish political system, to a certain extent, having been allowed to continue unchallenged during the occupation, even under the so-called 'Government through the heads of department', which officially led the administration of the Danish state from 29 August 1943 to 5 May 1945. If we wish to understand the central ground upon which the struggle took place, we need to incorporate far more the perception of politics by the occupying powers, and here the struggle over youth culture and body culture comes into focus.

Danish studies of the occupation tend to be *de facto* rather than *contra facto*, with the result that potential developments of a situation that lay in close proximity are not dwelt on to any extent, whilst what actually occurred acquires a slight air of inevitability. What is remarkable, however, is that the occupying powers did not set up a puppet government in Denmark as they did in other occupied countries. A perfectly relevant question, therefore, is what might have been the result of a Nazification of Denmark enforced from above.[9] The experience from other occupied countries shows that sport, the labour service and more generally youth work were central figures in the arena.

From the outset, the Nazis were clear that having power over a society depended on gaining the unprotected souls of the young, and to a great extent the best avenue was through gaining control of their bodies. Therefore, it is no wonder that sport was one of the first areas to attract Nazi interest in occupied countries.

Even the broad spectrum of sports studies has taken little interest in sport during the occupation. The only serious attempts to understand the role of DIF during the occupation are two masters-degree theses in history. Steen Rasmussen's central and pioneering work from the University of Copenhagen conserning "The Danish Sports Federation 1940-1945 – with particular interest in relations to Germany 1940-45", from 1981 has only been published as an article in the sports yearbook *Idrætshistorisk Årbog*, 1985. The masters thesis is markedly empirical and constructed mostly from the archives of DIF. Steen Rasmussen has a very sympathetic understanding of the difficult situation of the DIF leadership, which means that the actual dilemmas DIF faced step somewhat into the background.

In relation to Steen Rasmussen's thesis, the present study is based on a considerably broader source material that develops the perspective by drawing in interviews with players of the time and by considering the 1930s Danish fascination for German-Danish sport, professional sport, the issues of individuals, sports journalism, the 1942-45 period, sporting relations after the liberation, together with the visual side of those sporting relations throughout. However, there will still remain themes that are under-investigated after this present study, such as the actions of the various associations and unions, not least in relation to the creation of new organisational structures in a German-dominated Europe, archive material covering professional sportspeople as well as amateur cyclists, horse-racing undertaken through the Danish Jockey Club, Foreningen til Den Ædle Hesteavls Fremme, and unofficial German-Danish collaboration at club level.

In 2004, Martin Frei submitted his masters-degree thesis on the role of DIF during the occupation, with Claus Bryld and Hans Bonde as supervisors, at Roskilde University.[10] For the present study, Martin Frei has contributed his masters thesis as a base text and passed on his photocopies of source material to Hans Bonde. The masters thesis is chiefly founded on DIF's archives and comprises the back bone of this study's history of the development of DIF's role as an instrument of sport-and-politics. Frei's thesis provided a breakthrough, especially in relation to previous studies, with regard to 1) the treatment of the disturbances on Danish Constitution Day in 1941 that rocked collaborative sporting relations, together with the political ramifications, 2) the view taken by the illegal press on sporting relations with the Germans, 3) relations between DIF and Dansk Ungdomssamvirke [a coalition of pro-parliamentarian democratic Danish youth organisations and associations] and 4) the purgative years after the occupation. To a greater degree than previous studies, the thesis managed to draw out 1) that it was German authorities who eventually lost interest in these sporting relations, 2) that DIF closely followed the line taken by Sweden and declined to join a German-dominated European sports federation, and 3) that the chairman of the Danish Football Association, Dansk Boldspilunion, Leo Frederiksen represented a clear 'activistic' policy, and in many ways functioned as the strong man of DIF over this period.

In addition, major differences can be traced between various evaluations of sporting relations with Germany during the Second World War. The two German historians Hajo Bernett and H.J. Teichler consider that sporting relations both in the occupied countries and in neutral Sweden and Switzerland aided the Nazis' attempt to gain control over the whole of European sports. The Swedish historian Per Olof Holmäng resents the comparison between neutral Sweden's sporting cooperation and the collaboration with Germany in occupied Norway and Denmark. In contrast, he considers that Swedish cooperation was legitimate since the Swedish Government found it politically desirable, and he believes in consequence that it would have been to take a political decision had the Swedish sports leadership rejected collaborative sports with the Axis powers.[11]

# SPORTING RELATIONS IN THE 1930s

## Fascination

> For the Germans, sports and gymnastics have become an indispensable part of the popular and national revival movement. This fact can well cause a Danish folk high school teacher to begin to wonder. (Gymnastics instructor K. Kristensen on German mass displays of 4,000 gymnasts)[1]

That sporting relations of the 1930s and the fascination for German sports are given relatively close attention in the following chapter comes from a need to explain the weak immune system of sport in resisting 'football with the foe' after 9 April 1940.

It might well be that Danish sports leaders claimed sport had nothing to do with politics but the view was not shared by the Nazi sports authorities, who regarded sport's most important function as political. The top people of German sport became political ambassadors for the Third Reich. They were co-opted to present a good impression of their country by 'correct action', and their conduct abroad was watched and reported on by intelligence agents.[2]

The German expert in the history of Nazi football, Nils Havemann, has pointed out how sport was regarded by the Third Reich as an important political medium. "The leadership of Reich sports, the foreign ministry and the propaganda administration regarded international sporting events as a medium for drawing regions and states that were politically, militarily or geo-strategically interesting more deeply into the sphere of German influence; German football as well as the general body of German sports was seen as the finishing touch to an aggressive policy of expansion that, in the manner of a thrilling sporting event, was invested with a harmless, almost peaceful appearance."[3]

The clearest sign of the propaganda function of Nazi sport was that far more resources were channelled towards entertainments and propaganda than to the activities themselves. Nazi sports policy was firmly grounded in entertainment expenses and increased media awareness. The Reichssportführer, von Tschammer und Osten, took part in every large sporting event, and key figures in both the State and party often showed themselves at sporting arrangements, whilst Hitler's lacking interest in sport was partially effaced.

Even if the construction costs for the Olympic Stadium are ignored, along with the foundation work for a stadium with room for 400,000 spectators at Nürnberg, the cultural propaganda expenses at the German Olympics still out-stripped actual sporting activities, for example through the resumption of excavation at Olympia in Greece, the financing of Leni Riefenstahl's film of the Olympics, and the purchase of Myron's world-renowned classical statue of the discus thrower.

The money poured in for national and international sports festivals and congresses, often with considerable generosity towards the visiting sportspeople, such as undertaking all travel costs for the 1,200 foreign sportsmen and women to the Winter Olympics in 1940 at a time when a period of scarcity was beginning to bite. The Games, however, were cancelled. The sporting leaders, though, were impeccably dined and treated as important diplomatic emissaries. It is not strange that Danish sports competitors and heads of association might have difficulties resisting such a massive offensive to convince Danes how highly the new German nation valued sport in general and the Third Reich's sporting guests in particular.[4]

By comparison, the British Government did very little during the inter-war years to support elite sports in gaining international success. Elite sports training centres were not established, and neither was there state support for participating in either the Olympic Games or the 'Empire Games' (afterwards the Commonwealth Games), although leading British politicians were able to take part in fund raising on an independent basis. Against such a background, a British journalist could write after the Winter Olympics in Garmisch Partenkirchen in 1936 that the British skiers had competed against "state-funded gladiator skiers from the Alpine countries".[5]

However, England was a pioneer country in the professionalisation of football, and throughout the 1930s the British Government developed a growing strand of quiet diplomacy in the use of sport for political aims. Consequently, there was far greater support from the foreign ministry for football matches against Germany and Italy than against republican Spain or the Soviet Union, which in itself contributed to the sporting isolation of communist countries.[6]

In Denmark, too, there was no inter-war tradition of State funding for DIF. The federation, however, received the insignificant sum of DKK 35.000 in 1938. Generally, there was far from consensus reached about sport's positive social importance. In particular, many critical voices were raised against 'chasing records' and the participation of women and children in elite sports. Indeed, sport came under such heavy fire that, in October 1933, DIF was forced to publish a defensive paper entitled *The Danish Sports Federation and its Critics*.[7]

In January of the same year, the Nazi accession to power was underway in Germany, and it quickly became apparent that the Nazi regime privileged sports to new heights, both financially and ideologically.

For Danish sportspeople, Nazism could take on a positive face because of the Third Reich's prioritisation of physical culture and its cultivation of both anti-intellectualism and the vital body of its youth. In the shelter of an impression that sport and politics could be held apart, a deep fascination developed for Germany's enormous commitment to elite sport, sports education and sporting facilities.

In 1935, Hitler decided that the Nazi Swastika should fly above sporting events instead of the Wilhelmine flag, but with its background colours of black, white and red, that would signal continuity. A clear political symbol was thereby raised to the position of national symbol. Another amendment was that *Deutschland, Deutschland über alles*, with the ominous undertones of its first line, should be played at sporting events[8] often followed by the Nazi anthem, the *Horst Wessel-lied*, at arrangements on German soil. It was further expected that German sportsmen and women, and spectators, gave the 'heil' salute when the national anthem was played. There was no doubt about the politicisation of German sport through the Nazi symbolic language used in its cult of the Führer.

The German historian Hans Joachim Teicher has shown how, after the Nazis came to power in 1933, the Western democratic nations continued and even developed sporting relations with Germany, which in Teicher's opinion displays their weakness and lack of principle. The continued collaboration gave the regime – in far greater degree than the exceptional Olympics – "an appearance of normality and continuity". "Pragmatism and opportunism meant that international sport saw no reason for reducing or breaking off relations with unified German sport because of State terror and the revolution in Germany achieved through open violence."[9]

In 1933, the Danish sports leader who embodied most clearly the Danish public fascination for Nazism was the founder of a new internationally renowned gymnastics, Niels Bukh. Shortly after gaining power, the Nazi authorities were in need of international acknowledgement and a normalisation of relations to the outside world. Bukh's display in Berlin, in October 1933, was a welcome cultural exchange with a small 'Nordic brother-nation'. Bukh's success depended not least on his active support for the Nazi project in Germany and that he was able to deliver the archetypal image of the ideal Aryan youth. Bukh's support for the 'new Germany' led to Bukh and the Reichssportführer developing what they both described as a friendship. On returning home to Denmark after his German tour, Bukh began a campaign of glorification of Nazi ideology, using elements from racial theory, anti-Semitism, the cult of the Führer and even suggestions of the legitimacy of violence. In doing so, he plainly stepped beyond the limits of traditional Danish right-wing radicalism.[10]

In cycling, especially, a close partnership occurred between Germany and Denmark during the 1930s. On 2 February 1934, a private Danish-German consortium, its economics foundations assured by the Berlin business figure Walter Lindberg, could open the first winter cycle-track race, based on German initiatives, in the newly furbished Forum hall in Copenhagen. During a large six-day race in Berlin, the traditional Wiener Waltz *Wiener Praterleben* was rechristened the *six-day waltz*,

*Display by the internationally renowned gymnastics instructor and innovator Niels Bukh, at Østerbro stadium in July 1939. The Swastika (centre) is carried side by side with national flags from various countries where Bukh had recruited students: an ominous gesture, given that Bukh was known for his favourable attitude towards Hitler's Germany.*

heard in epidemic proportions throughout Denmark. In December 1934, spectator interest culminated in Copenhagen's second six-day race in which the team of Danish Willy Falck Hansen and German Victor Rausch won outright, with a Danish-Belgian team taking second place, and while a solely German team took third.

## The Nazi Olympics

The Olympic Games of 1936 was the foremost event that brought Danes closest to the Nazi commitment to organisation and order, and its attempts to create a strong common experience through aestheticised mass displays.

The German Reichssportführer, von Tschammer und Osten, did much to convince the Danish sports world about the excellence of the new German power. In 1934, a delegation came to Denmark that included Tschammer himself, the envoy Baron von Richthofen, Duckwitz, who was counsellor for the legation, Frielitz, the press attaché, and Dr Carl Diem. Tschammer had previously visited Denmark on several occasions and now was in the country to orient Danish sporting circles about preparations for the Olympic Games.[11] The Reich's sports *Führer* also invited Niels Bukh to present a display at the Olympics in Berlin, which took place quite independently of the Danish Olympic Committee, who were only consulted later.

Although Tschammer was not particularly active in the organisation of the Olympic Games, they nevertheless formed the high point of his career.[12] Instead, it was Carl Diem, the arbiter of leadership in sport before Nazism, who was the actual organiser in his role as General Secretary of the organising committee.

The summer Olympics were a major event for many young Danes. In the exultant phrases of a sports magazine, *Idrætsbladet*

> In the approaching summer holidays, there is one burning question everywhere, in offices and factories, and in schools and workplaces. Anyone who is able to take their holiday at the beginning of August daily counts the contents of their piggy bank and weighs the consequences, for and against, of travelling to the centre of world sport that Berlin will become.

Against such background, *Idrætsbladet* began a competition to

> … *try to help one or two young people make the journey* … In various competitions, we will be giving travel tickets to the Olympics as the prize; a trip where the adventures will pour in over the lucky winners, who don't need to be seasoned travellers or to know the language. *All difficulties will be taken care of by us – the winners of the trip can use the entire visit to see and enjoy, to learn and to reap experiences.*[13]

From Berlin, the rowing expert Axel Lundquist wrote

> My first walk this morning took me out to Grünau. It is incredible what the Germans had done last year out on the Lange See lake; but this year the scenery is even more impressive. In particular, the huge tribune out in the water – with room for more than 6,000 spectators – makes a colossal impact. It cost 150,000 Reich marks and will be pulled down again after the Games, but by then it's also paid for itself.

But not everyone took part in the chorus of praise for the Olympic Games. Among Danish Social Democrats and to a great extent Communists there were objections to the Berlin Games, which is of no surprise given that the Nazis had eliminated leftist-oriented sports movements. The leftist social-democratic Danish workers' sports association, Dansk Arbejder Idrætsforbund, in contrast to bourgeois sport and its press, took a strong stand against the Olympics. Niels Bukh was a special thorn in the side of both social-democratic and communist opinion. Concerning Tschammer's inviting Bukh to the Olympics, during a visit to Bukh's Gymnastics folk high school, the periodical *ArbejderIdræt* wrote "The Führer [Tschammer]" had held discussions that lasted 7 hours with "the Danish chief Nazi, Niels Bukh".[14]

*The Olympic Games provided opportunities for inventive shop-window displays throughout Denmark: a notable sign of a broad acceptance of the Olympic Games among Danish people.*

The Jewish sports association Hakoah, allied to the official Jewish congregation in Denmark, Mosaisk Troessamfund, decided to boycott the Games,[15] and Denmark lost the chance of a medal in wrestling as Abraham Kurland followed suit, as did also the Jewish master fencer Ivan Osiier.

In Denmark a protest movement developed amongst radical artists who tried to establish a boycott of a competition for sporting works of art, held at the Olympics. The Danish International Olympic Committee member Prince Axel was thereby forced to inquire into what were the criteria for taking part in an art competition at the Olympics. The answer he received from President for the German Olympics Committee Dr Theodor Lewald was as expected, that the entry requirements for taking part in the competition were open to all artists regardless of religious or racial background. The answer, however, did not convince the protesting artists, who were more concerned about the general German policy towards Jews, although some Danish artists nevertheless did take part.[16]

The Danish Olympic Committee (DOK) rejected that the Berlin Games would be used politically. In response to the 'artist protest' that was regarded as an untimely interference in sporting relations, DOK's punctated reply stated that

*Abraham Kurland who won silver at the Olympics in 1932. As a Jewish competitor, Kurland did not get the opportunity to repeat his triumph at the Berlin Olympics in 1936, in which he refused to compete.*

1) The Olympic Games have not changed character because they are held in Germany. They have no political purpose, merely sporting and cultural.
2) The phrase 'Hitler-Olympiad' is misleading and tendentious. The Games have been set in Germany by the International Olympic Committee, and the German organisers are obliged in every way to maintain to the letter the rules and spirit of the Games, and have provided the most thorough assurances in this regard.
3) A solid and friendly collaboration exists between Danish and German sports, for which Danish sportsmen and women are pleased. We hold regular sports matches involving numerous disciplines: in football, rowing, lawn tennis, wrestling, boxing, athletics, riding, swimming and so on. Considering that we obtain only dividends and delight from this collaboration with Germany, it would be completely meaningless to refrain from a world Games simply because they occur in Germany, where we always feel welcome, and also on this present occasion are sure to be well treated.
4) Denmark's absence from the Olympiad in Berlin would be regarded as a protest and an unfriendly act against our German sports colleagues. Danish sportsmen

have no wish to let political considerations influence this sporting collegiality. Should protests arise from the Danish side regarding certain German methods inside that country's borders, it would be sportsmen, having been met only with friendliness from Germany, who would be the last to invoke such protests.

At the same time as DOK's statement, a communication appeared from the chairman of the International Olympic Committee (IOC), the Belgian Count Henry Baillet-Latour, addressed to the collected National Olympic Committees. According to the Jutlandic sports magazine, *Jysk Idræts Blad*, Baillet-Latour had conducted an investigation and held consultations with Adolf Hitler, who had convinced Latour the boycott campaigns were "political, based on groundless statements whose falseness I have without difficulty exposed." [17]

The magazine came out purely in favour of participation in the Olympic Games in Berlin. Under the heading *A Word at the Right Time*, about "the workers' movement and the Olympic Games in Berlin …", it was emphasised that "the world over, the question of social democratic positions towards the Olympic Games in Berlin is still pressing. We take the liberty of citing an article from *Frihet*, the organ of Swedish social democracy … 'It should be said that the boycott of the Berlin Olympiad has won wide support within the social democratic international youth movement, and presumably will attract adherents from various youth associations.' …" [18]

The Danish magazine continued, "However, the leadership of the [Danish] social democratic youth federation has decidedly rejected such conduct. The motivation for this rejection, as with similar decisions taken on this question, based on long and positive experience, is a conviction that socialism's cause, too, is best served by remaining neutral."

*Idrætsbladet* believed that the Germans created an Olympics of peace, and the editorial surrendered itself completely to the grandiose Olympic air. In 1936, its editor Emil Andersen published a book[19] wherein he detailed eyewitness accounts of "the largest and most impressive festival of sport the world has yet seen." The book gave its readers an excellent glimpse into the importance of the Berlin Games. He believed it was a political act to boycott the Olympics and that including the Third Reich's "position on the Jewish problem" was itself a "political position". Although, when it came to the Danish top wrestler Abraham Kurland, the book claimed that as a Jew he "quite naturally" did not wish to participate.

Emil Andersen did, however, not try to conceal attempts by the Nazi regime to seduce the visiting athletes and the public.

> From every building and house, in squares and over streets, fly flags and banners. Afterwards, the official statistics spoke about what had been bought in

*Photo taken at the opening meeting of the International Olympic Committee (IOC) in Berlin 1936. Front row from the left: Wilhelm Frick, Levald, Hitler's deputy Rudolf Hess, President of the IOC Baillet-Latour, and the German Reichssportführer, Hans von Tschammer und Osten. Hitler's military-political aspirations are hardly concealed by Hess's appearance.*

respect of banners, by the Government and the council alone ... and it was no slight number.

'Mr Smile', the alias Andersen used, also described the "large 'German National Exhibition' that was visited in enormous numbers – over a million guests passed through its doors – and on the way out to the Reich Olympic Sports Grounds there was an entire exhibition village that the impressive organisation *Kraft durch Freude* [the Nazi leisure-time activities organisation 'Strength through Joy'] had set up." Anyone who did not have a ticket could nevertheless follow the athletic events because at "countless sites around Berlin, loudspeakers delivered radio transmissions about what was happening right now at the stadium ... and, if you stood on tip-toe, you could follow the Games in small 'television theatres'."

The military organisation behind the games was obvious. It was said about the Olympic village that the Germans "built a town on military land ... that would last,

*Athletes were escorted to the Berlin Olympics by the German envoy to Denmark, Cecil von Renthe-Fink (right of the flag with hat in hand). Renthe-Fink became plenipotentiary during the occupation and was the driving force in the German share of efforts to resume sporting relations between the two countries. Renthe-Fink here demonstrates an early appreciation for the propaganda value of sports.*

and after the games serve for another purpose: service as a military camp." A German officer was also attached to the Danish delegation, for general assistance. At the Stadium "everything was quiet, order and discipline, without noticing at all any bluntness or the so-called Prussian spirit. The supervisors were open and friendly, and the many uniforms seen (SA and SS troops) – were only *seen*, not felt, apart from when Hitler arrived at or left the Stadium and then everything was on alert." For the sailing sports at Kieler Förde "the Navy were very helpful. Each nation had a Marine officer at their disposal."

It was impossible not to notice the cult of the Führer

> Almost every day, Reich Chancellor Hitler came to the stadium. He arrived usually at 3pm. When the rumours spread that he was on the way, the public stormed into the south side of the stadium, out onto the terraces, to see their immortalised Führer entering. And as he took his seat in the dignitaries box, at the same time as gala-dressed Marines raised the gold-embroidered Reich banner over the enclosure, it was as though the entire stadium's attention was focused on his person; all the German spectators – surely always in the

*The interweaving of sporting and military ambitions was made clear at the Winter Olympics. Here, Hitler inspects troops before arriving at the ski stadium.*

majority – stood up and saluted him with outstretched arm, while their unified thundering 'heil' cut through the air.

During the entry march, spectators could not help noticing those countries whose delegates lifted their right arms in greeting were received "with special enthusiasm" despite that many of them "had no intention of using the German greeting, but simply used the wave they were accustomed to at parades." The Germans nevertheless saw their waves as "a declaration of sympathy towards Germany, perhaps a gesture of a political nature".

For many watching the entry march, it was noticeable that around 200 Frenchmen passed the dignitaries' tribune while they apparently gave the 'heil' salute in honour of Hitler, which incidentally can be seen in Leni Riefenstahl's film of the Olympics. But though the Frenchmen's salute could be regarded as a 'heil' to Hitler, they had a mitigating circumstance on their side in that the same gesture was an Olympic greeting, although they must have known that many would interpret this greeting in the context of the ever-too-present cult of the Führer. In using the Olympic greeting, the right hand should first be brought to the heart, and afterwards brought out horizontally to the side. At the Olympics in 1932, for example, the Norwegian delegation had greeted using the Olympic salute, which the following year "was annexed by the Nazis".[20]

Mr Smile concluded "there were admirable men who said about the Olympics in Berlin ... that they had stopped a world war." He had to acknowledge, however, that political propaganda was at work under the "uniform-wearing" Games with "the endless ranks of soldiers, all these uniforms, the Hitler idolisation, the restricted areas, the processions".

Apart from those features already described in the coverage from Berlin, there were naturally reports on the results. In the beginning, however, not much could be reported and in the respectable Danish press Niels Bukh's display became a redeeming feature, not least since no Danish medals had yet been won.[21]

Later on it was the swimming girls Ragnhild Hveger and Inge Sørensen, especially, who ensured Denmark took its share of the medals with their bronze and silver, despite Danes having expectations of a gold from the record-breaking Hveger.

The Olympics of 1936 provided the Nazi regime with a fantastic opportunity to affect an entire generation of young Danish elite sportspeople and their leaders. There were 135 Danish sports competitors apart from judges, referees, seconds, heads and congress representatives. The Berlin Games gave continuity to the Danish fascination for the Third Reich's sports culture that lasted long into the occupation. Many of the sports heads and sportspeople who came to compete against German athletes during the occupation had taken part in the Olympics of 1936. Among the more prominent athletes, Svend Aage Thomsen can be named and the long-distance runner Harry Siefert. Among boxers was Gerhard Pedersen, who won bronze in welterweight, as well as the twins Kaj and Viggo Frederiksen, and Poul Kops, while wrestling included Robert Voigt.

A pro-German head such as Jørgen Beyerholm, track leader and press officer for the Danish Bicycle Club (DBC), attended the Games and provided reports. The same was true of Hans Spanheimer, a later successful Danish middle-distance runner and journalist for the Nazi newspaper *Fædrelandet*, who enthusiastically reported from the international youth camp that the Germans had arranged, all expenses paid, for 30 participants from other European countries. The camp had been built by the military and all food was prepared by military personnel. On the opening day of the Games, the young visitors took part in an exclusively political event: the laying of wreaths on the tomb of the unknown soldier. Arranged, too, was an international student-sports camp for around 1,000 European participants, which included highlights such as displays of aeronautic gliding and parachuting.[22]

The 1936 Games were such a success in Denmark that the swimmer Inge Sørensen, who had won a bronze medal, was received on her homecoming by 30,000 people

*The Danish troupe were greeted with 'heil' salutes from the public, during their entry march into the Olympic Stadium in Berlin. The Danish Olympic committee, nevertheless, maintained that the games were quite a-political.*

*Bukh's gymnastics presented by blonde, blue-eyed beauties at the Olympics of 1936. Bukh's gymnastics were ensured positive attention in Germany through Bukh's friend, the German Reichssportführer.*

at Enghave Station, while Ragnhild Hveger was met by a 10,000-strong crowd at Helsingør.[23]

This intense Olympic atmosphere was graphically expressed in the daily press, which the Germans were aware of.[24] In the Danish Foreign Service, it was immediately noticed that the German authorities placed great importance on positive press coverage of the Games. The Danish legation in Berlin likewise registered how "particularly what is written on the Olympics abroad is studied by German interests, and how eagerly each acknowledging word is brought to the attention of German readers." As an example, the legation included cuttings from *Berliner Börsen-Zeitung*, from 8 February 1936, on "Copenhagen Reports", covering Danish newspaper articles by *Politiken* and *Berlingske Tidende* on the Winter Olympics in Garmisch-Partenkirchen.

Among the participants at the 1936 Olympics, too, no discordant notes can be traced. Within women's sport, too, there were examples of this deep fascination for the New Germany and "the greatest Games of our age". According to Ellen Paul-Petersen, one of the two chairpersons for the Danish women's gymnastics association, Dansk Kvinde-Gymnastikforening (DKG), who incidentally also competed with a team at a Danish-German gymnastics meeting in February 1941, the women competitors felt very satisfied with the women's camp Friesenhaus, and Tschammer's new sports facility, Haus des Deutschen Sports, where the surroundings both indoors and out were "ideal". Paul-Petersen wrote in her illustrated article "The Home of German Sport – a new centre-point for all of German body culture" that

*The Nazis were masters at propaganda. Here, Danish swimming stars Ragnhild Hveger and Inge Sørensen are taken care of.*

> As evidence of collective organisation and attempts at an across-the-board approach, which is undertaken in all areas of Germany, the new home for all body culture should be mentioned, which is the construction of Haus des Deutschen Sports, an example that calls out to be copied.

She approved of the Reichssport*führer's* efforts in creating an organisational monopoly by prohibiting alternative sports association to the Nazis', in which the aim was that Adolf Hitler's comprehensive 'body policy' should reach widely out into the German realm.

The fascination with German sports was no less felt when DKG and a broad section of German women's gymnastics was inspired by the new German gymnastics systems – especially that of Heinrich Medau – the interest in which appeared firmly in 1936. Medau's gymnastics is built on soft, flexible total movements, where every part of the body is involved elastically in each movement, and where exercises are carried out with equipment such as a ball. In the words of Ellen Paul-Petersen, "Let

*Ragnhild Hveger in close contact with Ruth Halbsguth during a Copenhagen–Berlin intercity competition in april 1939. In sport, people are allowed to be emotionally close. When these meetings involve representatives of a regime, it can mean that the interpersonal contact breaks down critical distance to the regime's propaganda.*

it be said right away, 'oh' there's so much that is wonderful and gloriously natural about German gymnastics." [25]

All in all, DIF did not react critically to the 'streamlining' of German sports. On the contrary, the wider Danish sporting world took part in a chorus of praise for the 1936 Olympics, despite a DIF-member organisation, the Jewish Hakoah, feeling itself to be particularly unwelcome in an anti-Semitic State, therefore choosing to stay away. An entire generation of talented Danish sports competitors and leaders were exposed at the Olympics to the Third Reich's exhaustive propaganda, which did not exactly enhance the Danish 'immune system for the spirit' against the German Reich and German sport, when Denmark was occupied three and a half years later. The rural shooting and gymnastics organisation DDSGI, with Arnth-Jensen and Niels Bukh as frontmen, showed strong sympathies for the Nazi-organised games, which as far as Bukh was concerned was part of a more thorough fascination for and collaboration with the Third Reich.

## From Olympic Games to War

At the end of the 1930s, the greatest Danish sporting stars were the women swimmers who came to play an important role in the course of events that the current study will examine. The women swimmers were some of the most popular sportspeople of the time, and attention was primarily focused on Ragnhild Hveger, Inge Sørensen and Jenny Kammersgaard. We will meet Hveger later. But in Denmark, the last-named, Jenny Kammersgaard, became the most prominent example of how the German authorities used sport to attract international 'Aryan' sports stars to the Third Reich.

Jenny Kammersgaard was born in 1918 and in 1934 became a member of Horsens Swimming Club and Gymnastics Association. Unlike Hveger, she distinguished herself not by a spectacular technique but through enormous willpower and endurance. In 1936 she completed her first long-distance swim in Horsens Fjord. She was impressive again in the following year in both distance and duration swimming.

In August 1937, taking some 29 hours, she swam across the Danish Kattegat, from Odden to Sangstrup Klint, north of Grenaa; linking the island-centre of Denmark, Sealand, with the Danish mainland. Afterwards she embarked on a veritable triumphal procession. The first stop was Copenhagen where she was accompanied by a following up to the *Politiken* newspaper offices in the city's main square, Rådhuspladsen, where the editor, Niels Hasager, and Valdemar Koppel played host. Emil Andersen, who had been at the editorial offices of *Idrætsbladet*, part of the *Politiken* concern, came down with a pile of letters and telegrams. [26]

> Among the pile, there was a telegram from Hitler. There was quite a fuss. My table companion said this was the first time ever that a Head of State

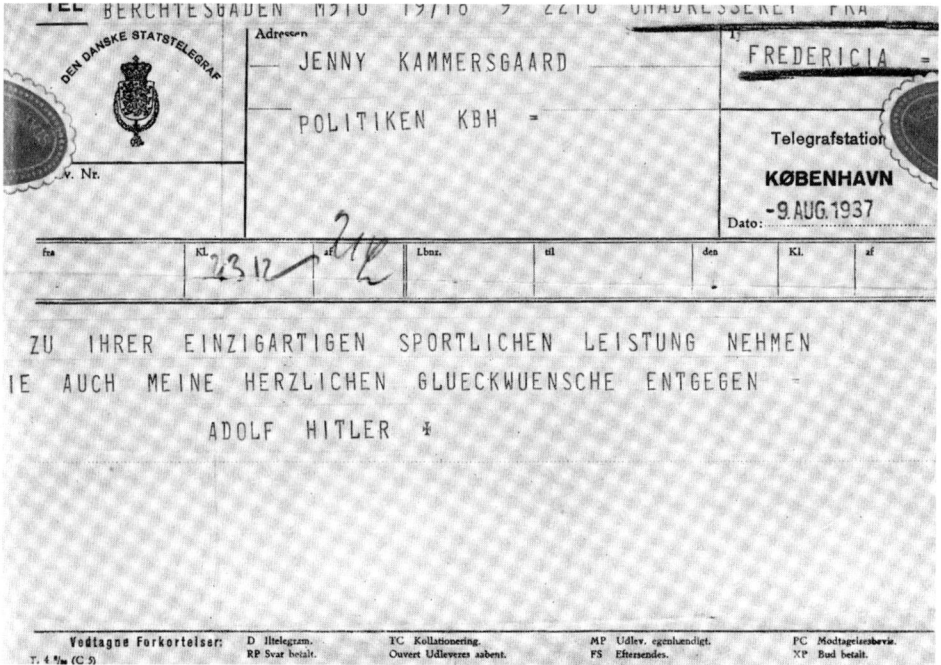

*"Receive, too, my heartiest congratulations for your outstanding sporting achievement," the German Führer wrote to Jenny Kammersgaard after her crossing of the Kattegat in August 1937. The Nazi regime launched a formidable 'charm' offensive, hoping to use the Danish swimming phenomena as its own symbol for the new German politics of the body.*

had sent a telegram to a sportswoman from another nation. I thought it was quite friendly of Hitler.

For the German Nazis, the almost supernatural achievement in water by a 'North Germanic' woman could be seen as a sign of the perfection of the Aryan race. In the telegram from Hitler, sent from his summer residence in Berchtesgarten, it said "Receive, too, my warmest congratulations for your unique sporting achievement."

As a result of her triumph, Jenny Kammersgaard was shortly after invited to Berlin by the German paper *Berliner Illustrierte Zeitung*. She was waved off by a gathering of Danes as she boarded the plane with Mr Smile, who followed her throughout her German tour. At the Tempelhof airport in Berlin she was met by a crowd, by journalists and press photographers who "fired away at me. It all happened so fast. In just a few minutes I was photographed a hundred times and talked on German radio, and I said – in Danish, of course – thank you for the telegram from Hitler and it was lovely to be in Berlin."

*Jenny Kammersgaard and the Reichssportführer, von Tschammer. The Nazi regime knew how to exploit Kammersgaard as a symbol of Danish-German unity. For the Nazi authorities, her swimming could be seen as a maritime 'welding together' of two Germanic peoples.*

Later Jenny Kammersgaard was picked up at her hotel by Reichssportführer Tschammer, who came "in this huge car that he drove himself. He was a smiling, healthy man. I sat right enough next to him, but I've no idea what he said but his smile and his eyes were easy to understand."

When they arrived at the Reich sports academy for physical education, Tschammer gave a speech in her honour, in which he passed on a greeting from the Führer, who had commented that with her impressive long distance swimming, she must be a fish. It was hereupon agreed that German doctors should examine Kammersgaard, the physiological wonder, although this could only be carried out a week later in Copenhagen. Von Tschammer gave her an album with "impressive images of the stadium and of the Olympiad" and other gifts, and assured her that in future she would always be welcome in Germany; which turned out to be ominously relevant.

The "many thousand people" at the Reich academy's swimming stadium wanted to see Jenny in the water, and a swimming costume was duly brought out so she

*Jenny Kammersgaard giving a gesture that the German propaganda machine knew how to exploit.*

could show off her technique in 'Kattegat swimming'. Later she was taken to dinner at Hotel Eden, and afterwards to a fashionable variety theatre, the Scala. Everywhere "people recognised me and called out, 'Kattegat Jenny'!"

The day after, Kammersgaard received an invitation to visit Munich from 'Reich Minister Dr Goebbels'. It "was a generous offer but it couldn't be done as I had to be in Horsens the next morning."

The enthusiastic attitude of the German authorities was hardly without bearing on Jenny Kammersgaard's decision in 1938 to swim south of the border. Her crossing of the Baltic, from Gedser in Denmark to Warnemünde, just north of Rostock, in Germany, a crossing of 110 km completed in 40 hours 30 minutes, 27-29 July 1938, again resonated both inside and outside Denmark, not least in Germany.

Towards the outbreak of war, the Nazi authorities capitalised on Jenny Kammersgaard's popularity in their efforts with Nazi sports, and tried to tie her closely to the regime. To all intents, the sympathy was mutual, given that she did much to emphasise her German connections and Hitler's sympathetic attitude and, as we will see later, this favourable disposition towards the Third Reich took deep root in this young woman.

In the period following the Games, a message was spread abroad about the vital, 'sporting' German nation. This was done through Leni Riefenstahl's aesthetic and technically ground-breaking film of the Games, *Olympia*, which had its premiere in Germany in 1938, on the Führer's birthday. An effective propaganda message was spread about Germany as a peaceful nation, in its acceptance of the multiculturalism of the Olympics and with Hitler as its father who stood out as a human figure, committed to modern competitive sports; which essentially he abhorred since in principle it gave all races the equal opportunity to win.

The Danish King, Christian X, attended the film's Danish premiere in Copenhagen. On the occasion *Berlingske Tidende* wrote

> It has been grand and wonderful to play a part, in these weeks, when the whole world of sport rallied together and without objection fought for sport's highest honour ... The Führer has been one of the most photogenic focal points, and we are taken very close to his private enclosure, which shows his intense excitement, his trepidation, his anxiety – as he continuously grinds his knee – and his deep engagement in his countrymen's struggles for first place. A dictator is seldom seen so intimately.[27]

There seems to be no trace of criticism of the Berlin Games from either Denmark's Olympic Committee or from the Danish member of the International Olympic Committee (IOC), Prince Axel. The IOC had shown itself to be extremely cooperative towards Germany. IOC could have changed its decision about awarding the Games to Berlin by referring to the point that the new powers in Berlin no longer

*The Danish King, Christian X, and Queen Alexandrine cast their lustre over an event to celebrate the first showing of Leni Riefenstahl's film Olympia, in Copenhagen, August 1938. The wide acceptance in Europe of Riefenstahl's film helped her in arguing after the war that bodily aesthetics and politics had no connection.*

satisfied conditions for the original award; through its acts such as excluding a large number of Jewish sportspeople from the German Olympic team. But IOC chose to turn a blind eye.[28]

After the Olympic Games, the collaboration with and fascination for German sport continued. It was a sign that Danish and German sportspeople could develop closer and friendlier relations that would continue into collaborative sporting relations during the occupation.

In the Nordic countries, it did not go unnoticed that throughout the 1930s Germany joined the European elite class in football and in boxing, and that the country was a leader in motor-cycle racing and speed-record flying, together with being placed strongly in cycle track racing, not least through the figures of W. Arend and W. Rütt. The same applied to horse riding, in which Germany took every gold medal at the 1936 Olympics. In motor sports, the motor manufacturers Mercedes-Benz and Auto-Union, from 1934 to 1939, dominated the European racetracks. The racing driver Bernd Rosemeyer, from 1936 to 1938, became a symbol for German control of the track. He beat several world speed records and was killed during a record attempt in 1938.[29]

In Danish wrestling, a national competition was agreed on with the Nazi sports authorities for 19 February 1939 in Nykøbing Falster, which resulted as expected in "an absolutely sure and well-deserved victory for the German colours with five matches won against two, a result that in view of the wrestling skills showed by the two competing teams on Sunday seems to be reasonable measure of their respective strengths." The athletics club Thor on behalf of the Danish athletics union was responsible for the event, which was marked by the German organisers' use of symbolic action, whereby the German team gave "a three-fold 'Sieg Heil' in honour of Danish wrestling and as a salute to Nykøbing Falster – and with that a fine warm-up ceremony, which was introduced by the two nations' respective national anthems, was over and the wrestling could begin."[30]

It was especially in the field of cycling that an intense collaboration developed between Denmark and Germany. Up until the Nazi accession to power in 1933, there had been amateur international track championships between Denmark and Germany in 1924, 1927, 1928 and 1932. From 1933 until 1939, these international matches happened annually. Germany became incomparably the most important international opponent for Denmark who, for example, did not compete against England at all after 1932.[31]

In spite of the Nazis' appetite for state-controlled sport, there were examples of privately organised professional sports in the Third Reich. Road-race cycling enjoyed an extremely close partnership. This took on new importance when, in 1937, four Danish riders were invited to the 'Preis der Nationen' at Bielefeld. It was "the first time a sign came from south of the border that Danish riders were really taken seriously." Around 20,000 German spectators could watch a dramatic race where the Danish riders were first announced as the winners, only to fall to second place when on closer inspection the German team appeared to be 3/5 of a second faster.[32]

In 1938, four Danish road racers took part. The best Dane was Arne Petersen, taking sixth place after the German race winner, Herman Schild. Arne Petersen repeated his success as best Dane, with his performance in 1939, coming in eighth, again after a German winner, Georg Umbenhauer, which was impressive since Petersen was not part of a group with other riders. Arne Petersen's achievement was particularly praised because he was not used to the tough conditions of the German road championships, Deutschland Tour, that were characterised by "20 stages in alternatively rain, icy cold and murderous heat, which all made enormous demands on the individual rider's physique, will power and strength of character." For his performance, Arne Petersen earned DKK 5,000, which was a considerable sum at the time.

After the 1939 race, as part of the post-match celebrations at the Berlin City Hall, negotiations were opened between Standartenführer Viktor Brack, an SS unit commander and chairman of the German cycling association, Deutscher Radfahrer-Verband, and the head of the Danish Bicycle Club, Jørgen Beyerholm, about whether the Danes should be allowed to compete next time with a six-man team, instead of having to take part in a combined Danish–Spanish–Dutch team. At the same meeting it was suggested that a 'revenge match' might be organised, at Ordrup track, in Denmark.[33]

Besides participating in the ordinary German road races, there were Danish riders who competed in the large stage race, Deutschland-Tour, with much coverage from the Danish press at home. In 1939 the collected prize totalled a staggering 100,000 Reichmarks, which made this road race the largest-prized cycle race in the world. That year, Arne Petersen came in sixth.

The three-day Berlin to Copenhagen stage race geographically and mentally bound the two nations together. The race was set up by the Danish Bicycle Club in collaboration with Deutcher Radfahrer-Verband and the newspaper *Berlingske Tidende*, and was held in 1937, 1938 and again in 1939, where Germany won all three races against the two other competing countries, Denmark and Sweden. The head of the track at Ordrup and the Winter Track, Jørgen Beyerholm, from the Dansk Bicycle Club, could announce that the German winners in 1937 were able to take home "one of the Reichssportführer Hans von Tschammer's own prize Meissen-porcelain vases."[34]

German cyclists could also be impressive on Danish tracks. Until 1936, only Danish racers had won the International Grand Prix Race in Aarhus, Denmark, but in June 1936 the German Purann became the first international Grand Prix winner. "This sympathetic German," wrote *Idrætsbladet*, won "in superior style"

*The Reichssportführer, Tschammer, in uniform, in conversation; including Jørgen Beyerholm (the tall figure on the left). Taken during the stage race Berlin–Copenhagen in 1938. Under Nazism, an aesthetics around male uniforms became an important signal for the splendours of the Party.*

and "the cheers that poured down on this handsome sportsman during his lap of honour proved the public knew they should value his splendid sporting accomplishment."[35]

In rowing, too, a close collaboration with Germany occurred, including 'tourist-oriented' rowing. An association of German long-distance rowers called Die Dänemarksfahrer aimed at furthering Danish-German cooperation. The association launched a cup, Die Dänemarksfahrers Pokal, which was presented annually to the Danish rowing club that had completed the longest trip in German waters.[36]

Germany was the only country Denmark competed against in an international match in 1938, before the occupation. The Danish crews were impressed that the match was part of a larger German commitment to rowing. It did not go unnoticed that Germany was planning in 1938 "a gigantic international match plan".[37]

In terms of handball, Germany provided the toughest national opponents, next to Sweden, in both field and indoor handball, from the Danish national team's debut in 1934 to 1939, with a match each year, except in 1936. On 4 June 1937, Denmark played Germany at field handball, at Frederiksberg stadium, in Copenhagen.

When it came to football, Denmark was oriented more towards Germany than England, throughout the 1930s. Germany was an important opponent for Denmark, playing eight international matches up until 1939, although not quite so prominently as the Nordic countries and Holland (twelve matches), but more so than England (five matches).[38] German footballers had a tight grip on the Danish national team; and on 16 May 1937, at the Hermann Göring Stadium in Breslau (now Wroclaw), the Danes were dealt a traumatic 8-0 defeat by extremely fit German players.

The Danish inferiority complex towards the German team proved to be a difficult one to get over, because for a long time afterwards the anxiety of running into a similar thrashing tortured the Danish press. *Idrætsbladet* almost declared the international defeat of 2-0 in 1939 as a semi-victory. In its headline, it said "Danish football took its moral revenge for the massacre in Breslau." "Several German players were about to topple with fatigue." "The goalkeeper deserves the honour of the German victory." Although it was admitted that "in the first half, our eleven men didn't manage to keep up with the precise and inspiring German play, in which the ball flowed beautifully from man to man, but in the second half our team performed the not so inconsiderable feat of throwing the Germans off balance and convincingly dominating play on the pitch."[39]

As can be seen from the previous sections, for a very major part of the Danish and international sporting world, there were few reservations about working together with Germany, and moreover, in a number of cases, there seemed to be a tendency towards glorification. But was this because the people involved did not know better or because they turned a blind eye?

## War and continuity

At the outbreak of war, the German Reichssportführer ordered that German sport should continue as before, since it was indispensable part of the preparatory work for young men to wage war. The Foreign Minister of Germany, Joachim von Ribbentrop,

*It was not difficult to identify German or German-friendly spectators at Idrætsparken on 7 October 1934, when Denmark played against Germany. It may possibly be Frits Clausen, leader of the Danish Nazi party, giving the 'heil' salute, to the furthest left of the picture.*

the ministry of the interior, and Reichssportführer von Tschammer all wished Germany to continue competing with neutral countries, as often as possible.

That Europe had now embarked on another large-scale war did not cause DIF executive-committee hands to tremble. At their executive committee meeting on 23 October 1939,[40] the DIF chairman general Holten Castenschiold stipulated that Denmark was neutral and that it maintained a relation of friendship towards Germany. Therefore, there was no reason for not keeping agreements on international matches, since Germany was "extremely sensitive towards any slight" and followed "our conduct closely". Only important reasons could "make us break our agreements." Castenschiold arranged with the Danish Ministry of Defence that those liable for national service who were called up could have leave of absence for games both at home and especially abroad.

The decision by DIF meant that Denmark became the only nation in the Nordic region that failed to boycott Germany from the outbreak of war in September 1939 until 9 April 1940. Denmark, thereby, gained optimal opportunities for meeting top-level German sportspeople. From 1933 to 1939, Denmark had not even featured in the German top-five placements for international opponents, but in the course of

1939 the country moved to fourth position, holding 10 international matches, only surpassed by Italy (14 matches), Sweden (15 matches) and Hungary (16 matches). The list of countries playing against Germany from the outbreak of war until 9 April 1940 included Hungary, Italy, Yugoslavia, Slovakia, Bulgaria and Romania, as well as the German-occupied Protectorate of Bohemia and Moravia.[41]

The Germans felt they had been hit hard by the international sports boycott, during the first year of the war, and did not try to hide it. In the Nazi sports magazine *NS-Sport*, there was both anger and threats made towards the presumptuous Swedes who had played 15 international matches against the Germans until World War Two, but who now refused.

The Danish teams lost so often that they could confirm feelings of superiority among Nazi sports authorities. Denmark lost an international match in handball on 8 October 1939 in Leipzig, in boxing on 2 December 1939 in Berlin, in wrestling on 7 January 1940 in Copenhagen and in tennis on 23 February, again in Copenhagen. The upper levels of the German sports leadership attached great importance to the handball match of 8 October 1939, which could be seen in the way the games were staged. The German Reichssportführer summoned 1,000 regional party functionaries and heads of association from the German sports federation (NSRL), together with personnel from various Nazi-party organisations including trumpet playing SS-youth, to a "sports assembly", to make them aware of the significance of their assignments. The games were hailed as "a great success for the public", bringing in around 12,000 spectators to watch Germany's victory. At the reception for the Danish guests held in the evening, the choir Leipziger Thomaschor – a choir steeped in tradition that boasted Johann Sebastian Bach as a former musical director – provided an "extremely impressive repertoire" in the shape of German folk songs such as *Heidenröslein* and *Heilig Vaterland*.[42]

*Idrætsbladet* did not play down the Nazi stage-management and in its headline could enthuse that "Denmark led by 4-3 against the German world champions":

> The match was played in Leipzig's newly renovated stadium, in front of 15,000 eager spectators, and ended with a German 11-7 victory; but the Danes could be entirely proud of their efforts against the world's supreme handball nation. The pre-match buildup was a delight. Young handball players made a guard of honour as the red-and-white Danish team came onto court, where they were greeted by a fanfare from the SS-youth and a deafening cheer from the public. After both national anthems had been played, the toss fell in favour of the Germans.[43]

That the German organisers spent much energy on impressive Nazi scenography can also be seen at a city fencing competition between the host city Hamburg and Copenhagen, on 20 May 1939. From the photographs covering the event, it can be seen clearly that the Swastika and the Danish flag Dannebrog are featured, with the German eagle centrally placed, and that there are banners, too, lettered in German gothic and held by officials.

Germany tried single-mindedly to maintain sporting relations with the outside world but their sporting old guard consisted of around 50 amateur sports men and women, who took care of sports activities during the first year of the war. The German sports authorities constantly had to struggle to save their sportspeople from being sent to the front.[44] For example, Rudolf Harbig, who had run off with a "fantastic world record" in 800 meters, in summer 1939, was enlisted to a strict tour of duty in occupied Poland. In a letter from October 1939, Harbig expressed his frustrations about being unable to prepare for the not-yet finalised Olympic Games in Helsingfors:

> In Gnesen, here, all we have is our guard duty. You can surely imagine my annoyance … I would much rather carry out other duties for the Fatherland in the nature of the great task sport has given me. I have to admit, though, that guard duty is more important for the State than a possible winner's place at the Olympics.[45]

During this early period, sporting relations with Germany concentrated especially on handball, swimming, wrestling, gymnastics, tennis and professional cycling. Although the Danish focus was on the sporting achievements of the Axis powers and particularly Germany, a newspaper such as *Politiken's Idrætsbladet* could also carry large news items on developments in English football, through a journalist by the name of Gunnar Henriksen. In October 1939, the paper also ran a photograph of Great Britain's best-known professional boxers, Len Harvey and Eddie Philips, training their soldier comrades in boxing.[46]

Professional cycling kept its home fires burning, spearheaded by Jørgen Beyerholm, sports director at both the Winter track and Ordrup track and press-secretary for Danish Bicycle-Club from 1941. In February 1940, an inter-city championship was held in which Copenhagen took part. Around 10,000 spectators were present at the track in a comfortably heated Deutschlandhalle, the large indoor arena in Berlin. There was no doubt about German political intentions, since the Danish riders were each given a gift of "a large bronze eagle on a stone plinth with the Swastika at its breast".[47]

All in all, throughout the 1930s until 9 April 1940, the Nazi regime managed to create a fascination for German sport among Danish sports competitors and its leadership, through its commitment to a massive, generous and stage-managed collaboration. In this way, the idea was established in Denmark before the occupation that the experience of Danish-German sports was forceful and positive, both on a personal as well as organisational level. The close contact and goodwill towards

German sport could not have avoided providing fertile soil for the comprehensive sporting relations that sprang up during the occupation.

In spite of the relatively large political room for manoeuvre afforded DIF, from the period covering the outbreak of war until 9 April 1940, Denmark was the only nation in Western Europe to continue its sporting relations with its large neighbour, whereafter Denmark's sports collaboration with Nazi Germany increased dramatically.

# DANISH SPORT UNDER SIEGE, 1940-41

On 9 April 1940 Denmark was occupied, thereby initiating one of the more unusual occupations in modern history. In contrast to other German-occupied nations, the Danes were subject to a 'peaceful occupation', which to a great extent made it possible to carry on as though nothing had happened. Apart from avoiding making public proclamations aimed against the occupying forces, society's various organising bodies were able to operate almost as before, which was exactly the aim of the Danish policy of collaboration: not least so that the parliamentary system, the life-blood for Danish politicians, could be preserved intact.

Danes therefore resigned themselves and tried to carry on with business as usual. Was the country on a war footing? Not according to the German propaganda minister Joseph Goebbels who, on 9 March 1941 in the conservative newspaper *Nationaltidende*, contended that Denmark should not be counted among occupied countries but on the contrary that it had reached a settlement with Germany. Or rather, in a pragmatic and much-criticised phrase from 1945 by Erik Scavenius, the Danish foreign minister and later Prime Minister, who said that if the Danes had been at war then it was rather lucky the Germans had never noticed.

On the day of the occupation, the German plenipotentiary, Cecil von Renthe-Fink, handed a memorandum to the Danish Government wherein Germany demanded an unconditional surrender but at the same time guaranteed that Denmark could retain its territorial integrity and political independence. Relations to Germany were arranged in such a way that the Danish Government could maintain the fiction of Danish neutrality. Collaboration between Denmark and the occupying forces therefore should be conducted through the offices of the foreign ministry, as between two sovereign nations.

Denmark positioned itself in a grey area between being a neutral country and an enforced German ally, which led to a comprehensive collaboration with the occupying forces, especially economically. The rationale behind this collaboration was a recognition that Denmark did not have the faintest chance of offering military resistance or to defend its territorial borders. A collaboration with the occupying forces, therefore, was regarded as being the only measure by which the Danish Government could retain as much power as possible in Danish hands.

For sports, the attempt to perpetuate the status quo itself produced a dilemma, in so far as competition between Danish and foreign teams became a point of contention. Against whom should occupied Denmark compete, since competitors were classified into aggressor, occupied and neutral countries? Danish sport entered a state of shock and initially all international sporting relations were brought to a halt.

## Ragnhild Hveger and German propaganda

The break in sporting relations meant that it was even more important for the Germans to secure positive gestures from well-known sporting figures to bear witness to continued positive relations between Germany and Denmark. The occupying forces' Nazi leadership wanted to give their soldiers in Denmark an impression that the soldiers were welcomed by 'their Aryan brothers'. It was therefore something of a propaganda coup when two of the best known Danes in Germany – Ragnhild Hveger, the swimmer, and gymnastics innovator and instructor Niels Bukh – both met the occupying forces with open arms, which for many Germans became a symbol of underlying Danish hospitality and consent.

Ragnhild Hveger was a member of the Helsingør Swimming Club, and worked as an office clerk in Helsingør. She was a highly unique freestyle swimmer, who combined a rhythmic stroke with extremely effective leg work. Hveger won a silver medal at the 1936 Olympics in Berlin and from 1936 to 1942 she achieved no less than 44 world records in crawl – although, despite supreme efforts, she never surpassed the most prestigious record (for the 100 meter crawl) set by Willy den Ouden, the Dutch woman swimmer, at 1:04.6. According to the swimming expert Alf Mørkeberg in 1941, Ragnhild Hveger was one of the last to be able to set so many records since "women's world records have now reached such a level that improvements only occur within a tenth of a second."[1]

Hveger became known as 'the golden torpedo' in *The Times*, when in 1938 the Danish women swimmers won five gold medals at the European championships at Wembley in London. The importance of these women for Danish national sentiments showed itself clearly on their homecoming, when they were received at the Copenhagen city-hall square, on a hastily built rostrum, cheered by "a sea of people" in what *Idrætsbladet* called "the greatest reception ever given to Danish sportsmen or women". According to The International Swimming Hall of Fame, the record books show that Hveger could well have won in the Olympics of 1940 and 1944, had they been held.[2] It was without doubt a great loss to Hveger that these two competitions were abandoned due to the war.

Ragnhild Hveger was the single most-discussed individual in the Danish sports press and by all accounts the first sporting star, in the modern sense of the term, to

*Ragnhild Hveger performing a turn. Denmark's most victorious sports star, ever, gave the occupation forces a positive welcome.*

have public interest gather around her whole person, including her private life and the emotional life of the star.[3] She was the daughter of a railway engine driver, V.A. Hveger, and was the youngest among five, her family playing an important role in forming her political convictions. Both parents and her brother were members of the Danish National-Socialist Workers Party. Her father features as a Nazi Party member, registered 6 January 1941,[4] while her brother fought for the Waffen SS. At the beginning of the war, Hveger's favourable experiences with German sports initiatives, such as during the 1936 Olympics, her family's Nazi background, and her position as a sports star with every opportunity for continuing her raids on the world's swimming records, proved to be one of the worst cocktails imaginable for any resistance to German appeals to compete south of the Danish border. By 1 December 1940, Ragnhild Hveger had taken part in 587 races, achieving first place on no less than 427 occasions. All in all, she took part in 98 competitions outside of Denmark, of which the majority (30 in all) were held in Germany, with 14 in Berlin.[5]

In the wake of the occupation, it was evidently important for German journalists to secure German-friendly signals from Hveger as soon as possible, who because of DIF's initial embargo at that point was not training much apart from a little canoeing and participation in a gymnastics course at Copenhagen. A well-edited

*It was first with Danish champion swimmer Ragnhild Hveger that the tendency to incorporate details from a sports star's private life became an important ingredient in Denmark. The photograph shows a scene from Ragnhild's birthday. Her father's political orientation combined with the temptations of the Nazi sports world proved to be a dangerous cocktail for Ragnhild Hveger.*

and generously composed magazine for occupying soldiers *Kopenhagener Soldatenzeitschrift* came out as early as July 1940 with a double-page, fully-illustrated portrait interview with the Danish swimmer, who with her current 32 world records was characterised as "the world's most successful sportswoman".[6]

The article went through Hveger's impressive career from child star to adult elite sportswoman, intimating that German soldiers were also sportsmen and as such amiably placed in respect to Danish sporting circles. Soldiers were simply sportsmen in uniform and sport was a bridge for creating a broad mutual understanding between occupiers and the occupied. The interview was presented as resulting from a visit to Hveger paid by a group of German soldiers on duty in Denmark, one of whom was the article's author. The interview clearly aimed at getting German soldiers to feel well received in Denmark with the help of a world-renowned swimmer, who spoke a passable German, besides.

At that time, erotic undertones to the reception of the Wehrmacht's soldiers by Danish girls were heavily played on.[7] Throughout the *Kopenhagener* magazine, there were a great many pictures, reports and cartoon sketches of meetings between beautiful young Danish girls and uniformed German soldiers. Photographs from Bellevue and other bathing beaches north of Copenhagen were printed, of bathing beauties in conversation with uniformed Germans, while Ragnhild Hveger was shown off in a swimming costume between two of "our German boys" as "the best swimmer in the world" who undeniably "feels right at home sitting in the middle". She was also featured in several pictures in a swimming costume with a hat and fur wrap, in a signed medallion photo. The interview also carried a report and photographs of a swimming race between a sun-tanned, athletic German soldier and Ragnhild Hveger, and their paired dive from the five-meter board, in the pool at Helsingør stadium. One picture shows the soldiers holding Ragnhild's arm from behind, flanked by smiling Danish children in swimming costumes.

A German journalist, visiting Ragnhild Hveger supposedly during 'spring cleaning' at her mother's house in Helsingør, concluded that "Ragnhild looks stunning in her long work trousers, her red pullover and a blue ribbon in her blonde hair. From the tomboy image, which we were used to seeing in pictures brought in newspapers and magazines around the world, there has grown up *an exceptionally female creature* – a blossoming young woman of 18 years. Her young girl's shyness at the sight of three soldiers, unexpectedly turning up, disappears as quickly as the purpose of their sudden visit becomes known."

Beyond eroticism, the interview highlights Hveger's sympathy for the German cause. Her 30 trips to Germany had "besides the field of sport, given her an understanding and a sympathy for the New Germany" and she felt "a close bond to her German sports colleagues … who nearly all are now at the front." She sent them her best wishes, and the magazine carried a reprinted letter in German from Hveger to the Wehrmacht's soldiers.

> I'd like to wish all the German soldiers in Denmark welcome and I remember with much happiness all the fine times among German sporting friends I've had the pleasure of, during my many visits and competitions in Germany. All I'm looking forward to now is the day when I can again step up to the starting line in Germany.

Under the headline *Ragnhild and the War*, "the Danish world champion" described how she "with an open mind and with great personal involvement follows the course of the war". She is "constantly in communication by letter with her German fellow sports friends who today bear the honoured grey uniform, fighting for Germany's freedom." "Ragnhild Hveger *humbly puts her own needs behind her* in this great

# Ragnhild Hveger erzählt

Soldatenbesuch bei dem erfolgreichsten Sportmädel der Welt
Ein Kind erschwamm 32 Weltrekorde für Dänemark

nach Paris, nach Brüssel, nach Stockholm, nach Prag, nach Amsterdam und schwimmt alles in Grund und Boden, was sich ihr entgegenstellt. In ihrer engeren Heimat, in Dänemark, hat sie seit langem keine auch nur annähernd gleichwertigen Gegner mehr. Die dänischen Schwimmer weigern sich, mit dem Schulmädel zusammen an den Start zu gehen, weil sie in diesem ungleichen Wettkampf keine Erfolgsmöglichkeiten für sich sehen. Ragnhild wird geschlagen! Dem erfolgreichsten Sportmädel der Welt entgeht der längst verdiente Lorbeer seiner so jungen, aber so unwahrscheinlich steil ansteigenden schwimmerischen Laufbahn. Wie das möglich war? Eine Stirnhöhlenentzündung unmittelbar nach dem Düsseldorfer Start, die eine Operation bedingte, hatte Ragnhild derartig geschwächt, dass sie bei den Olympischen Spielen bei weitem ihre Form nicht er-

*Hveger was a big name in Germany. For the occupying powers, Hveger's warm welcome to German troops and sporting colleagues was an important signal.*

campaign, even though the war has cost her biggest chances of victory in events such as the now-cancelled 1940 Olympic Games in Helsingfors," and despite that "the Danish sports authorities have ceased all international cooperation because of the war."

The article's clinching point was the revelation of Ragnhild Hveger's dream of a future career as a swimming coach in Germany: "Germany for her is the country that can fulfil an until-now unrealised dream. She desperately wants to perform as coach in the German national socialist Reich federation for physical training (NSRL), or at one of the large associations for women's swimming." Hveger believed she had reached a peak as an elite swimmer and now wished to prepare the way for her appearance as a paid coach in German swimming by pointing out that Germany must "try to give its youth an even more systematic sports training. Tiny Denmark with its barely five million inhabitants has with its exemplary selection and training methods brought on almost a dozen girls under the age of fifteen, who are very close to being able to set new world records." Accordingly, Germany must be "a true goldmine" of sporting talent, waiting simply to be identified and trained rationally and at an earlier age than has been the custom in Germany.

The interview was excellent advertising material for Germany. But, as already mentioned, Ragnhild Hveger was not the only one to assist in German propaganda. Niels Bukh, too, was interviewed in a lengthy richly-illustrated article for the German soldier's magazine.

## The propaganda of military sports

That the German leadership in Denmark should so emphatically intend to re-establish sporting relations with Denmark was a result of a strategy by Hitler and Goebbels for how best to win over the Danish people for the epoch's New Order. Included were a list of propaganda measures such as "outdoor concerts with German military bands, Danish-German sports events, loud-speaker trucks carrying German news and comment, and 'open days' to the German Wehrmacht for the Danish public." The aim was to turn the Danish population away from Anglo-American cultural sources of inspiration and instead towards Germanic-Nordic cultural values.[8] As far as this concerned sport, it meant a mental move away from Great Britain, the birthplace of modern sports and football, to instead regarding Germany as the new international power centre and motive force behind sport.

In the late summer of both 1940 and 1941, a large sports event was held with the participation of the Wehrmacht's Copenhagen guard battalion. In August 1940, chief officers from the German and Danish military met to watch the competitions, together with representatives from the German colony in Denmark and various Danish guests. At the entry march, the German athletes were dressed in only shorts and running shoes, with torsos bare. The programme ranged wide, including the 'Machine Gunners Company competition', relay races by riders on horse, on cycle and by runners, 'light athletics', a Bukh-inspired mass gymnastics display, handball, football and a relay race in uniform: all in all, a clear symbol of sport's military value. In handball, the Copenhagen battalion played against men from a German sports association, *Deutscher Turnverein*, who were mostly staff from the German embassy and which included the embassy secretary Dr Gustav Meissner.

There were other German enterprises, too. The head of the German Navy in Denmark, Vice-Admiral Mewis, took the initiative to hold a tournament and training course in boxing for beginners from the Navy, which was held at the end of February 1941.[9] Many of the sailors fought so enthusiastically that they completely forgot to block incoming punches. The German soldiers' *Kopenhagener* magazine encouraged other military units to follow this successful evening and to arrange other boxing competitions, which "more than any other sport demands a wholehearted commitment."

For the Wehrmacht, it was important to show that the soldier and the sportsman were two sides of the same figure. The *Kopenhagener* published a double-page article[10] on German sports stars serving in the forces. In a pictorial cavalcade, the athletes were shown in sports outfits and in uniform. Involved were stars such as Rudolf Harbig, the runner and now an NCO; Henner Henkel, the tennis player, who had just won the German wartime championships from 1940 and who had toured in Japan to show off the high level of German sport; Hans Fömming, the jockey, who astounded the German public by continuing to win trotting races whilst still in military service; hurdle racer and NCO Kaindl, who served on an anti-aircraft battery on the Western front; Fischer, a professional soldier and German 100-meter record holder; Rudolf Hasenörl, the rower, who came second at singles sculling in the 1936 Berlin Olympics; and the German champion in 1500-meter crawl, NCO Heinz Ahrendt, who together with his sister Gisela "were known beyond the borders of the Reich and especially in Denmark".

The sports hero and soldier most talked about was Max Schmeling, the boxer, often appearing in German war propaganda directed at servicemen in Denmark, and who naturally had "renounced his collected championship titles in order to serve the Fatherland in the paratroops." Schmeling became simply the most powerful symbol of the invincible, mighty, toughened German soldier, pictured in situations such as in a paratroopers' transportation plane or standing on Cretan soil with a parachute under his arm. In triumph, the soldiers' *Kopenhagener* could announce that during the Battle of Crete the foreign press had declared Schmeling dead but in reality he was only wounded and now at a camp hospital.[11]

Schmeling was a trump card as a symbol of German invincibility, and in the forces it proved difficult to avoid idolisation and the autograph hunting whenever the boxer appeared. The Battle of Crete could be presented through the eyes of Max Schmeling, "always a friend" who noted that "The English ignored the rules of engagement", for example, by mistreating German prisoners.[12] This naturally offended Max Schmeling who as a top boxer "knew everything about fair play". Through sport the Germans were presented as a people who were in accordance with the norms of fair play evading any understanding of the real face of the cruel Nazi war politics.

Taken broadly, sport became an important link in Hitler's and Goebbels's strategy for winning over the Danish people to German thinking. Through public sporting events, the occupying forces attempted to present themselves to a Danish audience as an open nation of dynamic sports enthusiasts, and at all costs not as gun-loving fanatics. However, there is little indication that these games were a runaway success with the people of Copenhagen.

## Pressure from the Reich plenipotentiary

In the first days after 9 April, DIF was in a state of bewilderment about the future of international engagements for Danish sport. After a motion from the chairman, Major-General Holten Castenschiold, a boxing match was postponed provisionally until May. In fact, there are hints that the DIF leadership may even have believed a tour by the Danish football club Fremad to Berlin, planned for the Whitsun holidays, together with an inter-city football match between Berlin and Copenhagen, could actually go ahead.[13]

Over the following period, it was difficult for DIF to find room to manoeuvre. On 13 April 1940, the federation's executive committee met two days in advance of a board meeting.[14] The day before, Castenschiold received a clear point of view from a board member representing Funen, a barrister, Ernst Petersen, who was unable to attend the board meeting but who wished to bring the board's attention to information he had learnt through the press that negotiations with Germany had been resumed after 9 April. He pointed out that, so long as there was a war on and Denmark was occupied any sporting relations with Germany were quite undesirable and must be regarded as a "slap in the face". To play against Germany would be a provocation against the Danish people and "our Nordic sporting friends", by which without doubt he implied occupied Norway, especially since there was still fighting in that country. A Danish match against Germany would unavoidably be used as political propaganda to highlight the "warmest relations" between the two countries, which directly contradicted opinions held by the people of Denmark.

Castenschiold apparently agreed with Ernst Petersen's rejection of engaging in sporting relations. He likewise informed the executive committee at its meeting that the letter from Petersen "fell in line with my opinion." Castenschiold, however, proffered another argument for discontinuing sporting relations than that used by Ernst Petersen and also introduced the idea of a time schedule. DIF ought to break off any contact with Germany "at least provisionally" since it could not be guaranteed that anti-German demonstrations from the public could be avoided, and that it was still questionable whether Danish sportspeople would demonstrate against the occupation by refusing to turn up. In this respect, Castenschiold was concerned the Germans would hold DIF responsible for any disturbance. The prevailing mood was that DIF "neither can nor will hold official matches against Germany". But, it was fear of the reaction from Danish sportspeople that worried the chairman and not a decision as to whether 'collaboration' with the enemy was ethically wrong, as Ernst Petersen believed. The executive committee backed Castenschiold's position and it was decided that he should contact the Ministry of Foreign Affairs of

Denmark to hear whether support from the Government could be expected for DIF's agreed position.[15] In spite of this, the question still refused to be resolved. Two days later, Petersen's opinion was again brought up at the board meeting on 15 April, whereupon Castenschiold maintained that cooperation with Germany should cease since no-one wished to "harm the position of sport among the country's populace". Under particular scrutiny were games held in Denmark with the participation of sports representatives from the occupying powers, as well as the participation of Danish sportspeople in games against the Axis powers and especially Germany. It was unanimously agreed to recommend to the unions and associations that all cooperation with German representatives should cease.

Before their referral to the foreign ministry, however, the leadership of DIF altered the wording from 'rejecting collaboration with Germany' to 'a rejection of cooperation with all belligerent countries', so that the German authorities should not feel the decision was directed solely against them. With this amendment, DIF had ensured they could play against a neutral country such as Sweden and at the same time avoid playing Germany or other teams from the Axis alliance, which could have provoked a negative reaction among the Danish people, who were still in a state of shock about 9 April, and whose reactions were unpredictable.

Before any official press release was sent, Castenschiold attended a meeting at the Danish Parliament buildings, in Christiansborg, with Otto Carl Mohr,[16] who until spring 1941 was the powerful Permanent Secretary of State for Foreign Affairs, after which time – because of a conflict with Erik Scavenius, then Minister for Foreign Affairs – Mohr passed over the position to Nils Svenningsen to become Danish ambassador in Berlin. Mohr was centrally placed given that together with the foreign minister he planned foreign policy.[17]

To understand the position of the Danish foreign ministry, it is important to be aware that both Mohr and P. Munch – the foreign minister of the time until the change of government on 8 July 1940, when he was succeeded by Scavenius – both subscribed to a high degree to the so-called 'German School' of thought (as did Svenningsen, and Scavenius). The German School applied a geo-political viewpoint to Denmark that stressed the weak economic position of a small State and its military position in the international world order. Denmark, therefore, needed to draw its lines of foreign policy under careful consideration for its large neighbour to the South. As already indicated, the core position of the foreign ministry regarding Germany rested on a fiction of neutrality that required cooperation to take place as though between two sovereign nations. To maintain that condition, it was important for the Ministry of Foreign Affairs of Denmark to build up goodwill with the occupying powers and ensure that collaboration between Danes and Germans be carried out with as little friction as possible. The result of this way of thinking was that in contrast to many party politicians civil servants supported an active collaboration policy, as occurred during Scavenius' term as foreign minister from 8 July 1940 until 29 August 1943, and as Prime Minister between 1942 and 1943.[18]

At the Christiansborg meeting, Castenschiold presented a draft of the press release to Mohr who immediately pointed to the expression 'belligerent countries', arguing that in respect of German interests this should be amended to 'foreign nations'. It was obviously Mohr's not-illogical opinion that the Germans would regard the expression 'belligerent countries' as a one-sided attempt to boycott games against them. For DIF, the problem was that the amended wording would also exclude games against free, neutral countries, which in practice would mean Sweden, and thereby an already arranged international football match the following month. Mohr, however, would not be moved, and Major-General Castenschiold was forced to accept. It did not exactly cause jubilation when Castenschiold conveyed the news to his Vice-Chairman, head of the influential Danish Football Association, Leo Frederiksen; particularly given the approaching football match against Sweden.

Rejecting collaborative sports with the occupying forces, though, was no simple matter. For the German plenipotentiary, Renthe-Fink, a resumption of Danish-German sporting activities would soften the Danish public's negative attitude towards the occupying power. Renthe-Fink had been the German Ambassador in Copenhagen since 1936 and on 9 April, as plenipotentiary, had assumed political responsibility for German occupation policy in Denmark.[19]

On 29 April 1940, Castenschiold and Leo Frederiksen met with Secretary Mohr, Renthe-Fink, and Frielitz, the press attaché, at the offices of the Danish foreign ministry.[20] The official purpose of the meeting is apparent from the minutes, written in German, for the use of Renthe-Fink's staff. By way of introduction, Castenschiold pointed out that he had done what he could to cooperate with the Germans since the outbreak of war until 9 April 1940, but that the occupation had frozen any collaboration with foreign nations and thereby also with Germany.[21] Their decision had been taken in light of the general opinion among the Danish people, and because of both the King and the Prime Minister's inducement to correct and dignified conduct. Since the Danish public was not positively disposed toward German-Danish sporting events, there was a danger of demonstrations, which could threaten relations between the two countries. Furthermore, since sport was a voluntary activity, DIF could not guarantee that competitors would indeed turn up for these types of games.

That Castenschiold had hold of a convincing argument here can be seen in the way the German occupying authorities in Holland did *not* undertake international games in that country, despite the Dutch people in line with Danes being considered to be racially matched with Germany – although there was a measure of exchange through the participation of Dutch women swimmers at competitions in Germany.

The Reichssportführer Tschammer had argued that no Dutch-German international matches should be held in Holland since they might "bring the tempers of the Dutch supporters to boil, so they turn to political demonstration." As a rule, the German authorities did not intervene in the internal organisation of Dutch sports that continued at full tilt, since the attitude of the appointed Reich Commissioner, Arthur Seyss-Inquart, was "those who compete in sports don't sin." Dutch sporting associations were encouraged, however, to set up a single comprehensive federation, which continues to the present; while the decisive German intervention was that participation by Jewish sportspeople was outlawed. Over the course of 1941, Dutch Jews were removed from community life and a ban against Jewish participation in sport did not bring forth any great protest from other sporting circles.[22]

Nevertheless, Renthe-Fink was not inclined to sympathise with DIF's decision. He maintained that Germany had occupied Denmark to assist and protect the country, and he was convinced that the future would offer even closer ties between the two countries – also in the field of sport. He therefore hoped that the DIF leadership would resist any hostile attitude towards Germany instead of supporting it. If DIF was so afraid of demonstrations, one could always go ahead with a trial event. Why not test whether it was such an explosive proposition by continuing with a cancelled international fencing match? Since this would not be expected to attract a large crowd of spectators, and the match would be held indoors, then surely no great disturbance need be anticipated?

Castenschiold countered that a change of decision could not be carried out without informing all of the board members, as well as the various unions, and that DIF would therefore be obliged to account for the reasons behind the change. The only way a 'climb down' could be explained was that it "occurred under force of the German authorities". Renthe-Fink promptly replied that he was adverse to applying force and suggested that they all wait until the end of May, and thereafter overturn the decision. Castenschiold considered this to be unwise and underlined DIF's need to "insist" the issue only be brought up again after the end of summer.

Against such a background, the plenipotentiary could only conclude that the two parties were no nearer than before. Conversely, the discussion had now been simplified to a question of not *if* but *when* the new decision would come into force. Renthe-Fink reported back to the German foreign ministry that the ban on sporting relations was retained "due to the wishes of the Danish King."[23]

On 1 May, negotiations were conducted between Leo Frederiksen and the German football executive Dr Xandry, and it was officially decided to postpone matches until further notice. Hans Joachim Teichler, the German historian, has meanwhile shown that an internal agreement was reached between Frederiksen and the German executive that a match would be held between Germany and Denmark in the autumn, which became a reality on 17 November 1940.

On the home front, the Danish sport leadership apparently managed to resist

*In Holland and France, German occupying forces took charge of the various sports facilities and put them to use in their own tournaments and games. Such a situation is seen here from a football match in Paris at the prestigious Parc des Princes, on 8 August 1940, where Germany and Italy played on conquered French soil: a clear humiliation of a defeated enemy. In the photograph, a German officer congratulates the Italians on their 1-0 victory.*

German diplomatic pressure by referring to fears that Danish sportspeople would turn unfavourably against collaborative sports via demonstrations and boycotts. In the meantime, cracks were beginning to appear in their defence: partly through the way the question of when sporting relations would be resumed was slowly being reduced to a question of when the Danish people would mentally accept meeting German players on the sports field; and partly because Leo Frederiksen had already made a private agreement with the German football association that relations would be re-established by the autumn.

## The hard line begins to bend

The question of holding local matches against Germans became embarrassingly pertinent with a previously arranged match between a German team and a team from the Danish town of Holstebro. Holstebro football club had taken part in the Jutland championship division since 1933, and was a large club with some 350 members.[24]

The intention was to play the German team, but the local representative of DIF (from the West-coast town of Varde), P. Friis, who was also a committee member of the Danish Football Association (DBU), had imposed an injunction in the last moments before the match. The local German commandant then complained about the obstruction. So serious was the protest that it reached ears within the Danish foreign ministry. On 9 May, Major-General Castenschiold contacted the head of the press office for the foreign ministry, Karl Eskelund, who was responsible for censorship within the Danish press. To understand Eskelund's political inclinations, it should be mentioned that almost half a year later, in the winter of 1940-41, Eskelund made himself notable by proposing legislation for tighter restrictions on existing press regulations that would remove most of the press's remaining freedom. After heavy criticism, however, the proposal was turned down.[25]

Eskelund reported on the conflict in Holstebro with the clear intention of encouraging cooperation. Castenschiold replied that in his opinion the participation by German players in the club's daily activities was not unlawful, but that he would like to discuss the problem with Leo Frederiksen. Frederiksen agreed. It was not these kinds of low-key, everyday matches that DIF were so much against. It was more the pomp and ceremony at high-level sports events with music and national symbols that should be deterred. In short, it can be inferred that DIF's leadership were acknowledging that an unofficial match could be regarded uncontroversially, in terms of Danish public reaction. Leo Frederiksen could thereby reassure the "irate" Eskelund that the ban imposed by DBU only applied to matches between Danish clubs and German military teams with an official distinction. DBU could not hinder and had nothing against matches that took place in "an unobtrusive manner", nor against Germans training for Danish teams. This answer satisfied Eskelund who could convey the decision to the parties in Holstebro.

On 23 May, Castenschiold was contacted by Count Bent Holstein, who until 1922 had been a Conservative politician and afterwards an independent. Bent Holstein was closely connected to several top figures in the Danish Nazi Party and spoke at a number of their meetings. He was a contributor to the Nazi newspaper *Fædrelandet* [Fatherland] and in that capacity wrote a series of articles in 1939 that turned against the Danish Constitution as a French imported foreign element into Danish culture.[26]

At a board meeting on 7 June, Castenschiold gave an account of his meeting at the Danish foreign ministry with Renthe-Fink and related DBU's position that local matches between Germans and Danes were allowed. This gave no immediate grounds for raised eyebrows. Representatives from the provinces had sent in written declarations that a frictionless cooperation with the occupying powers was underway.[27] Th. A. Klostergaard from Aarhus stressed outright that German

*A Danish–German football match just one month after 9 April 1940. Football can open the doors for close contact and friendship between competitors, and can break down the 'mental and spiritual immune system' towards a totalitarian regime.*

military personnel using their facilities (such as their athletics track) behaved "in an exemplary manner", and the representative from Thisted, Marius Jørgensen, reported that certain clubs in his region had already accepted Germans as members, which allowed them opportunities for both training and appearing in club matches, all without rise to any contention. It can therefore be explicitly asserted that at an early stage, and before any change of course had been authorised by DIF, German soldiers were active in Danish clubs and associations.

Though there seemed to be a consensus within the DIF board, there were some objections. Ernst Petersen from Odense, as the only representative from the provinces to attend in person, came to the board meeting to challenge the prevailing authority. He later showed himself to be the sole member of DIF's inner circle to represent a counter position. He worked both on an illegal resistance publication, *Frit Denmark*,[28] and for a Danish democratic youth umbrella organisation, Dansk Ungdomssamvirke, supporting in November 1941 protests by Dansk Ungdomssamvirke against the Danish Government's signing of the Anti-Comintern Pact between Germany, Italy and Japan together with a number of German satellite States.[29]

Ernst Petersen also found other ways of protesting. In October 1940, he was instrumental in the founding of Odense Terrænsportsforening, an orienteering club practising semi-military exercises, which later became a recruitment source for the resistance movement.[30] Previous to the 7 June board meeting, Petersen had consulted his sports membership and ascertained "quite decisively" there was no wish to either train with or play against German troops. In his region, the position was that occupying forces were working exclusively to achieve propaganda effects. A sporting collaboration – just as with any other form of collaboration – would disguise the fact that the German occupation was "humiliating and tragic" and it would entail that both Danes and the international community would resign themselves to Denmark's fate in becoming a German protectorate.

This was not what the board wanted to hear, and Castenschiold placed a quick lid on any subsequent discussion. They should "in this matter leave behind their private feelings and instead concentrate on what is of benefit to us all." They would consider the matter further (but not with Ernst Petersen).

The timing of an opening up of attitudes by DIF towards Germany was hardly arbitrary. Germany embarked on the Western offensive in May 1940, and in the first days of June British soldiers had to evacuate from Dunkirk. The mental context had been adjusted far more to a sense of Denmark featuring in a Europe that had Germany as its uncontested principal superpower. DIF had gone over to adapting their organisation to the new situation, and it was up to individual associations to define how far they would go in terms of collaboration with the occupying powers. Through a decentralisation of sporting relations, DIF's top rid itself of its ethical obligations and no longer needed to make political decisions concerning concrete sporting events but rather leave this to the member organisations.

## "Fruit must not be picked until it is ripe"

By 8 June, the day after the board meeting, Renthe-Fink with some impatience paid a visit to Secretary Mohr at the Danish foreign ministry. The German plenipotentiary urged a memo onto the foreign minister, P. Munch, in which he called for action in the removal of DIF's ban against mutual sporting relations. According to Renthe-Fink, there was dissatisfaction in Danish sporting circles about DIF's restrictive policy. A new meeting for Renthe-Fink at the Ministry of Foreign Affairs was agreed on, for 27 June, in which Castenschiold's presence was also requested. At a previous meeting between Castenschiold and Mohr, Castenschiold claimed DIF was now placed in an intolerable situation, and demanded that the foreign ministry provide clarification: either the foreign ministry officially backed DIF or else it should accept the consequences of maintaining another position. Castenschiold would no longer take responsibility alone and therefore requested a written statement from the minister that he could put forward to his board: "a verbal expression of intention is no longer enough." If the foreign ministry believed it "lacked the authority to provide such recommendations to a voluntary organisation" or else did not believe that it was advisable to follow Renthe-Fink's wishes, then DIF intended to pursue its current course. In the autumn, according to their plan, DIF would then reopen negotiations concerning official games.

Castenschiold received no precise answer to this request. Mohr replied that since DIF was a voluntary organisation the foreign ministry could only contribute in an advisory capacity. He believed, however, that advice in this matter was difficult to give. Firstly, no-one in DIF could know the extent of the pressure Renthe-Fink might apply to remove the ban. According to Mohr, Renthe-Fink set great store by establishing good relations between Danes and Germans, and considered sport as a contributing factor. Secondly, the foreign ministry was unclear about how great would be the "animosity" in Danish sporting circles towards such a removal. If sporting relations were re-established too quickly, it might well be counter-productive. Secretary Mohr was direct in suggesting that good relations with Germany in the field of sport could have wider effects. Compliance could have a bearing on "the question of South Jutland"[31] as a resort against demands by Germanized Danes for the reunification of the South Jutlandic region with Germany: and it was essential that Renthe-Fink did not judge that they had rejected "an outstretched hand".

The opposing forces were thereby lined up for a decisive final meeting at the foreign ministry.[32] Castenschiold and Frederiksen attended, representing DIF. From the Danish foreign ministry there was Mohr and the head of the ministry's political-juridical department, Nils Svenningsen (who later became the ministry's Permanent Secretary). German interests were represented by Renthe-Fink and the attaché from the German embassy, Gebhard Seelos. Not surprisingly, the German delegation and DIF adopted widely opposing positions. Castenschiold maintained that a removal of the ban at the present could easily lead to a split in the Danish sporting movement. In which case he could not give any guarantees against demonstrations and "expressions of discontent" from either the public or via a boycott mounted by competitors. If this happened, DIF would be left looking like the proverbial black sheep. A premature removal would therefore – as Castenschiold put it – only damage that which "we both wish for." If the ban were dismantled here and now, then it could only be achieved, in Castenschiold's opinion, through a direct order from the German forces, for which Renthe-Fink had previously professed his reluctance.

Nevertheless, it now appeared clear that DIF and the German representatives no longer disagreed over the substance of the issue, but alone over the schedule for a relaxation of restrictions in sport. In DIF's new interpretation of its earlier declaration, Castenschiold claimed that DIF was already under way with joint activities that could be regarded as preparation for later unrestricted collaboration. The federation had thereby demonstrated its good will but as its chairman now put it "fruit must not be picked until it is ripe." He suggested again "in earnest" a postponement of negotiations until the autumn. But it was not going to be so easy for DIF, and the German negotiators (as previously in their dealings) now tried to drive a wedge between DIF and its membership. Renthe-Fink had, in his memo to P. Munch, pointed to dissatisfaction for the ban in Danish sporting circles. Castenschiold wished to know the details of who were specifically involved, and was told that the dissatisfaction comprised individuals from the boxing, wrestling, handball, swimming and cycling associations.[33] And so the pressure was squeezed up a notch. According to

Seelos, the DIF ban was actually the expression of a "plainly-put resistance towards Germany" and "it would be extremely unfortunate if they were forced to report to Berlin that no resolution had been forthcoming."

Castenschiold then asked, quite reasonably, whether this should be regarded as a threat, which Seelos denied. But Renthe-Fink, too, began to tighten the thumbscrews. He suggested it would be wise for DIF – before it was too late – to acknowledge that Germany and Denmark would be far more closely joined in the future. The plenipotentiary therefore, with regret, repeated that he must tell Berlin that no progress had been made since the meeting of 29 May.

It looked bleak for the DIF leadership, until Leo Frederiksen broke the deadlock. He reported that the Swedish football association had requested that negotiations be opened up for the resumption of sporting relations with Denmark, at a congress in Stockholm. He suggested, therefore, that they wait for the result of these negotiations. Renthe-Fink was apparently satisfied, and must have considered this an assurance that after a match against Sweden the path was clear for an international match against Germany. It was agreed that when negotiations with Sweden were closed and submitted to the DIF board, they would address the issue once again.

As became apparent, DIF's top chiefs were being pushed from both below by their own associations who wished to resume sporting collaboration, and from above by the occupying powers. The struggle was now over who would be left holding the baby, or in other words who would have to assume responsibility for the resumption: the foreign ministry via a directive; the occupying powers through threats and force; DIF's local unions or the DIF leadership itself. This ugly dance then took its first steps.

## "The Führer would be furious"

In Germany, developments were followed closely. The Reichssportführer, Tschammer, was so eager for the Danish and Swedish negotiations to turn out well that he asked the German Embassy in Stockholm to help the process along.[34] The 'carrot' in front of both the Danish and Swedish negotiators was that future games against Germany and the Axis powers could be better justified to opinion at home if matches between Nordic sister nations were taking place in parallel.

Following the football congress, Leo Frederiksen reported to Castenschiold on 12 July 1940. The Swedish delegates hoped that a match between the two countries could be arranged for 6 October to be held in Sweden, with a return match in Copenhagen two weeks later. If an international match against Germany should follow the Swedish matches, then Denmark would not be able to meet Germany until the latter half of November, since an international match required two months' preparation. Frederiksen and Castenschiold now planned a board meeting for 5 August,[35] with the aim of removing the ban; which they duly reported to Secretary Mohr.

DIF's peace of mind, however, did not last long. Already on the day following the two DIF leaders' meeting, Leo Frederiksen was invited to lunch at the fashionable Nimb restaurant by Seelos, the German press attaché, and Kurt Volkmann, who was responsible for German radio sports transmissions from Denmark.[36] The two Germans undoubtedly regarded Frederiksen as more manageable than his DIF chairman. It quickly became apparent, as expected, that the meeting was aimed at an immediate removal of the ban, especially in respect of swimming, for which the Germans hosts would dearly love to have Danish swimmers along for a competition in Germany, set for 7 August 1940.

Frederiksen's German dining companions had apparently got wind of the planned removal, since they stressed that the competition would take place two days after the expected lifting of the ban, which would be too late to plan Danish participation at the contest. Seelos implied that the president for the Danish swimming association, Niels Bruun Jagd, a civil engineer, was interested in Danish participation but was obliged to reject the German initiative in reference to DIF's decision.

Seelos explained that he dared not report back on DIF's position to his superiors in Germany. In fact, the issue was so important that "the Führer would be furious. In view of the consequences, it would be foolish of Denmark not to support Germany." It was evident that Seelos felt his standpoint was strong since he then pointed out that, if Scavenius had been Minister at the last meeting, another result entirely would have emerged, and that Mohr, too, was critical of DIF. According to Seelos, the war would be over by 1 September, and if Denmark had not allied itself with Germany by then it would be too late.

### The ban is raised

Castenschiold was acutely aware that the board was left with a major issue. He opened the board meeting on 5 August 1940,[37] stressing the proceedings were confidential, after which he stated that German patience was coming to an end. In an attempt to bring up pressure from below for a resumption of sporting relations, he then asked if any of the associations had received "calls from either Danish or German interests for cooperation with Germany".

The problem for Castenschiold was simply that although some of his heads of association had doubtless given Germans an impression of Danish interest in resuming full sporting relations they nevertheless were wise enough not to promote the point to the board, thereby pulling off on a course that would undermine DIF.

The head of the swimming association, Niels Bruun Jagd, could not be cajoled into giving an opinion since he had not turned up. Castenschiold instead turned to Jagd's deputy, Svend Nørregaard, who revealed that Kurt Volkmann had indeed approached him regarding a swimming tournament in Germany, but Nørregaard had rejected the approach, referring to both DIF's stance and the fact that the swimmers had not been permitted by their parents – the last claim being of interest since it may indicate that the swimming association had indeed discussed the possibility of attending. Volkmann had replied that DIF's stance could certainly be changed and referred to Leo Frederiksen, but Nørregaard had subsequently heard nothing more from Volkmann.

Castenschiold did not pursue this tack further. Instead he gave a report on developments since their previous board meeting, saying the actual problem was the degree to which the ban should be lifted; their standpoint towards Germany being "crucial". At the same time, the chairman explained that it would be unwise to resist Germany's repeated advances. He then put forward a proposal by the executive committee for a new decision in which DIF would leave "individual associations freely enfranchised in respect of sporting collaboration with other nations." Castenschiold hereby precluded the DIF leadership from becoming the motive force behind and guarantor for specific collaborative events, responsibility for which would now be passed over to the associations. He urged that the first match to take place on Danish soil should be against a country other than Germany, and that the remaining associations postpone any Danish-German collaboration until after the football match between Denmark and Sweden in October.

What worried the board members most, apparently, was not an ethical slide in the direction of collaboration with the Germans but rather how Danish supporters would react to official matches against Germany. The leadership stressed its belief in the population's understanding that any wish to resume international sports would unavoidably involve matches against Germany: moreover, they had already agreed on two dates for matches between Denmark and Sweden, and a further match against Germany set for November 1940. Castenschiold assured them Renthe-Fink approved of the procedure of first playing Sweden and only then Germany. Leo Frederiksen, too, argued for the importance of only embarking on sports with Germany until after the match against Sweden on 6 October.

It was an obvious sign that the board had been reduced to the job of rubber stamping the process. But there was resistance. As expected it came from Ernst Petersen, and again his was the only voice. If the decision was approved then he would resign from the board. Castenschiold replied that he and Leo Frederiksen were convinced a removal of the ban was the only correct procedure and that they would not take responsibility for it remaining in place alone. Furthermore, if Ernst Petersen wanted to resign his seat, it should not happen as a demonstration but be calmly and quietly handed in at the next representatives' meeting in the autumn. To do otherwise risked serious knock-on effects among the various associations and unions.

This brought the other board members out of their seats. In principle, they agreed with Ernst Petersen but in their capacity as board members they were obliged to put their feelings to one side and think of the best interests of sport and the country.

After the meeting, the approved decision was sent to the press office of the foreign ministry and thereafter to the Ritzaus Bureau news agency. By 7 August, the Royal Danish Embassy in Berlin could inform the Danish foreign ministry of German press announcements, from the same day, of a resumption of collaboration with Danish sports. Football and handball matches between Denmark, Sweden and Germany could soon be expected. The Danish foreign ministry confirmed in a letter to DIF two days later that desires for recommencing the collaboration had been pushed forward by German sources "with great force". On 11 August, Castenschiold received a letter of appreciation from Renthe-Fink in which he expressed his pleasure at the DIF decision.[38]

German interests wished for the resumed games to begin in Germany, as Castenschiold's warnings of spectator disturbances were taken seriously; and the German people were in need of a moment of normality through sporting entertainment.[39] The DIF leadership ended by assuming formal responsibility for the collaboration, although the business of actual events was left entirely to individual unions and associations.

At last there was an opportunity to gauge fairly how sporting circles would react to a revival of competitions against Germany. The newspaper *Socialdemokraten* told its readers that football matches against both Sweden and Germany could be expected,[40] while *Idrætsbladet* received the news with a cheer.[41]

Many of the individual unions supported the decision. DBU, especially, showed "the greatest interest for resuming our international sporting relations." Kristian Middelboe, the Danish football pioneer, former national coach and DBU vice-chairman, could report that "an international match will be negotiated as soon as possible with the German football association," but it was as yet unclear whether the match would be held at home or in Germany. Middelboe was particularly pleased since international matches were once "DBU's economic ballast and in pure sporting terms it is utterly necessary to compete between nations." Others followed in this wake. The treasurer of the boxing association, Alfred Overgaard, who had also been a judge at the Berlin Olympics in 1936, announced that a postponed tournament against Germany was the first item on their programme. He was also frank enough to add "in all honesty, we have hoped for some time to re-establish our connections to the outside world."

The athletics association gave a positive response. This was not so surprising, since its head from 1940 to 1943, Svend Jensen, was an organised Nazi.[42] He naturally greeted "with pleasure" the opportunity to resume international relations but regretted the late timing: "We only have planned arrangements with two international opponents in athletics – Norway and Germany – and we should have competed against them, at away matches, this year. The Norwegians informed us a while ago they were unable to hold an international games this year, and we've heard nothing from Germany." It would soon become apparent that the Germans were more than interested.[43]

# THE STRUGGLE FOR DENMARK'S YOUTH

Germany wished to show a human face, and Denmark's role as advertising space for this attempt meant that of all the occupied countries Denmark had the best chance to preserve remnants of its independence in a newly organised Europe. But everything, of course, proceeded only by the grace of the Führer.

The DIF leadership decision to resume sporting relations with Germany could have been impelled by anxieties about a Nazi accession to Government in Denmark, and thereby to a Nazification of sport along similar lines to Norway. In Castenschiold's words, from 5 August 1940, it was undeniably preferable to remain at the negotiation table with Germany and according to him "the bow was now bent so far backwards that it cannot be pulled further without breaking." With this comment he undoubtedly referred to fears of direct German intervention. On the one hand, such threats became more realistic some time after DIF had reached its decision. To all intents, it was chiefly the astounding German victory and the prospects of a generation-long occupation that made DIF consider collaboration. In contrast, plans for sports drawn up by Danish Nazis become interesting on two points: they show how Nazi sports might have turned out, and also, according to Nazi papers for the reorganisation of sport, how several well-regarded heads of sport gave the plans their support.

Around 1 August 1940, Hitler approved a proposal from the German foreign ministry to provide the National Socialist Workers' Party of Denmark (DNSAP) with an economic injection to prepare for an accession to Government in Denmark. In the same year, on 22 October, Renthe-Fink formally called for a change of Government. Thus encouraged, Danish Nazis began an offensive that in November culminated in a large-scale meeting at the Forum hall and a march to *Den Lille Hornblæser* statue in the city square, in Copenhagen.

The National Socialist Workers' Party of Denmark was founded in 1930 by the co-founder of the Danish boy scouts association, Cay Lembcke, a Captain in the Danish Horse Guards.[1]

The structure and politics of DNSAP was all but a direct copy of the German party. Political dialogue was to be replaced by corporal manifestations, such as parades and mass rallies with the aesthetics of uniforms and banners, which as a rule ended up looking fairly pitiful because of the party's weak support.

Danish Nazis pursued a strategy of agitation towards the youth of Denmark involved in sports, with a result that the board of the Danish boxing association advised clubs to avoid political discussions. A Danish Nazi and trainer for the association, Valdemar Haakonsen, who travelled throughout Denmark, offering free trips to Germany and German-occupied Holland, was thereby relieved of his position as a trainer but not excluded from the association.[2]

In the late summer of 1940, the DNSAP sent 250-300 young Danish men on a six-month programme, to Klagenfurt in the Austrian Alps, provoking a reaction from DIF board member Ernst Petersen. The programme turned out to be nothing less than a training camp for "Waffen SS" and 5/6 of the participants went home again. In all likelihood, no DIF members took part, but members did participate from the South Jutlandic sports organisation Sønderjysk Idrætsforening. According to the historian Jørgen Hæstrup, the Danish Nazi aim was to infiltrate Danish youth and sports organisations. As a counter-measure, Castenschiold opened discussions with the education ministry about implementing a course in athletics instruction, which would take place that same year:[3] but changes in the national political climate began to have an influence.

The autumn of 1940 was coloured by rumours of an impending Danish Nazi seizure of power, and this may have reinforced DIF's conviction in its decision to resume sporting competitions with the occupying forces. Danish Nazis were also putting pressure on DIF. In the sports section of their paper *Fædrelandet*, the criticism of DIF was bitter, and the threat of a Nazi takeover of Danish sport was a recurring theme. By 16 and 17 August 1940, the federation had already been accused of being a most "irrelevant, dilettante 'administration'". A warning was issued that when the DNSAP leader Frits Clausen ran the country then "Danish national socialist sports groups with their membership, already in the thousands" would step into each and every post throughout Danish sport.[4]

All through the autumn, DNSAP stepped up its sports campaign. On 6 September and again on 15 October 1940, they published an invitation to a film screening, presenting lectures by well-known "medical advisers, sports instructors and heads of sport" to make members aware of the party programme for sport. The two articles were signed 'head of sport' and Poul Olsen, respectively, which later proved to be the same person. The *Fædrelandet* articles included sketched designs for a completely new structuring of the Danish sports system. It was claimed that the various sports associations had witnessed a "colossal intake" over the recent weeks, and included among the membership were "nationally if not internationally renowned Danish sports men and women".

To better understand the Danish Nazis and thereby the pressure against DIF, it is necessary to look a little more closely at the nature of Nazism itself. Involved in Nazism was both the idea of a Hitler-oriented subjugating imperialism intent on creating a Greater Germany with its *Lebensraum* to the East, as well as a more 'romantic' idea – but one that became less politically influential over the duration of the Third Reich – centring on of a *völkisch* conception of the people and the Aryan people's right to exercise their innate power and realise their potential. However unrealistic, the Danish Nazis were attracted to the romantic *völkisch* variant of Nazism, which also left room for organising sport on a national level. Against this background, plans for a new structuring of sports were drawn up by Poul Olsen.[5]

The plans were to be approved by Frits Clausen. They were confidential: "it could lead to the greatest detriment if these papers fell into the wrong hands or their contents became known by unwelcome interests," and thereby complicate further work. The plan was put together between 9 and 10 January 1941,[6] at a point when DNSAP's route to power was turning out to be long, rocky and even impassable. It is also apparent that the political climate had not reached a point whereby heads of sport could openly display sympathy for National Socialism. They would be "ostracised, and we are not in the least well-served by such a development at the current time." The plans were to be put before a small Nazi group meeting, for whom short papers would be presented by four invited heads of sport: providing us with a good picture of how sport in Nazi Denmark was to be structured. The head of the Copenhagen athletics association, Johannes Bojesen Barsøe, the main leadership figure from cycling, Jørgen Beyerholm [Senior], and the chairman of the capital's main rowing club, Københavns Roklub, Poul Kragh, were credited as authors for a portion of the presentation, under the title "heads of sport to be". The archives mention nothing relevant for the last-named, but Bojesen Barsøe was secretary of the Danish Athletics Federation 1932-42, chairman of the athletics association in Copenhagen and the sports editor of *Kristeligt Dagblad*, from 1935. A talented athlete himself, Bojesen Barsøe also showed great initiative as an organiser, arranging competitions between Oslo and Copenhagen, and the Danish provinces and Copenhagen.

In short, the people present were all important for their particular sporting disciplines. Bojesen Barsøe and Beyerholm were also contributing authors of articles for the Danish encyclopaedia of sport, *Dansk Sportsleksikon*, from 1945 but presumably written in 1943, in which they were the only authors to include pictures of German athletes wearing the swastika and German eagle emblems on their shirts. In the passage from the same encyclopaedia edited by Beyerholm about the Berlin to Copenhagen cycle races, the only photographs of the Nazi swastika can be found.[7] In another work on the history of the Danish Bicycle Club, from 1941, it is also apparent that it was hardly an anti-German feeling he cultivated. One of the images shows Danish cyclists wearing the winners' wreath bearing a swastika, and there is likewise a picture of Beyerholm in conversation with the Reichssportführer.

These two heads of sport – Bojesen Barsøe and Jørgen Beyerholm – featured in plans from different motivations. Bojesen Barsøe was considered by Poul Olsen to be an important player in the start-up of a new order in that unlike anyone else he would "be able to gather all the sports disciplines together into a common productive collaboration." He was the only head in Denmark who could "get each and every organiser and competitor to cooperate with the new Government already from day one," and his name was a guarantee for the plan's good intentions, creating a "smooth succession" for the new national federation. Jørgen Beyerholm was considered the person to have most public appeal. As the head of Dansk Bicycle Club he had organised cycle races with German competitors at the track at Ordrup both before and during the occupation.[8]

The plan would be implemented as soon as DNSAP had taken charge of Denmark. The plan was structured on a model for "current" and future national socialist countries, so to avoid any "divergences". Besides DIF, DDG and DDSGI (the Danish gymnastics, and the shooting, gymnastics and athletics associations) would also be dissolved and instead brought in under a federation for the Danish Realm. According to the proposal, the incorporated DIF would have no real influence in the day-to-day business of sport, which would now be run top-down on a national basis and be subject to "the firmest control and leadership".

In contrast to DIF, which at the time had no special legislative articles on its social function,[9] the new order would instead use sport as an instrument to promote health and hygiene amongst the Danish population. By transforming sport into a people's movement "Denmark's state of health would be raised by an enormous degree."

All sports – including professional sports – would be organised under a new ministry for health, in which a national head of sport would have overall command. Their plans went beyond authorisations that the Nazi party had otherwise conferred on national-level leadership, as the party would "monitor, investigate and control legislative work within the ministry." Their plans also clearly surpassed the party's intentions about a ministry of health, which did not prioritise sport over other health-related areas and included "nursing, child care, pharmaceuticals, dietary issues, hygiene, sports, etc."[10] The national head of sport in the new order was to be a DNSAP member, and should have thorough knowledge of sporting organisations, for which the plan recommended the same Poul Olsen. Under his leadership, there would be five chiefs of sport, each with thorough knowledge of their respective sports disciplines, each with responsibility for a "department". Four of the five had, supposedly, already agreed to step up in the new federation. According to the plan, sport would become financially independent, by measures such as introducing legislation to allow bookmaking; which was actually introduced but only in 1948. The sports leadership would receive its income from and be trained at the German Nazi national academy for physical education in Berlin.

Details of the plan[11] were that Department 1 would be responsible for ball games, including football, handball, tennis, badminton, cricket, hockey and golf. Its chief was to be a former player for the Copenhagen top club KB, and a barrister, Jørgen Cold, who was also earlier a member of the KB board. As KB organised several ball-game disciplines, Cold was claimed to enjoy great trust among the various relevant sports, and was one of Denmark's "most well-thought-of leaders within ball games." Department 2 would cover boxing, wrestling, weight lifting, fencing and athletics. Its chief would be Bojesen Barsøe. Department 3 dealt with about all of the important field then covered by Danish rural gymnastics and shooting associations. It would have responsibility for gymnastics, shooting, training of coaches, hygiene and sports training colleges. Within this department, the State gymnastics institute, today the Copenhagen University Department of Exercise and Sport Sciences, Institut for Idræt, would be allocated a place. The head of sports would be Dr Viggo Munck, a general practitioner and sports physician for various worker's sports groups. Over many years, he had worked as a sports physician and his connections to democratic circles and organisations was considered by Olsen to be crucial on "the day he steps up publicly as a sports chief among our ranks." Furthermore, Munck had written on the best conditions for fostering National Socialism in *Nationalsocialismens Opdragelsesprincipper*, in 1934, and was therefore well known as an important part of "our sporting endeavour".

Viggo Munck also knew rural gymnastics from his days as a teacher, from 1921 to 1927, at Niels Bukh's gymnastics folk high school in Ollerup. He wrote enthusiastically in various sports magazines about the Nazi programme for youth education, not least its use of sport. He sensed parallels between an important Danish people's countryside movement, known as Grundtvigianism, and Nazism in its impression of "a German country and landscape, a German people's character, German life and its conditions, German work, its history, its rights and its culture." From these principles "conclusions should be drawn and acted on, to be made fruitful in raising the German people. We cannot help but notice a fellowship between these thoughts and Grundtvig's plans for science-based academies, with the people and the people's culture at their centre." Munck was also affected by Nazi ideas about 'the organism' and said at one point that "national socialism puts the people above the individual, in the same way as the body is more than its single parts."[12]

Department 4, headed by Beyerholm, took care of professional sports such as cycling, both track and road racing, horseracing, both trotting and race, and pigeon racing. Department 5 was concerned with those sports disciplines that had a certain 'privileged class' flavour and included rowing, sailing, kayaking, skating, riding and swimming. The department chief was to be Poul Kragh, chairman of Københavns Roklub, who had been chosen because of his ability.

These concrete plans, including the names of heads and departments, remained secret throughout the occupation. Poul Olsen, however, never concealed the intentions behind them. In *Fædrelandet*, on 16 March 1941, a full-page interview with him was published entitled "How sports and athletics will be organised in the New Denmark".[13] The piece reproduced a summary of the plan with an additional comment that sport should get rid of certain "unlucky elements" within its leadership. Furthermore, the press would function as an "information conduit to the people". To ensure that journalists were up to their task, the Nazis sports groups would organise "a form of school for would-be sports journalists". A comparable arrangement was proposed for sports photographers. The title of sports instructor would be achievable in the same way as in the forces, so only the "most entirely-suitable people" could take part in instructor training.

Although the chances of the plan being carried out were small, DIF took them seriously. Partly this was to do with the details, and partly the political situation was so unstable because of the occupation that it was deemed necessary to be prepared well in advance. On the whole, the leadership of DIF were highly well-informed and it is therefore likely that the article in *Fædrelandet* had come to their attention. At a board meeting on 3 March 1941,[14] Castenschiold mentioned "The Danish national socialist sports groups" whom he nevertheless refused to enter into collaboration with since they "belong to a political party".

The ambitions of the Danish Nazis to play a role in Danish Government was, however, an illusion. Although Renthe-Fink spoke again and again for the admission of Nazis to Government, he was in reality highly sceptical of DNSAP. Wisely, he kept his scepticism to himself, so as not to give away a trump card into the hands of the Danish authorities. An attempt to seize power by DNSAP was planned to take place on 17 November 1940, where a large demonstration with Frits Clausen at its head would lay a wreath dedicated to the fallen from 9 April beneath *Den Lille Hornblæser* in the main city square. It ended, however, with a somewhat dismal defeat and street fighting whereby numerous Nazis were given a severe beating by furious Copenhageners. Almost a month later, Danish Nazis were involved in fighting with Danish police in Haderslev, and in February 1941 Renthe-Fink was able to report to the German foreign ministry on DNSAP ambitions, assessing however that Denmark run by the DNSAP would not especially assist German interests any more than the present Danish coalition Government did. And apart from a show of temper by Hitler over the so-called 'telegram crisis' in the winter of 1942, DNSAP retained a marginal place in the plans of the occupying powers.[15] But if the German choice was between the Danish Nazis and the Danish authorities, it was not always certain whether the Germans would play their trump card, should they find relations with their tiny neighbour to be a nuisance. But after the general election in March 1943, in which DNSAP failed to make significant headway, any plans for a seizure of power by Danish Nazis were simply judged to be totally unrealistic.

The Danish Nazis' plans for sport never came to anything. But even if the DNSAP had taken power, events would never have gone as they planned. By all accounts, Frits Clausen was not convinced of the value of either Olsen as a national administrator or his initiatives. Accordingly, Olsen was not among the many national leaders named in February 1941. Perhaps Clausen had realised the dilettante nature of having a ministry of health led by a national head of sport, organised around sports departments. In addition, the individual sports groups were never big enough to provide the proper stage-set for the party leadership, on a level that could even suggest that of the German sister party.[16] Conversely, it must have been satisfying to have a pair of active heads of sport from both professional and amateur levels apparently lining up under the party banner. The sports plans must have remained a sensitive issue for insiders up until 1943, however, since Bojesen Barsøe did not put forward his plans for bookmaking, or proposals for his own position as a head of sport in a new federation, until as late as March the same year, at an athletics association committee meeting; at a time when most Danes realised that Germany could never win the war.[17] As an organisation, DIF kept the Danish Nazis at arm's length throughout the occupation. The only direct contact consisted of an application, at the end of 1943, by the youth wing of the Danish National Socialist Party to become members of DIF, turned down on the grounds that DIF did not accept political organisations. The same refusal and the same grounds were given to the Conservative youth wing for a similar inquiry in 1944.[18]

In his studies of Danish cultural life under the occupation, Hans Hertel, professor of the sociology of literature, has shown that pro-Nazi groups and individuals cannot be dismissed as harmless even though, according to Hertel, a large section of these should be considered marginalised, frustrated 'small fry': they nevertheless commanded "a large network of institutions, subsidiaries and potentials capable of effecting opinion – and had a considerable reserve force of also-rans and passive sympathisers, who in a particular situation, as during a Nazi takeover, could have filled the positions of education and cultural policy administration."[19] Shedding light on these groups and individuals who, like Niels Bukh, found themselves in a grey area between Nazism and the traditional radical right wing,[20] appears to be an important task for our understanding of collaboration in Denmark.

# ENGLISH OPPOSITION TO COLLABORATION

The important Danish sports magazine *Idrætsbladet* reported positively on Danish-German joint activities up until the cessation of sporting relations at the beginning of 1942, but continued to cover sports events in Germany for a year more. Sports news in the main Danish newspapers such as *Politiken*, *Socialdemokraten* and *Berlingske Tidende*, too, did not fail to cover Danish-German events, all described with pride and veneration.[1] It would have been difficult to advance negative remarks about matches because of censorship, meaning that any critical articles or readers' letters would have been screened. Even the Communist newspaper *Arbejderbladet*, still active due to the German-Soviet Non-Aggression Pact from 1939 to June 1941, could yield up column space for a number of Danish-German sports events in its rather limited sports section.[2]

Altogether, the press was generally uncritical of Germany in its sports coverage. And the press could have chosen to tone down its reports on sporting collaboration with the occupying forces, of its own volition.

Only one sports periodical turned out against collaborative sporting relations with Germany. From January until March 1941, a magazine was issued called *Fodbold – hele landets magasin* [Football – a magazine for the whole country], with a subtitle proclaiming "The magazine you've been waiting for", and on the first page a large drawing of a football inscribed with the English word "Improved".[3] The English inscription was hardly a coincidence, given that the editor was Harold Philipson, of British extraction. To a great degree, the motivation for this opposition to collaborative relations was an affinity for Great Britain, as was the case with the Danish hockey association and its chairman, George Peel Harvey, a civil engineer, who as part of the DIF board refused to vote for the removal of the ban on Danish-German collaborative sports. Philipson attempted to mobilise the pleasure Danes took from the football game invented by the British, to turn Danes away from collaboration with the Germans and instead channel their interest into matches, internally, between Danish clubs, or into a Nordic community feeling, embodied in Swedish football. "Danish football will get all the space it needs in *Fodbold,* as our regional staff will be writing about what's going on in exactly their area." "International football: contact to the outside world will not be missing and, to the extent that it is possible at the current time, international football will also have its place in *Fodbold*. First and foremost, this means our friends across the Danish-Swedish Sound."[4] And not

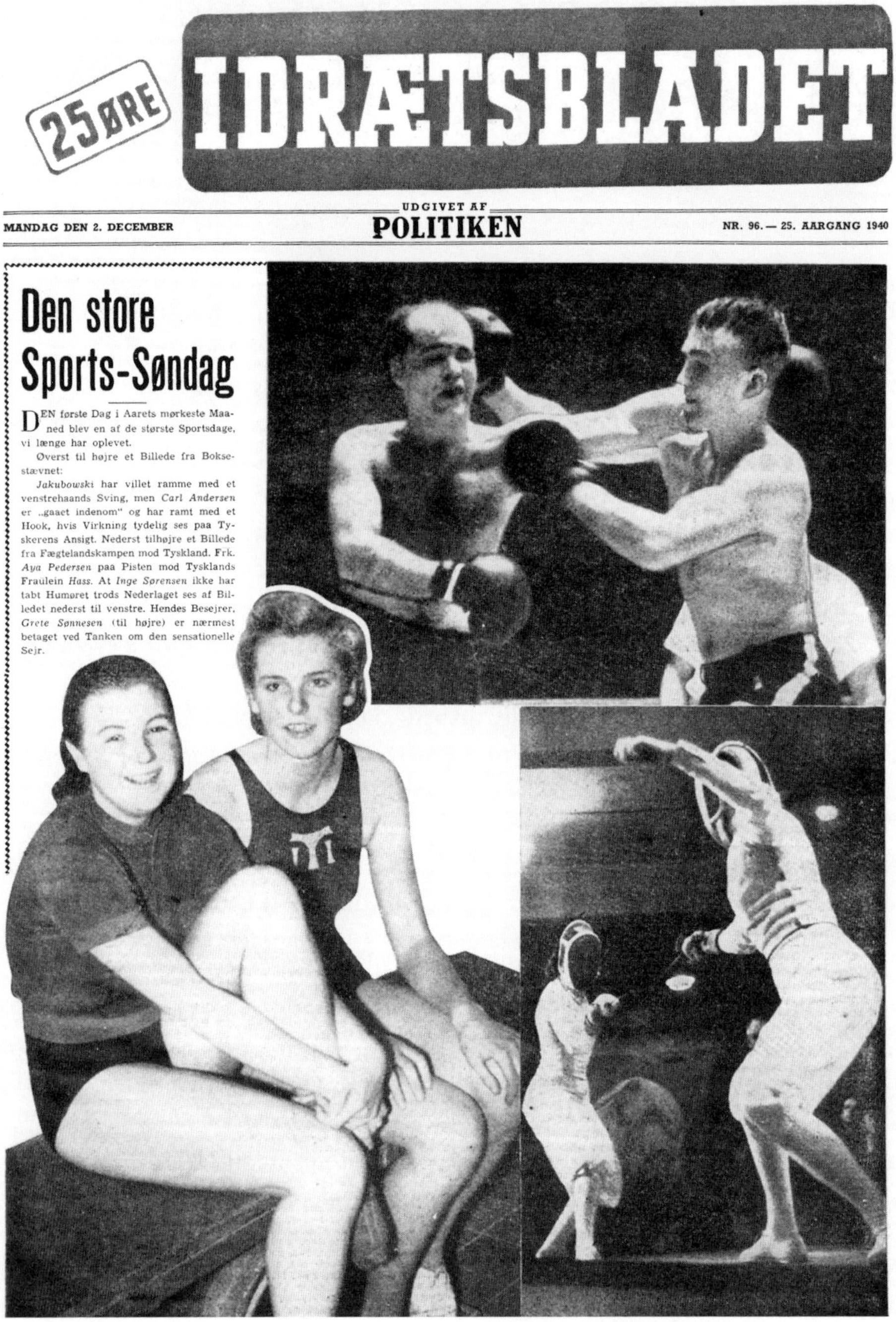

25 ØRE

# IDRÆTSBLADET

MANDAG DEN 2. DECEMBER — UDGIVET AF POLITIKEN — NR. 96. — 25. AARGANG 1940

## Den store Sports-Søndag

DEN første Dag i Aarets mørkeste Maaned blev en af de største Sportsdage, vi længe har oplevet.

Øverst til højre et Billede fra Boksestævnet:

*Jakubowski* har villet ramme med et venstrehaands Sving, men *Carl Andersen* er „gaaet indenom" og har ramt med et Hook, hvis Virkning tydelig ses paa Tyskerens Ansigt. Nederst tilhøjre et Billede fra Fægtelandskampen mod Tyskland. Frk. *Aya Pedersen* paa Pisten mod Tysklands Fraülein *Hass*. At *Inge Sørensen* ikke har tabt Humøret trods Nederlaget ses af Billedet nederst til venstre. Hendes Besejrer, *Grete Sønnesen* (til højre) er nærmest betaget ved Tanken om den sensationelle Sejr.

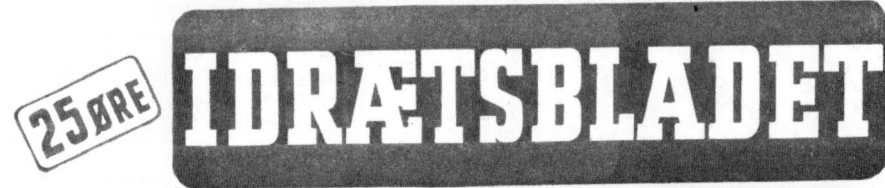

Idrætsbladet *was Denmark's largest sports newspaper, with an increasing circulation during the first years of the war. The paper knew how to spread an enthusiasm for sport during the dark days of the war. Here, for example, in December 1940, where "the first day in the darkest time of the year became one of the greatest sports days we've seen in a long while" with Danish–German collaborative sports in boxing and fencing.*

*Advertisements for sports goods available from a Reich sport fair in Leipzig in autumn of 1941 and spring 1942 – with special trains organised, departing from Copenhagen. Collaborative sporting relations between Denmark and Germany included sports wear and equipment, too.*

only were Danish-Swedish competitions covered but also "the continuing Swedish league" that "Steve" had already reported on, in the first number.

Harold Philipson's life-long passion, however, was not football but that quintessentially English game cricket. He had played in approximately 200 matches in the Danish first division, had organised several visits by English cricket teams and in 1926 was responsible for a Gentlemen of Denmark cricket tour of England. In addition, he had been the editor of a periodical, *Cricket*, during the 1930s, but by 1941 had realised that the struggle over the political direction of sport was taking place around football.

It would hardly have been Philipson's 'cup of tea' when his competitor, Gunnar Hansen, editor of *Idrætsbladet*, was able to report in May 1941 that Danish cricketers would soon be playing with German 'stolen goods'. There had been some concern in Danish cricketing circles "at how to acquire new equipment, but it now seems that a large consignment of bats and balls is on its way from Germany: an estimated 60 balls and around two hundred bats. The British goods, on their way

*During censorship, sympathies towards great Britain found subtle expression. A football bearing English print, used as the front page of the footballing magazine* Fodbold, *from January 1941. This magazine was the only publication wherein traces of opposition to collaborative sporting relations with Germany could be traced.*

from England to India, or vice versa, did not get any further than Berlin. And they don't play cricket in Germany."[5]

As a sign of the British orientation for the new magazine, great emphasis was placed on 'fair play' and the referee's rulebook. A series was also included on the memoirs of a popular Danish football player, Carl 'Shoemaker' Hansen, covering his time as a professional for the Scottish club Glasgow Rangers. Incidentally, Carl 'Shoemaker' was notable during the occupation for a prison term he received for "beating up a German civilian" in October 1943.[6]

Niels Middelboe, who had played in the English league, including a period as striker for Chelsea until 1922, and who had lived in London from 1913 to 1936, was given the job of writing a history of football that, because of the game's development, focused to a great extent on its British roots. Even Philipson wrote a series on "The language of football" that unsurprisingly pointed out its English origins. Philipson made use of the occasion to argue for the close kinship between Danish and English, and that an English glossary had become a natural part of the Danish language. The Germans, too, believed that the struggle over language was important and can be seen from attempts in the Fatherland to remove English sporting terms such as 'match', 'kicker' and 'kick'. In occupied Holland, the German authorities banned the use of English sports terminology, and in games such as cricket or tennis scores were not allowed to be given in English. The Dutch tennis player Hans van Swol received several minutes' applause when, in a match in 1941, he repeated the scores that the judge had given in Dutch, but in English.[7]

There was also a 'readers' letters' page in Philipson's periodical that the editors had given an English twist from the beginning, by publishing anonymous questions from "people from around the country who have heard that *Fodbold* was on its way." The first question asked "couldn't the planned football magazine do an article on the English club Arsenal, that we're all interested in, in our area?"[8] Because of censorship, it was not always easy to print direct sentiments that were friendly towards England, and the magazine ceased publication altogether after only three months. Whether this was a result of censorship, or from a lack of adequate interest in football is not known; or whether it was because the Danish public found no excitement in a magazine that toned down Danish games against German competitors?

# PROFESSIONAL SPORT

Danish sport was not especially professionalised in the first half of the twentieth century: what professional sports there were at the time occurring chiefly in boxing and cycling. So when the wider European market became curtailed after the beginning of the occupation, German professional sports became even more important for Danish cycle riders and boxers. An interest and pleasure can be noted in the Danish press because of the recognition from German sources given to professional Danish athletes. Perhaps one reason why no concern can be traced about competing in collaborative sports against the occupying forces is that professional sportspeople thought of themselves in the same way as in any other field cooperating on an economic basis.[1] Sport was just another professional vocation – despite the rare symbolic value sport could have, and that many doubtless had the opportunity to find alternative employment – so it all came down to a question of earning a living.

## Cycling

Among international cyclists, the victorious German road racer Harry Saagar was especially celebrated in Danish quarters. In May 1941, a professional race, the Rudersdalløb, was staged by the Dansk Bicycle Club. As in the previous year, the race was held in bad weather and although around 5,000 Danish spectators turned out to watch there were probably more who stayed away because of the rain and cold that continued throughout the day. The Danish riders had the advantage of being able to support each other in contrast to the two German riders; and as Emil Schöpflin retired early from the race, Harry Saagar was left alone. 50 metres from the finish line, Rudolf Rasmussen, the previous year's winner, led the field in a nerve-racking climax in front of an ecstatic Danish crowd, but then Saagar pressured him on the inside and passed him, and in the final dash the German held onto an easy 1-meter advantage all the way to the finish line.

*Idrætsbladet* was extremely enthusiastic about Saagar, who for his part also spoke well of the Danish competitors. Under the title "Winner of the Rudersdalløb: a tough road race and fine tactical ride by the Danish cyclists". In the same way as the year before, the magazine ran a photograph of the winner wearing the characteristic eagle and swastika badge on his jersey, with Saagar clearly surrounded by a crowd, wanting to get close to their cycling hero. Saagar's countryman, too, was interviewed and talked about the injury that had forced him to drop out. When German riders were in Denmark, they happily took part in more than just one race, and at the end of May Harry Saagar again beat the whole of Danish elite cycling by winning the Storstrømsbro race, again outdistancing Rudolf Rasmussen over the last meter.[2]

Among Danish riders, the big trump card over the first half of the occupation period was Willy Falck Hansen, a track racer and the most successful Danish professional of the period. The great breakthrough in professional collaborative sports with Germany under the occupation came when he won the sprint competitions between Germany, Italy and Denmark, in Berlin towards the end of 1940.

*Idrætsbladet* came out with a front page saluting "Willy Falck Hansen's major triumph in Deutschlandhalle". In the final half minute, Falck Hansen – also called Scout because as a boy he had raced in scout uniform – broke away from a strong competition that included the Italian Astolfi, and the two Germans Tony Merkens (OL gold medallist in sprint, in 1936) and Jean Schorn. The competition gave German fans an opportunity to show their appreciation of a small occupied country in the North. Spectators "cheered on the Dane until hoarse with excitement, the man who was oldest of the group but fastest of them all." Falck Hansen was also cheered on by hundreds of Danish workers at the German Siemens factories. Other Danish riders, too, performed well. Mogens Danholt won an international points race over 20 stages, in front of the Italian Bergomi.[3]

Eventually, as the winter season of 1940-41 rolled on, Falck Hansen, along with Knud Jacobsen whose main strength was not in track but road racing, took part in further races; but not quite reaching the same heights. To give an example, they lost a pair's match but were able to gain some consolation, according to the Nazi newspaper *Fædrelandet*, because the two winning German riders "were very unpopular due to their unfair racing" whereas "the Danish pair were the object of an enormous ovation."[4]

To use a phrase from shares trading, both boxers and cyclists could make a bomb out of the market for foreign professionals in Germany. Knud Jacobsen and Peter Hansen, both cyclists, were in Germany from the end of May 1941 for three weeks and, according to themselves, their sizable earning turned out to be 'very satisfactory'. Knud Jacobsen was a notable rider. When still an amateur, he won 60 important Danish road races and the Nordic championships in 1936. Subsequently, he competed in the German road championships, Deutschland Tour, as well as in the Berlin Olympics, after which he turned professional in October 1936.[5]

When the winter track season was over, in which Jacobsen performed without great success, he competed in a number of German road races. In these he performed slightly better. He won a race in Magdeburg, finished eighth at a championships in Dortmund that was won by Majerus of Luxembourg, and was placed in two further races. Peter Hansen cut less of a figure over the four races he competed in.[6] Despite the not-quite stunningly good results, the Danes were engaged by a German company-sponsored team, which must be taken as an indication of healthy war-time market conditions for Danish riders.

From the Danish point of view, professional cycling was eager for an intense Danish-German collaboration. On 11 February 1941, five top leaders from Dansk Bicycle Union watched the track races at Deutschlandhalle, where Willy Falck Hansen was competing. More to the point, the five leaders were in Berlin for negotiations held at a meeting of the International Cycling Union in the city's winter sports venue, Sportspalast. The International Union's administration had been brought to Berlin "so that the great range of continuing business can be satisfactorily dealt with whilst the war in Europe is on." According to *Fædrelandet*, the German cycling federation, Deutscher Radfahrer Verbände, had announced in December 1940 that the International Cycling Union (UCI) had permanently moved its head office to Berlin. In the opinion of Sports-Bladet, readers would have to "wait with interest to see what our delegation could get out of their Berlin trip. Hopefully, it will turn out that foreign riders can be brought here, for track races at Ordrup, as well as international names to take part in the big road races planned for this summer."[7]

Danish delegates to the Berlin meeting included DBC chairman Svend Thorsen, the vice-chairman, Søren Levring, the association's head of sport, Jørgen Beyerholm, the President of Dansk Cycle Union, Knud Danielsen, as well as the head of road racing, Henry Hansen, who together with Beyerholm had led Danish efforts at the Berlin Olympics. Some of the aims of the meeting were to "settle questions of payment and to discuss records". An international track race between Denmark and Germany, for example, was arranged for 24 August 1941 at Ordrup.[8] But, as will become apparent, the continuation of collaborative sports would become more difficult due to forces beyond the professional sports' realm.

Not least because of his win in Germany, Willy Falck Hansen became the most popular professional sportsman in Denmark, throughout the first half of the occupation. The positive attitude that grew up in Denmark around the talented road racer Harry Saagar shows how sport could create a special atmosphere wherein the realities of the occupation could be momentarily put aside for the benefit of taking pleasure in "pure sport", which unnoticed provided the Germans with a seat by the fireside, and which helped to break down the Danish 'mental immune system'.

## The boxers

Although collaboration with the Germans through sport might have solely pecuniary advantages, there were other professional sportspeople who threw themselves into German arms from feelings of ideological affinity. One example is the boxer Hans Holdt, who joined the Danish Nazi Party in June 1942.[9] He had actually retired from a professional boxing career in March 1940, when he narrowly beat the German Georg Sporer on points at a farewell fight in front of a home crowd from the provinces.[10] But in the beginning of June 1940, *Idrætsbladet* could come out with "the great news" that Holdt "has been invited to fight in Berlin against Wallner or the German champion Besselmann." *Idrætsbladet* followed Holdt's energetic preparations in his club Thor and at the end of the month they could assure readers that he was now in full training for his German tour. That Holdt was able to re-start his career must be attributable to the war, which reduced competition from European boxing to comprise chiefly German, Italian, Finnish and Swedish fighters.

After long and difficult negotiations, a middleweight match was arranged between Hans Holdt and Josef Besselmann, to be held at Deutschlandhalle, on Sunday 26 January 1941. Following a war of nerves waged against the German organisers, the Danish side clinched a deal for 1000 marks and travel expenses paid to Berlin.[11]

The huge Deutschlandhalle venue was filled to capacity on the big day for professional boxing. Before the fight, Max Schmeling stepped into the ring and welcomed both Holdt and Besselmann. Many Danes working in Germany had arrived to cheer on their countryman, but the fight did not go exactly in Denmark's favour as Besselmann exploited his longer reach, keeping the Dane at a distance. At the end of the third round, Holt intensified his attack, without result; by the fifth he was shaken and in the sixth round he went down for the count and wisely stayed there.[12]

Although Holdt had been able to kick-start his career again, he was never the most successful Danish boxer during the occupation, as the fight against Besselmann suggests. That place went to Carl Andersen, who, at a large bout in December 1940 beat the German Herbert Jarubowski. Jarubowski was stopped in the 9th round by the Danish judge, the ex-European champion Knud Larsen: a decision that the German fighter was far from pleased about, and he seemed to make a move in anger towards the referee who had left the ring. Carl Andersen, however, darted over with a big smile and pushed his winners' bouquet of flowers under the nose of a bitter Jarubowski, who in his surprise was thereby disarmed. "As a gentlemanly boxer, he [Jarubowski] suddenly remembered that it was customary to share flowers presented in the ring with the opponent. Thoughts on this point of boxing etiquette occupied him so much that he forgot his rage."[13]

In January 1941, the famous Danish sports journalist Gunnar Hansen was able to announce after discussions with the German head of boxing, Hans Hieronymus, that if the European lightweight Championship between Carl Andersen and Blaho became a reality, on 16 February 1941, it would certainly be fought at Sportpalast on Potsdamer Strasse in Berlin, which could seat 8,000 spectators.[14]

Over several numbers, Idrætsbladet closely followed the build-up to the fight, treating, too, the question of a revenge bout. Both of the magazine's editors, Magnus Simonsen and Gunner Hansen, travelled together with Carl Andersen to Berlin. Gunnar Hansen's main job was to send a radio broadcast of the fight, and with great excitement he could inform readers that his microphone would be placed near Andersen's corner. According to Hansen, Dr Thoma of the German Box-Sport magazine was the driving force behind the arrangement, organising everything to do with contracts, the weigh-in, and relevant explanations to international boxers. He had informed Carl Andersen that "the German boxing public was definitely against every unfair boxing tactic."[15] Aage Krøll was the Danish referee, the second referee would be an Italian and Ernst Pipo, a German, would be the chief judge, since the Swiss judge had not arrived in time.

The fifteen-round bout, however, was something of a tame affair, as neither Blaho nor Carl Andersen staked everything they had, which is what the Danish challenger would be expected to do. The German heavyweight Otto Nispel, who "in his time was well-known in Denmark" criticised the contest for being "a bad fight between two boxers who were just too clever." The fight drew criticism from other quarters, too. The Nazi party's newspaper Völkischer Beobachter criticised Andersen for not attacking more, which the challenger had a "moral obligation" to do. However, 12 Uhr Abendblatt also criticised Blaho who, as the title holder, had not shown enough daring.[16]

In May 1941, Carl Andersen fought against Gustav Eder. Eder had lost his European Championship title to the Belgian Felix Wouters, who in turn lost it to the Frenchman Marcel Cerdan, whereafter Eder had been deprived of the opportunity to regain his title because of the war. Idrætsbladet was well-disposed towards Eder, publishing many pictures of him.

Before Andersen was to meet Eder, another Danish boxer, welterweight Hans Drescher met the German ex-champion at the beginning of May 1941. The fight was hardly noticed by the Danish press. According to the German sports magazine Box-Sport, Drescher went into the fight without respecting Eder's long record of wins, and much to Eder's surprise went at it with 'all guns blazing'. Drescher dominated the beginning of the bout with 'out fighting', and in the second round was ahead on points. But, true-to-form, Eder kept his cool and waited until the seventh round before launching his offensive.

> Gustav Eder, the personification of ice-cool composure and superiority,

counters his attacking opponent with a finely calculated right to the jaw. Drescher sways on his knees, still goes forward, goes down for 6, and is afterwards mercilessly attacked like by a big panther with a succession of punches, high and deep, so to all intents he is beaten standing. His seconds realise what's happened and throw the towel into the ring.[17]

Andersen's main bout was planned for 21:15, after several Danish-German amateur fights, so that "businessmen, too, had a chance to join in." In the last minutes, Danish radio broadcasting managed to set up a broadcast of the "Eder fight". It would not be broadcast direct but was a recording of the opening and finish of the fight, which would be broadcast at 22:30, so that listeners could re-live the outcome at home.

At this "prize fight" in KB-Hallen in Copenhagen, Carl Andersen showed another side to his boxing, most probably because his new trainer, Knud Larsen, had been working on his boxing technique and tactics. Gustav Eder played a waiting game, delaying his counter attack until he felt that Andersen had been softened up. Naturally enough, Andersen did really well for the first five rounds, while Eder's continued passiveness started to irritate the crowd that, by the tenth round, began to lose patience. In the twelfth and last round, Andersen was hit in the temple and went down for the count of nine, but then quickly got back into the fight. After the last round, Carl Andersen raised Eder's arm in the air, as a sign that he believed Eder had won, so both boxers were astonished when the fight was declared a draw, leaving Eder extremely unhappy. The Danish boxing public, on the other hand, jeered the decision since they thought Andersen should have won. A contributing factor to Andersen's propitious draw may have been that there was only one points judge at the fight, chairman of the boxing union of Copenhagen, Johannes Christensen.

Altogether, favourable market conditions combined with weakened competition from the war-time European boxing scene provided Danish boxers with opportunities to travel to Germany, and gave renewed life to the careers of boxers such as Hans Drescher and Hans Holdt. Despite the European boxing system being put out of action because of the war, the Danish boxers' fights against German champions were staged as "European Championships". Carl Andersen's draw against the ex-European champion Gustav Eder, especially, attracted great attention in Denmark.

# AMATEUR SPORTS

Elite non-professional Danish sportspeople within DIF ranks were eager to take part in collaborative sports, too. Over 10 months – from 5 August 1940 until the anniversary of the Constitution, Grundlovsdag, on 5 June, 1941 – there was a special boost in Danish amateur sports against Germany and Sweden. Reports received from the various DIF member associations and unions after the occupation revealed that 13 of these groups had officially worked together with the occupying forces: eight declaring they had never cooperated.[1] The eight member groups not to cooperate were not necessarily more patriotic, not to say more inclined towards resistance, but rather they were relatively small in terms of their respective publics and thereby not so interesting to the German competition.

The German organisers took a great deal of trouble with these sporting events to give the impression of friendly, sociable relations between Danes and Germans, not just within football. The Danish competitors were extremely well treated, undoubtedly with the intention that they should later spread the news about the nice Germans, when they returned home. To increase interest in collaborative sports, the Germans often promised to cover all expenses incurred in a German trip, but they were promises that were not always kept. In June 1942, the Copenhagen club Sparta had not yet received compensation for their boxing team, to which the boxing association chairman suggested that they ask for 'payment in kind' to solve the problem.[2]

Following a football match in Hamburg, in November 1940, for example, a dinner was held for Danish and German players and executives, involving "many fine speeches". The Danish players were each presented with "an elegant silver pencil, a folder and an artistic etching".[3]

German organisers were also able to draw in Danish sportspeople by providing support from among the comprehensive ranks of German sports experts. An Austrian skiing coach gave instruction in Copenhagen, during the winter of 1940, German trainers came to Denmark, and Danish competitors were sponsored to travel to Germany, which included competitors such as Ragnhild Hveger, and which always provoked a delighted response in sections of the Danish press.[4]

Top German representatives also tried to get involved in Danish sports, via the head of the German Navy in Denmark, Vice-Admiral Mewis, a sports enthusiast, who

*The Commander-in-Chief of the German Navy in Denmark, Vice Admiral Raul Mewis, took a lively interest in sport. In 1941, he took the initiative to set up tournaments in boxing, along with training courses for beginners, for the German Navy. Here Vice Admiral Mewis hands over the 'Admiral's Cup' to the winner of the so-called Furesø regatta in autumn 1940.*

with his naval base in Kiel had done much to integrate competitive sailing as part of naval training.[5] As part of the Danish Furesø sailing-club regatta for junior and senior teams, in the autumn of 1940, Mewis included an 'Admiral's Cup', which was used in German propaganda.

# ATHLETICS TAKE THE LEAD

## The first games with the Germans

As was made clear in the earlier chapters, the DIF leadership wished to avoid official sporting relations with Germany until after the international match against Sweden, arranged for 20 October 1940. But their decision was not whole-heartedly welcomed in every quarter, and in the late summer DIF's intentions were for the first time knocked off course.

Nazi-inspired groups within Danish sport caught the scent of a new morning and could not wait to begin collaboration. The athletics association of Copenhagen (KAF), with Johannes Bojesen Barsøe at its head, became the first association to organise an event with German competitors. Unfortunately, the archives of the Copenhagen athletics associations are unable to shed light on the situation leading up to these games, as the minutes taken from the relevant board meetings wherein precisely these games were discussed are, hardly coincidentally, missing from the archive.

A suitable date for the games turned out to be 22 August 1940. Despite a pessimistic comment from the chairman of the athletics association, Svend Jensen, that is was somewhat late in the season, preparations got into full swing. The major interest shown by the occupying powers in getting collaborative sports underway can be demonstrated from how a team of notable German athletes was quickly put together. Throughout the entire early epoch of Nazi-governed sport, there had been close collaboration between German and Danish athletics at national-team level. That helps to explain why, perhaps, resumed collaboration was so quickly achieved after 9 April 1940. *Idrætsbladet* completely bypassed the point that the games contravened the wishes of the DIF leadership that a resumption should begin with a Swedish international match in football. The magazine, in fact, began discussing the games only a week after the DIF ban had been rescinded.

As a way of indicating the unproblematic attitude held towards collaborative sports in the Danish press, it can be seen how *Socialdemokraten* published an article on the KAF games on 20 August, under the headline "First International Games". On 21 August, they included a photo of the German competitors with the caption "three more Germans". By 22 August, they announced "Tonight – international athletics – no Swedish competitors but still exciting." On 23 August, under the headline "Danes and Germans share the victory", it was described how there were "outstanding people" among the German competitors. However, the current study, rather than going through newspaper reports from the daily press, will instead place its emphasis on coverage in the sporting press.

On the day itself, 22 August, the games were front page material for *Idrætsbladet*, which also included three large photographs of German athletes during training at Østerbro stadium.[1] What was most exciting about the participation of German athletes was the chance that tough competition might drive the Danish athletes to set new Danish records. The headlines enticing people to the games read "German athletics stars should mean Danish records at the stadium".

The Danish papers reported that the first international games of the year with participation of German athletes was now a reality.[2] Thirteen competitors from the club Berliner Luftwaffe Sport Verein, with a Major Reuter in charge, were flown in especially – indicating direct cooperation with the German Wehrmacht. The German military Commander-in-Chief General Lüdke – who had also visited Niels Bukh's gymnastics academy on 2 June 1940 – was also present at the stadium, together with the plenipotentiary Renthe-Fink; the German military and political heads thereby demonstrating the importance placed on collaborative sports, through their presence.

The games were an outstretched hand from German to Danish athletics and, via its new concept for a games, launched to create maximum spectator appeal by "showing us in those disciplines where we are strongest: in the events where the chances for setting records are greatest. Therefore, and because eight out of nine competitions are track races, the programme will especially appeal to the crowd, who will experience so many moments of excitement over the tense climax to each race. It will all be done with in just over an hour, but it's likely more will happen in that hour than during most drawn-out competitions."[3]

Further along in the coverage, potential Danish record breakers in the various distances were detailed. Of special interest was a Danish middle-distance runner of international calibre, Harry Siefert. The Copenhagen athletics association's head, Bojesen Barsøe, a pro-German, watched the German training and was extremely satisfied "with their speed and fitness": "the Danes will now have a chance to show what they're made of. In this company, it's got to mean a few new records," he announced exuberantly.

Although it was not an official international competition, a German orchestra played the national anthems of both countries while the spectators, according to the Nazi newspaper *Fædrelandet* "stood with their heads bared, but the real atmosphere was when the runners lined up for the 100-metre hurdles." This event was "a great win for Ole Dorph Jensen". The first German place was fourth, but he was "one of the German team's weakest men".[4]

Generally, the German runners "set the pace". However, it would not have displeased German guests when the Danish 800-metre runner Hans Spanheimer won "after a highly tactical race in a tight struggle against the German, Grau". Spanheimer worked as a journalist for the Nazi newspaper *Fædrelandet* and was sports editor of the Danish radio.[5] He ran the best Scandinavian time that year; at 1:54.6.[6] What *Idrætsbladet* did not know at the time was that Spanheimer was on his way to run for a German club. His race at Østerbro stadium was a wonderful place to show off his talents to German scouts. But the German athletes, too, received glowing words, not least the two "superb Berlin sprinters, Mellerowicz and Bönecke, were supreme and their times excellent."

In the picture archive of the Danish newspaper *Politiken*, a photograph of Spanheimer's win has been preserved. On the rear face, the name of Kurt E.W. Volkmann is stamped, who was a German journalist and sports diplomat, along with his address, which indicates that this German propaganda specialist made sure that *Idrætsbladet* got the right, constructive pictures of Danish-German cooperation.[7]

Almost as an omen for the long-term future of Danish-German collaborative sports, the games were drowned out in a torrential shower, which washed away any possible record attempts with it. Nevertheless, *Idrætsbladet* regarded the games as a success, emphasising the first-rate performances and the skill of the German competitors. The magazine estimated the paying crowd to be around 4,000, plus a good many courtesy guests. *Fædrelandet* characterised the games as "a huge success!" highlighting that 6,000 spectators had turned out in such bad weather. Renthe-Fink proudly reported back to the German foreign ministry that a total of 8,000 spectators had watched the games and he could impart that the Danish press had responded to the games with enthusiasm. Renthe-Fink clearly placed great emphasis on this resumption of sporting relations since he sent a film taken of the games to Berlin, showing just how well everything had gone.[8]

On the whole, the games were effectively used by German propaganda. A Danish radio broadcast was included as part of a German programme called Deutschdänische Sportveranstaltung im Kopenhagener Stadion. True to form, it was Kurt Volkmann who was their man on the spot. On German radio, coverage of the games was transmitted as part of German sports radio.[9]

The multi-talented phenomenon Svend Aage Thomsen was singled out, praised for his "exceptional abilities" and "outstanding victory in the 100-metre hurdles". Thomsen was a master of a number of athletics disciplines, besides apparatus gymnastics and the decathlon, in which he won the Danish championships from 1940-42. Thomsen had attended Niels Bukh's school of gymnastics, he had taken part in athletics events at the Berlin Olympics, and could easily challenge the Germans for precedence on the athletics field. In 1938, he won both hurdles and pole jumping in international competitions against Norway and Germany. Svend Aage Thomsen retired in 1943, at 34 years of age, devoting himself to setting up a Jutlandic sports school, Den Jyske Idrætsskole, at Vejle, which was a result of his initiative, and where he became the first principal.

In the build-up to the games in Copenhagen, Thomsen could play a role in German propaganda, in a pictorial from the stadium at Aarhus, showing him in training with the well-known German high jumper Martens, who recently had taken on Thomsen's main discipline, decathlon, with some success. The friendly relations between the two elite sportsmen were taken as an obvious indication that "in the realm of sport, collaboration between Denmark and Germany throughout this war has become a valuable link in the friendship between two neighbouring peoples."

The DIF leadership wished to imbue collaborative sports with a neutral tone, beginning with a football match against Sweden, but their decentralisation of the decision-making process regarding international joint sporting events allowed that tone to be completely taken over by Nazi sports leaders within Danish athletics. In

*German propaganda could make good use of Svend Aage Thomsen (left) training against the German boxer Martens. Svend Aage Thomsen was one of Denmark's most skilled, all-round international athletes, so his willingness to enter into a close training partnership in September 1940 was welcomed by the German authorities.*

*Per Lie from Norway, Rudolf Harbig from Germany, and Hans Spanheimer from Denmark at the large Berlin indoor sports arena, Deutschlandhalle, March 1941, where they ran 800 metres, coming in fourth, first and last respectively. Harbig's enthusiasm at having just won a bust of Hitler seems less than overwhelming, but for the Nazis any displays of brotherhood between three 'Germanic' nations was a scoop.*

the presence of German high ranks, the German organisers had the opportunity to put their fresh slant on the resumption of joint sports with military music, broadcasts through both Danish and German radio, and film coverage for the powers in Berlin, so Renthe-Fink could reassure his superiors about how well collaboration policies were going in Denmark.

In addition, there turned out to be good opportunities for Danish elite sportspeople to 'try out' for German clubs. The opportunity was taken by the pride of Frederiksberg athletics association, Hans Spanheimer. From the beginning of 1941, he was able to compete for Hannover Sportverein, secure in a new job at a graphic arts studio in Germany.[10] Spanheimer set a new Danish record in 800 meters, in 1940, and in 1000 meters, in 1941. Speaking to *Idrætsbladet*, "our fabulous runner" described his first win for his new club and the excellent conditions in German elite athletics, which were often linked to military facilities.[11]

By march 1941, Spanheimer had moved to Berlin, where he was to train together with two track stars, Dieter Giesen and Ludwig Kaindl. Sports journalist Gunnar Hansen concluded that if "Spanheimer doesn't learn to run 1,500 meters in under 4 minutes with such guides, then he'll never learn it."[12]

*German press photograph with the caption "Seidenschnur from Kiel gets in front of Danish Spanheimer", June 1941. There is clearly a close contact between the two (Spanheimer, second from the left). In German propaganda, pictures of young Germans and Danes showing mutual appreciation had a high priority.*

Membership of the Berlin club was obviously decisive for Spanheimer, and in June 1941, at "an evening festival of sport", at the Momsen stadium in Berlin, he ran to second place, becoming the first Danish record of the year by running 1,000 metres in 2:28.2, which was the fifth-best international time that year.[13] Before that, Spanheimer won a 3,000-metre cross country race in Brandenburg.[14] *Idrætsbladet* championed him with the words "Hopefully, this victory will bring Spanheimer further onto track so he can bring home even more wins, bringing lustre to Danish athletics." In Denmark's most important sports periodical, no sign could be traced of any reservation in coming forward for the occupying powers; and Hans Spanheimer's accomplishments in Germany continued to be reported on in *Idrætsbladet*, regardless that Spanheimer was also editorial secretary and sports correspondent for the Nazi *Fædrelandet*.

## Athletics championships in Germany
The administrative leadership of Danish athletics did not sit idly by, but continued to exploit the favourable conditions to compete against the best German athletes. An opportunity now appeared to meet German champions on a German track, and athletics again made the front page of *Idrætsbladet* in March 1941.[15] The sensation was

that Hans Spanheimer would not only meet "the elite of the world" at Deutschlandhalle in Berlin but he would also compete against the athletics star Rudolf Harbig, who again was shown on the magazine cover with his swastika-emblazoned jersey. Given how many countries that had suspended collaborative sports due to war and occupation, perhaps "elite of the world" was somewhat overstated, but the magazine did not feel the need to reflect over this claim. Neither did *Idrætsbladet* mention that two English runners, L.F. Roberts and A.G.K. Brown (recently killed in the line of duty), had both achieved positions among the world's five fastest in 400 metres. Spanheimer and Harbig's opponents were Per Lie, a Norwegian who in fact broke the Norwegian sports boycott against the Nazified sport organisations, Lennart Nielsson from Sweden and the powerful German runners Giesen and Grau. Svend Aage Thomsen and Harry Siefert were also to line up. Siefert told journalist Gunnar Hansen that the German organisers placed great importance on Danish participation, arranging for flights both to and from the championships.[16]

Siefert's most renowned opponent over 300 metres was Miklos Szabo, from Hungary, which was part of the Axis alliance, having joined the tripartite pact between Germany, Italy and Japan in November 1940. Szabo was one of the world's most versatile runners and achieved numerous titles including European Champion over 800 meters; he set the world record for two miles (3,218 meters); and he had run 10,000 meters in under 31 minutes. The championships were a big disappointment for Denmark. Both Seifert and Spanheimer took last place in their respective races. Only Svend Aage Thomsen cut a decent figure over the 70-meter hurdles by winning his preliminary heat, to thereafter give the Swedish favourite Håkon Lidman a close-fought contest in the final, in which Thomsen took second place in front of the German competition. *Idrætsbladet* wrote that "it was the most exciting hurdles race ever to be held in Deutschlandhalle." According to *Fædrelandet*, Thomsen was so thrilled about the preliminaries that he "amazed the 8,000-strong Berlin crowd with a pair of somersaults".[17]

Spanheimer was overtaken by both the three German runners and the two Scandinavian. The headline in *Idrætsbladet*, though, stated "No-one could follow Harbig in Berlin", with his time of 2:28.4, in which "the German runner touched his personal record, while Spanheimer, Svend Aage Thompsen and Seifert all produced an honourable performance."

Harbig's race "clearly shows that all of Germany's adored 'Rudy' is most likely embarking on his best season yet. In Denmark, too, there is a buzz around Rudolf Harbig. The Danish national coach, Svend Lundgren, wrote the best part of a serial for *Idrætsbladet* on Dr Woldemar Gerschler's [Harbig's coach] 'excellent' and 'captivating' book *Harbigs Aufstieg zum Weltrekord*.[18] When Lundgren turns to Harbig as a role-model, it is partly because of the intense relationship between trainer and athlete, the 'slavish care whereby Harbig follows his coach's advice and direction.' In addition, there is Harbig's psychological preparation, which reveals itself 'in the purity and toughness about everything he does in his life, not least in the iron-bound discipline of his training and his robust enthusiasm for athletics.'"

However, Harbig was not so untouchable that American athletes, still unaffected by the war, could not threaten his position. During the American championships in the summer of 1941, Grover Klemmer already touched Harbig's record by running 400 metres in 46 seconds flat. Nevertheless, *Idrætsbladet* introduced this piece of news with a picture of the Italian runner Mario Lanzi and a large "fabulous" picture of Rudolf Harbig in action, who was now being called world champion, although he was only a record holder. Again, Harbig's body was brought into focus. "We see the wonderful stretch he commands, the fantastic hip work that characterises all of his races."[19]

Other Danish athletes took part in athletics competitions at the very highest elite levels during the spring of 1941, in Germany. In addition to a number of athletes already mentioned, there were Danish sportspeople such as the country's best race walker Viggo Ingvorsen from the Danish club Sparta.[20]

By the end of the occupation, Ingvorsen had won the national Danish championships no less than 12 times, setting 8 Danish national records; and from the period between October 1940 to March 1941 he was also a member of the Danish Nazi Party. There were also plans that Ingvorsen should be accompanied to Hamburg by his Sparta club colleague Poul Theisen. These plans came to nothing and, according to *Idrætsbladet*, Ingvorsen also had to pull out of the Berlin race fairly quickly, but perhaps he had been used as a 'pace-setter', instead. At any rate, he could be pleased that he had taken part in a field that contributed to Hermann Schmidt from Hamburg setting a new world record of 2 hours, 20 minutes and 33.6 seconds. The field included "several of Germany and Italy's best race walkers."[21]

Danish athletes were given further opportunities to meet the supreme stars of German athletics on German soil, which could be used by German propaganda to create images of German-Nordic unity under the swastika. Judging by the coverage in *Idrætsbladet*, the contact also contributed to a fascination with the masculine running phenomenon Rudolf Harbig.

The Nazi-influenced leadership of Danish athletics, and their comprehensive collaboration with German sport did not seem to worry the large brewery-backed Tuborg Foundation, which donated DKK 10,000 in May 1941. The editorial column of *Idrætsbladet* believed the award indicated "perspectives that go much deeper than the simple job of promoting Danish athletics. What is remarkable about the Tuborg Foundation award, which in effect provides a kind of stamp of approval, is the fact that for the first time Danish sport has been positioned alongside a number of other cultural pursuits, such as art and science, to name but two." Sport was therefore regarded as "having won recognition within circles

*Victory for the German athletics star Harbig, in front of the German runner Giesen and Bergsten from Denmark, at a games in Copenhagen, May 1941. It felt something of a coup for the Danish sporting world that they could now attract world-class names such as Harbig to Denmark.*

that have the power and finance to lend a helping hand, which is what matters", as *Idrætsbladet* put it.[22]

On 27 May 1941, the athletics association held yet another large competition with German participation, in Copenhagen. Six of Germany's best runners performed in front of 4.000 spectators. The great sensation was that Rudolf Harbig was coming to Denmark where he was treated like a super star by the Danish sports press.

During the initial period of occupation, Danish athletics experienced a large upsurge in activities and their association, especially a particular coterie of pro-German heads, actively participated. But, as will be shown, although sporting relations with Germany were very quickly restarted, athletics people were not the only ones to start out against DIF's wishes.

# BOXING

Non-professional boxers came quickly out of their corners, and the Danish boxing association must be given prominence as one of the most activistic organisations. The head of the Sparta club boxing team, Georg Schmidt, a wholesaler, was suspected by the DIF leadership of having too close relations with German interests at a time when there was still a ban against sporting relations with international opponents; with Sparta, especially, becoming deeply embroiled in collaborative sports with the occupying powers. In contrast to other sporting disciplines that had all built up sporting relations with Germany throughout the 1930s, the situation with Danish amateur boxing was somewhat different.

In 1930 and 1932, international boxing matches against Germany had taken place, but during the period of the Third Reich leading up to the outbreak of war it had not been possible to entice the formidable German boxers to an international match in Denmark. Although Gerhard Pedersen – a rare trump card – had won a bronze medal at the Berlin Olympics, the team's respective strengths were in complete imbalance. But following the outbreak of war, the time was ripe for an intensification of mutual boxing activities, culminating in the ring with an international match held on 3 December 1939, in Berlin, together with two further matches during the occupation.[1] Boxing was one of the few sports Hitler took an interest in, and the German authorities became very generous about sending boxers to Denmark. In addition to the international matches, Denmark's capital city also became the stage for a great number of boxing competitions with German participation. Perhaps there were those in the Danish crowd who relieved a sadistic compulsion to see Germans being thrashed, but on the vast majority of occasions they would go home disappointed. As a rule, it was the Danish boxing trainers who had to throw in the towel.

## Danish clubs

By 17 August 1940 – only five days after the DIF leadership decided to resume collaborative sports – *Fædrelandet* reported that Sparta's "energetic head of boxing, Mr Georg Schmidt" was bringing six German boxers to take part in an international tournament at Idrætshuset in Copenhagen, to be held on 11 and 13 September 1940. The board of this large club was pleased about the ban being raised. In the club magazine *The Spartan*, members could read "we received our first invitation abroad only a few days after being released from 'serfdom'."[2]

*Idrætsbladet* warmed up to the tournament with the headline "Europe's best middleweights at Sparta's panorama games".[3] Rudi Pepper, the unbeaten German champion for over three years, was to fight alongside other German boxers apparently all of national-team class, although there were many new names who were being tried out. According to Schmidt, the German team as a whole was "absolutely dazzling". The tournament was a near sell out and, presumably to avoid trouble with the Danish public during this trial run, the organisers omitted the usual presentation line-up of the teams that would have produced the obligatory Nazi salute from the German athletes.

In spite of this – as seen in a photograph of the tournament, published in *Fædrelandet* – the organisers must have accepted that the matches be fought under a huge Swastika flag.[4] Neither did it stop *Idrætsbladet* from concluding that the event was the biggest Danish success in boxing for many years, the German boxers being praised especially for their fine technique. No-one noticed that one of the German team members (Kurt Krause) did not represent the German boxing federation, nor even a German club, but rather represented the German Wehrmacht since he was a German soldier stationed in Denmark.[5]

Throughout three richly-illustrated pages, the magazine's boxing specialist, Jack Xmas, attempted to recreate the red-hot setting: "A sports complex, a packed atmosphere, and great excitement at five German boxers who would show us boxing culture in all its purity." Altogether, there was a highly satisfied response to the German fighters. The star attraction of the evening, Rudi Pepper, delivered the goods against a strong local fighter, Otto Winther. According to the rules, the fights were to be staged over three rounds, but Winther never got back into the ring after the second and had to give up, with a bad hand. Possibly, there was nothing wrong with his hand, and the problem may have been Winther catching his breath: unsurprising since Pepper had been relentless in attacking the Dane's midriff.

*Idrætsbladet* took the opportunity to put out a picture and interview with the two top German boxing leaders, who thought the arrangement had gone off without a hitch and that the matches had been good throughout. One of the seconds, the ex-European champion Hans Ziglarski, highlighting the continuity in German-Danish boxing, said "I know Danish boxing well, from my own time as a fighter. I was here first time in 1927 and finally in 1933 as a boxer, and I was here in '37 again as a second. I think Danish boxing's alright and the Danish crowd is pretty fair. And about all the wins, as a German, you can only be satisfied."

Ziglarski was not quite so satisfied, however, with the decision taken in the only fight the Danes won, and he had good reason for further dissatisfaction at the next match against Sparta, two days later, when only Pepper and the light-heavyweight Otto Umar won. The Danish public was delighted at the Danish victories, in contrast to the great many German spectators, most of whom were German soldiers. *Idrætsbladet's* otherwise so-enthusiastic boxing correspondent – in the interests of truth – had to cover Ziglarski's criticism as the main story from the contest, but the German second was still cited in the conclusion as saying "we'll gladly come back."

It may be that the relative mildness of the German response to partisan decisions from the judges, coupled to German promises to return, resulted from the main goal of the competition being a political one. The organisers had to ensure that these first games went off smoothly, without disturbance from Danish spectators, so that further collaborative events could quietly be set in motion and become a normal procedure for meetings between the occupiers and the occupied. If a few unfair Danish wins contributed, then it was no great concern.

After the Copenhagen tournament, the German boxers continued onto the Danish town of Odense, to fight two days later in their third match in less than a week. The event was put together by three local clubs, Odense's amateur boxing club (OABK), Olympia and Skjold. The fights were held at Forum, the premier venue for boxing in Funen, in front of a 1,600-strong "boxing-starved" crowd from Odense.

After the tour, boxing went from strength to strength. In October 1940, Sparta again organised a tournament with German participation, where a sense of pride can be detected among club members for being able to attract so many good German fighters to Denmark, to inspire Danish boxing. Others joined the bandwagon, too. On 8 November 1940, Søborg sports association, with its 800 members, organised a tournament in Idrætshuset, at Østerbro in Copenhagen, in which four German fighters took part. *Idrætsbladet* summed up its pre-fight appraisal by judging that with so few German boxers "Søborg had to win."[6]

There was a lively exchange in other parts of the country, too. Esbjerg Boxing and athletics club, on the Danish west coast, organised a competition for December 1940, where 1,500 spectators could enjoy watching three boxers from Hamburg. Without doubt, many of the crowd would have been fishermen, who had an excellent market in Germany, as well as Danish labourers who helped build the many concrete bunkers at Søndervig, and other places along the west coast.

In this way, club boxing in Denmark quickly mobilised an enthusiasm for Danish-German games, both in Copenhagen and in the provinces. They were not slow to turn an eye towards German-occupied Norway either, with the entire period from 5 August 1940 until the end of that year producing six tournaments with German competitors, under the aegis of the Danish boxing association. These competitions took place at club level, which was a situation that was about to change.

## Denmark vs. Germany

In 1941, international boxing between Denmark and Germany finally got underway: and more besides. Danish boxing judges were also helping German colleagues in their matches against other countries, and the former chairman of the boxing association, Henrik Meincke, a barrister, was thereby invited to judge a match between Germany and Finland, in February 1941.[7]

During 1941, a total of two Danish international tournaments were fought against Germany, on 19 January 1941 in Copenhagen, and again on 22 November 1941 in Munich. In these cases, particularly, there is clear evidence that the resumption of sporting relations with the occupying forces led to a distinct increase in the number of Danish-German matches.

The international tournament of January 1941 was the first fought on Danish ground since 1930, when Denmark and Germany had competed to a tie, in Aarhus. In the intervening period, international bouts had only been held in Germany, of which Denmark had only won one.

Over two pages in *Idrætsbladet*, Denmark's chances of victory were evaluated, including featherweight, among other classes, in which the German opponent was Schimansky, the German military champion. Six of the eight German boxers were military personnel and the heavyweight Adolf Kleinholdermann turned up in full uniform, because his leave of absence had come through late and he had only reached the plane to Denmark in a last minute dash. With great devotion, *Idrætsbladet* could inform its readers that Kleinholdermann belonged "to Adolf Hitler's bodyguard regiment [Leibstandarte SS Adolf Hitler], serving in its 4th unit. To serve in the first unit requires a minimum height of 1.95 meters."[8]

The German team was presented first. Afterwards the Danish team was presented "in which Viggo Frederiksen received the greatest applause, but nonetheless you could easily sense the boxers were very warmly received by the crowd. After this, the national anthems of both countries were played. The Danish fans tried to sing along to *Der er et yndigt land* and *Kong Christian* but it was difficult since the gramophone was set up to play so quickly that it finished four lines before the public." Playing the two Danish national anthems would most likely mean that the German team was also allowed two songs, most usually this would include the Nazi anthem, the *Horst Wessel Lied*.[9]

Although Germany had arrived with reserve boxers in four weight classes, they dominated so much in the heavier weights that "When half of a fight's first round was gone, you knew for sure how the rest of the bout would go, and that doesn't keep up the excitement with the crowd." To make matters worse, the Danish welterweight Poul Kops broke his thumb and had to be treated on the spot by the renowned Danish sports physician Dr Ove Bøje.[10]

Despite the imbalance between the sides in the heavyweight classes, the Danish boxing association did well out of the event in other ways. Idrætshuset was sold out, but moreover there were "many more seats in use than usual", to give a grand total of some 2,600 spectators. The association gained a good advertising opportunity, too. *Idrætsbladet* covered the event with a frontpage, two whole pages and two half pages of photographs. After the competitions, a banquet was held at Parkrestauranten, which signalled a veritable shower of gifts between the various Danish and German boxing representatives. "Speeches were held, songs sung and a lot of attention paid." German boxing's "head of sport for the Reich" Dr Metzner was presented with a badge of honour, while Hans Hieronymus, the German coach, Hans Ziglarski, the second, and Kurt Volkmann from the German embassy were also presented with gifts. The German association honoured the Danish organisation with "a beautiful set of Meissner porcelain", while Lauritz Jensen from the Danish boxing association and Aage Krøll, whom the Germans had wanted for a referee, also received gifts. Finally, the competitors each received a present.

Although the international tournament was a high point, there were other competitions in other places, and Odense and Esbjerg were not the only provincial centres to join in. On 21 January 1941, the sports association of Nykøbing Falster organised a Danish-German competition at the Hotel Baltic, involving seven German fighters.[11] The event was organised around the German national boxing team on its way home after the Copenhagen tournament, who would fight a selection of Danish boxers, put together to avoid any repetitions of the Copenhagen bouts. In *Idrætsbladet*, it could be read "the framework to these bouts will naturally be as festive as possible, and the arrangement has every chance of becoming Nykøbing's biggest sporting event yet" – convincing testimony that the Germans commanded significant appeal in the area of sports culture.

To the great relief of Danish boxing, the final results stood at 4-3 to Denmark, achieved in a packed house as revenge for the defeat in Copenhagen.[12] Nobody seemed too concerned that the German boxers must have been drained, having fought only two days previously.

It should now be apparent from the earlier sections of this study that a high level of activity and an intensive collaboration with Germany took place within boxing. Initially, professional boxing was described, which showed a good deal of activity, but this was surpassed in the field of amateur boxing, where many came out of their corners very swiftly, only too delighted to accept an outstretched German hand. Boxing was thereby one domain that quickly helped to move the borders of what was acceptable in terms of collaboration. But there were other sporting disciplines that helped to move borders. One of the most notable will be investigated more closely in the following section.

# SWIMMING WITH THE TIDE

The special intensity of the contact between German and Danish swimmers during the occupation was solely due to the Danish women swimmers and their international reputation – in particular Ragnhild Hveger, due to the number of records she achieved and because her intense wish was to travel out of Denmark. In the early period of the occupation, Hveger was still an important feature of Danish swimming. Internationally, she competed for the Danish swimming federation, Dansk Svømmeforbund (DS), that reported enthusiastically on the development of German swimming, on its high levels of ability, and on items such as Hungarian water polo, whose national team Denmark hoped to compete against in an international competition arranged for the end of July 1941.[1]

## Soldiers in swimming trunks

If a closer look is taken at the initiatives of DS, it appears they had an extremely unproblematic relationship to Germany and the stage management that the Third Reich made use of within the world of sport. When the federation's 'Official Announcement' reported excitedly on a forthcoming German championships, based on information from the journal *Der Schwimmer*, they made no secret of the fact that many of the German male swimmers were also soldiers.[2]

The swimming magazine also reported on fallen Finnish and German soldiers, such as the Finnish 1931 European champion at 200 meters breaststroke, Tolvo Reingold, who in 1941, during the Continuation War in alliance with Germany, "died for his country in fighting on the Ladoga front," and Herman Heibel, his club colleague from Bremischer Schwimm Verband, a German champion sprinter, who also "died for the Fatherland after being badly wounded at Leningrad."[3]

On the whole, international sport in the journal was completely dominated by the continuing swimming activities in Germany and its sphere of influence. In December 1941, the *Der Schwimmer* had reported very favourably on "a German 16-man team visit to Sweden".

The team comprised German swimmers "all from Luftwaffe Sportverein. The divers provoked special attention ... A dazzling, skilful dive, in beautiful freestyle, was on show. And their comedy dives brought on a huge round of applause." Above this column, there was a list of many new records achieved in Franco's Spain.[4] There were also comments to be found on Norwegian Nazified sports, which were written up in quite neutral phrases; it being noted that in January 1942 "the Norwegian Swimming Association has a new chairman, Einar Thomassed, director for the communal swimming baths at Drammen."[5] About the German swimming championships, it could be read in July 1942 that

> The competition was marked by a military presence. And the ten winners among the men's 13 classes were also from the military, of which far from all had the opportunity for decent training. Indeed Heinz Ahrendt, who was second in the 1,500 meters freestyle, had not swum for several months.

The magazine could follow the wartime progress of the German swimmers with anxiety. In December 1942, it stated "Our good friend at the Eastern front Werner Plath has been wounded in the upper arm by a shot. He is now laying in hospital with his arm in splints, but claims that he is now on the mend."[6]

With official notifications citing the above material, it is no surprise that the federation fully supported the swimmers' tour to Germany: but that a swimmer like Ragnhild Hveger was exceptionally interested also plays a pertinent role.

## Ragnhild Hveger and Jenny Kammersgaard

The scaling down of international sporting relations was a major loss for Ragnhild Hveger. In March 1941, she was interviewed by *Idrætsbladet* in a full front-page feature that carried a large portrait photograph, and here her frustrations can easily be sensed. To a question about a possible coming trip to Germany, she answered "Yes. What about it? I'd love to go. I'm in just the right form to go down there and compete, and show that in Denmark we can still keep up, but I've heard something about the invitation coming to nothing because Inge and Grete Tilda aren't allowed to by their parents."[7]

These were tough times with many hindrances for an absolutely top world-class swimmer, but Ragnhild Hveger compensated by becoming the Danish athlete to compete most in Germany. Altogether, in the occupation period from 1940 to 1942, she took part in 10 competitions.[8] In the winter of 1940-41, she also undertook a month of training at Mönchengladbach, to where she returned several times, and at the end of 1941 she received the offer of a coaching job in Kiel, which she took up for a period.[9]

During the occupation, Hveger continued her attempts to set new records. She was furious when the international swimming federation, FINA, refused to recognise her record in 1,500 meters, in November 1940, because she had swum with a male pace-setter (Poul Petersen) – incidentally, after the Danish men swimmers had denied her entrance to their 1,500 meter competition at the Danish championships.[10] Thereby, she held 'merely' 35 world records. Hveger believed it was Swedish representatives who had contrived to have her record disallowed, out of envy. With pleasure, therefore, she would take part in a further record attempt in Hungary, then an Axis power, so that the FINA head Leo Donath could see for himself that everything was in the strictest order.

Other swimmers were less willing to compete in games with the occupying forces. Apart from Ragnhild Hveger's first tour to Berlin in October 1940, when another woman swimmer, Lykke Larsen, accompanied her, Hveger was the only swimmer to take part in competitions in Germany. One of the other great Danish swimmers was the breaststroke champion Inge Sørensen, whom Gunnar Hansen had passionately christened on radio at the Olympics "little captivating Inge". In 1940, she was only 16 years old and quite sensibly had not been allowed by her parents to travel to a country that was at war. *Fædrelandet* wrote in August that Hveger wished to go, but Inge Sørensen would not, and the German organisers wished that besides an exhibition in crawl by Ragnhild Hveger their event should include a race between Inge Sørensen and the German champion Annie Kapell.[11]

In September 1940, Ragnhild Hveger began a triumphal crossing of the Reich swimming front, in her tour of Germany. On the first day, she swam to victory in Mönchengladbach in both the 100-meter and 400-meter crawl, as well as in 100-meter backstroke. Lykke Larsen came second in breaststroke, after the German star Annie Kapell. For the occasion, *Idrætsbladet* published a large photograph of the two girls with the heading "Abroad at last!" "It's clear from Ragnhild's face, she's thrilled to be finally getting her international trip."[12]

The Danish girls' contests in Germany marked a turning point for German women's swimming, which was patently taking advantage of the low levels of competitiveness among belligerent and occupied countries. Three German women now managed to swim 200-metres breaststroke in under three minutes. The editor of *Idrætsbladet*, Magnus Simonsen, concluded about the "downright astounding" progress of the German swimmers that "All said, it's a powerful impression you get of German sports, wherever you come in contact with it, whether it's in competitive sports or ordinary sports exercise."

On the home front, there was star-dust waiting to be sprinkled over sports swimming in general and Copenhagen's swimming club in particular, and fairly quickly an international competition was organised for 6 October 1940, to be held with the participation of six German swimmers at the Østerbro pool, with room for 1,200 spectators.

The German competitors won every race they entered. Even though the German European diving champion, Kurt Weiss, had not been able to take part, his stand-in,

Fritz Haster, impressed with his "elegant somersaults" that put Denmark's otherwise supreme Thomas Christiansen completely in the shade. In the words of *Idrætsbladet*, "A superb victory by the Germans", "handsome Werner Plath"[13] "paddled" to victory in the 100 and 400-metres crawl; with the magazine printing a full close-up picture of him. Generally, in the sports journalism of the time, there is an unmistakable fixation with not only the techniques and beauty in the patterns of movement by the German sportsmen, but also a broader aesthetics of the masculine body.

Ragnhild Hveger unsurprisingly won every race she entered: despite having let a laugh slip out during the start of the 400 meters, for her earlier false start, and she had got off late when it mattered. Hveger took the opportunity to announce that she would not swim professionally, as a number of her colleagues who had also turned professional were currently without employment. A month later, she was on tour again in Germany. In a press release from the Reichssportführer von Tschammer, there was a lengthy piece in which it was claimed that Ragnhild could fill swimming halls, and thereby bring income to the event organisers.

> Over the last year, the name Ragnhild has been said more often than any other. Regardless of where the 20-year old Dane appears, the reputation of her 37 world records proceeds her. Swimming halls and their cash registers are filled.

Other sections of the press were also active. The *Völkischer Beobachter* of the Nazi Party used a whole column for its "enthusiastic cheer" for the Danish swimmer, claiming that Hveger had refused an offer from USA: "There have been many offers from 'dollar-country' made to the young Danish girl, but she held firm, and the more tempting the American sums became, the stronger she became in her resistance."[14]

In March 1941, led this time by Grethe Møller, Hveger again embarked on another German tour. She took part in a number of competitions, in which swimmers from occupied Holland also competed. At the time, both Holland and Denmark were considered to be leading countries for women's swimming. Hveger told *Fædrelandet* with a smile "I'm glad to be up against tough competition again." However, she warned against over-optimism, as "it's not always easy to get the right harmony between arms and legs, so you mustn't expect too splendid results when I'm down there."[15]

Splendid results, though, were achieved in several events. In Krefeld, Hveger beat the new Dutch swimming talent Altje Styl in that year's best-yet noted time. Annie Kapell, the German star, took the same opportunity to beat the German record in 200-meter breaststroke.[16] In Düsseldorf, Hveger lost to Altje Styl in 100-meter crawl, but won a decisive victory in the 400-meter crawl, winning over her nearest

German contenders, Mirbach and Schäferkordt. Holland beat Germany in the relay event, and at the same venue Annie Kapell set a new world record in 200-metre breaststroke. After this, Hveger travelled on to Mönchengladbach, where she beat Mirbach at 400-metre crawl, as well as beating Styl, again, at 100-metre crawl in 1:05.6.[17] These excellent times for 100 meters were achievable, however, because the pool was only 20 metres long. Kapell won again at breaststroke. According to Hveger, however, it went "all wrong with my turns and my starts as well. I noticed it during the German tour. They weren't half as good as before and, in the competition with Altje Styl in a short pool, it was a serious drawback."

On her homecoming, Hveger was interviewed by the Nazi newspaper *Fædrelandet* who wrote that she and her tour leader Grethe Møller were "extremely glad for such a delightful tour. Everywhere, they were generously treated, stayed in all sorts of places as guests of the town, attending receptions at their town halls. Every mayor was a sports enthusiast and took a lively interest in our swimming ambassador's conduct."[18]

Danish swimming, however, involved more than just Ragnhild Hveger. Denmark's second star, Jenny Kammersgaard, turned her sights South, in precisely the same way as she had done in the build-up to the occupation. After Denmark was occupied, Jenny Kammersgaard travelled to Berlin in June 1940, to study to be a full swimming instructor, taking swimming as her main subject, at Friedrich Wilhelms Universität. Not that this was the source of any surprise. In 1937, after swimming the Kattegat, she had, in her own words, already received "an offer from Germany to study in Berlin, without cost."[19]

The famous Danish journalist Gunnar Hansen included a picture in *Idrætsbladet*, in October 1940, of a smiling Jenny Kammersgaard with the caption "'Baltic' Jenny is a swimming teacher." It was taken at the Reichssportfeld in Berlin, where she "has recently concluded her swimming instructor's examinations". Kammersgaard was now supposed to take up coaching in Berlin, where she "will stay for the meantime", "having enough to get on with". Whenever a teaching position became available in Denmark, she would immediately travel home to Horsens.

# OTHER SPORTING DISCIPLINES

## International handball

By the late summer of 1940, arrangements were in motion in many sports disciplines for matches against Germany. The handball association managed to organise two international games against Germany in the short but intensive period in which sporting relations were at their height. An international match in field handball was set for 17 November 1940 in Copenhagen. *Idrætsbladet* warmed up with a headline saying "Our handball players, the best in Europe?"[1] But the Danes were defeated.

The handball association were not to be outdone by their fellow associations, and by May 1941 another Copenhagen international match against Germany was staged. This time the guests won 5-1. After the match, the German embassy's sports press attaché, Kurt Volkmann, had arranged a dinner. Volkmann was also adept at ensuring German military music at several handball events.[2]

Collaboration in Danish–German handball occurred precisely as with other sporting disciplines, also at the level of judging, where the Danish national coach, Aksel Pedersen, in the wake of Denmark's match against Sweden in January 1941, was invited to judge at a Sweden-Germany match in Göteborg. Gunnar Hansen could report that the match was won 16-15 by Germany, after the Swedish players had led by four goals only four minutes before the end: "These were exciting minutes." In the following year, too, in January 1942, Aksel Pedersen was a judge at another match between Sweden and Germany, held in Sweden.[3]

## Wrestling

Wrestling involved itself quickly in occupation-period collaborative sports. However, the sole wrestler who was the pre-match favourite against whichever opponent was unable to take part. He was Abraham Kurland from the Jewish Hakoah club in Copenhagen, who would hardly wish to compete against Germans, but probably neither would he have been allowed by the German authorities. Furthermore, the affiliations of Hakoah club members was obvious from the Star of David symbol worn on their sportswear. Kurland had won a silver medal at the Olympics in 1932, at just 19 years of age. On his homecoming to Copenhagen's Central Station with the other Danish competitors, a large crowd welcomed "the popular Danish sportspeople with their fine results", and Abraham Kurland was one of those to be "chaired through the crowd".[4]

In spite of one of the best Danish wrestlers being omitted, competition against the Germans nevertheless went ahead. On 1 December 1940, the Danish national wrestling team took part in an international tournament in Munich, under the leadership of Ølgaard Rasmussen from the Copenhagen club Sparta. According to a probably exaggerated estimate in *Fædrelandet*, around 4,000 spectators watched the Danes struggle to an honourable defeat of 4-3.[5] Afterwards, friendly matches were held against a Berlin city team. More alarmingly, there were also plans to appear in occupied Prague. Ølgaard Rasmussen stated that this leg of the tour was only organised by the time of the Berlin city competition.

The lavish way in which the tour was presented is an indication of the great propaganda value the tour had for the German authorities. In Berlin, the troupe was received by "our old friend Willy Steputat, together with other heads from sports wrestling, who led us through Berlin's black-out to Hotel Nordischer Hof." In Munich, they were greeted "at the Station's Prince's Suite by City Education Officer Bauer, amid a large commotion, with speeches and shouts of 'heil.'" The Danish Consul, Karl Lindberg, gave a speech. After "this extravagant welcome, where we all stood our straightest in the splendid surroundings, we were lodged at the Hotel Excelsior, where Mussolini, Daladier and Chamberlain had stayed during the conference for the Munich agreement" in 1938, between Germany, Italy, Great Britain and France, about which Chamberlain announced famously 'Peace in our time'.

The international contest took place at "the colossal" Krone Circus building, and speeches were given from the circus ring, along with national anthems. Fritz Sørensen, a Danish wrestler, suggested that "the popularity of the Danish contestants" could be felt immediately, "because we were applauded so loudly by the crowd." Sørensen was disappointed, however, because against expectations he was not able to meet the local Munich wrestler Ehr, who was "a big crowd-puller", but Ehr who "was a soldier in France, could not make it in time." Instead, Sørensen would meet the European champion Schäfer, which was a distinct blow to the Danish team's chances.

The Danish wrestlers harboured hopes that the opposition might not be in such good condition as usual, which proved true. The games took a dramatic turn when the best Danish hope, Gunnar Nielsen, in the light-heavyweight class, beat his opponent, bringing the tournament score to 3-3. It quickly became an anti-climax for the Danes, however, when the German heavyweight, "our old friend" Hornfischer, threw his Danish opponent with "a beautiful waist move" before a minute had gone.

After the bouts there was "a large banquet; three courses and ice cream". Later, more speeches were given and "we received a beautiful engraving, together with a splendid bound book on Munich and its history." At night, the troupe had to take cover in an air-raid shelter, when the sirens sounded. The day after, the local newspaper *Münchener Neueste Nachrichten* showered praise on the Danish wrestlers for their abilities.[6]

On 5 March 1941, two clubs, Dan and Hermod, held a new Danish-German wrestling match. The contest was "strangely, not a sell out, but presumably many just assumed that it would be over-filled. The German team fielded a group of German champions, and won decisively. The German member of the resistance movement and an icon on wrestling Werner Seelenbinder was there, too, on the German team, winning a lightening victory, but frustrated that he did not get a chance for a revenge match against Gunnar Nielsen, who had not taken part this time." In late November 1941 in an international match in Stuttgart between Germany, Croatia and Denmark Gunnar Larsen again defeated Seelenbinder.

Altogether, Danish-German collaborative wrestling reached its crowning moments in the first year of the occupation, because they were able to directly compete against Germany in international matches, and because the icon of all wrestling, Werner Seelenbinder, was finally beaten by a Dane.

## Heydrich in international fencing

As discussed earlier in this study, Renthe-Fink had pushed for a fencing tournament to be held between Denmark and Germany, a plan that came to fruition on 30 November and 1 December 1940, in Copenhagen. Traditionally, England would have provided the important opposing team but, due to the occupation, an international match was arranged for the first time against Germany.[7]

It was predicted that the Danish chances were poor, as the German team were fielding both men and women fencers all of whom could produce awe-inspiring results, many of them with place positions at the Olympics and the World championships.[8] The Danish women were also obliged to compete without their champion fencers, Grete Olsen and Karen Lachmann, as the former was not in training and the latter was experiencing problems with her arm. Another related reason for Lachmann's absence may have been because as a child she had been adopted by a wealthy Jewish family, when her mother married for a second time, to Aksel Lachmann, a lithographer. It is also probable that Grete Olsen's withdrawal was an act of sympathy towards Karen. The two fencers established a close sporting partnership after the war, in which they won the world championships for team fencing in both 1948 and 1949. Lachmann, as an individual fencer, was also a finalist at the Olympics in London in 1948 and at the world championships in 1949, but lost both times.[9] The German fencers won the Copenhagen competition convincingly.[10] The Danish fencing association, nevertheless, was so pleased with the event that they had a small squared bronze plaque made, engraved with the name of the association, 'Dansk Fægte Forbund', and 'Germany–Denmark 1940'.

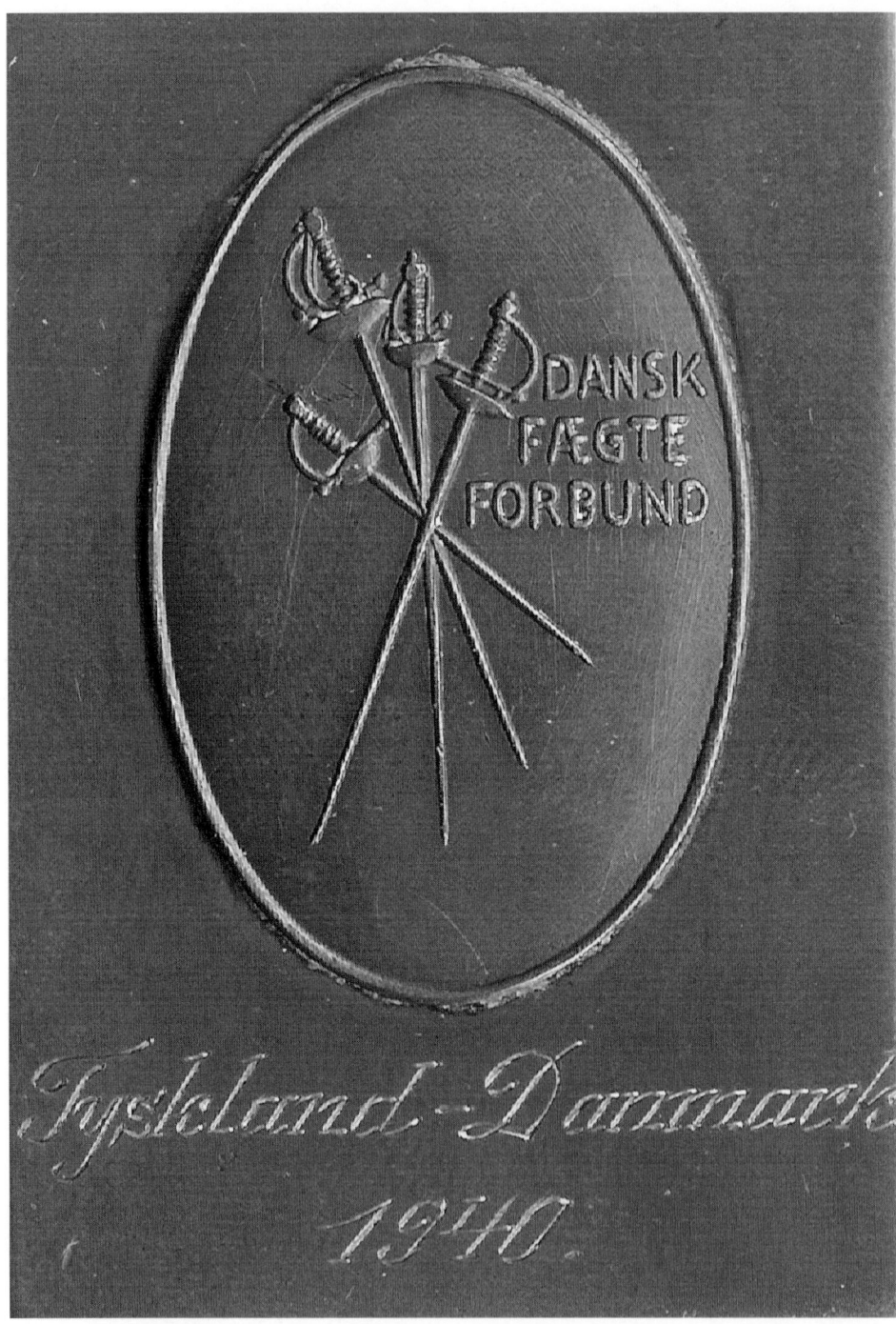

*Commemorative plaque made by the Danish fencing association to commemorate participation in an international fencing match against Germany in December 1940. The bronze plaque must have led Germans to believe that Danes placed great emphasis on their collaborative relations in fencing with Germany.*

*The salute was an obligatory ritual to be performed during the national anthem. Reinhard Heydrich sits among the spectators.*

One of the fencers present was Reinhard Heydrich, a member of the absolute highest levels of the Nazi party, an SS General and Chief of the *Reichssicherheitshauptamt*, the Reich Security Main Office (which included the Gestapo, SD and Kripo Nazi Police forces). Heydrich was also the main organiser of the Wannsee Conference and its "final solution to the Jewish problem". He was also involved, in September 1939, in a "Polish attack" on a German radio station that gave Hitler the excuse to invade Poland. Later on, he was made Reichsprotektor of the Czech puppet State of Bohemia and Moravia, but was assassinated by local partisans in 1942, leading to one of the worst reprisals of the Second World War, namely the liquidation of a Czech village, Lidice, and the murder or deportation of its entire population.

During the war, Heydrich's comprehensive sporting ambitions showed themselves in his attempt to have himself made president of the newly organised German and Italian-dominated European fencing federation. The Italians, however, had a strong opposing candidate, the former Olympic champion, IOC member and Minister of Finance, Paolo Thaon di Revel, and thereby frustrated Heydrich's ambitions.[11]

The Danish sports press rarely used images that were directly part of German propaganda, presumably to maintain the illusion that collaborative sports were non-political, and not to frighten off readers who were against mixing sport and politics, or who may have been decidedly anti-German. Nevertheless, a body of striking visual material is extant, kept by the daughter of one of the fencers of the Danish team. In the photographs of the international competition, the Swastika and Dannebrog are clearly seen, as are the German fencers who during the playing of the national anthems present a 'heil' salute direct towards the Danish national team: the team, thereby, during the traditional playing of anthems, receiving an explicit political gesture aimed at themselves.

To the right at the Danish team stands a fencer, Raimondo Carnera: who incidentally was a cousin of one of Mussolini's greatest sporting aces, the colossal 2.04-metre tall Italian heavyweight boxer Primo Carnera, world champion in 1933-34. Raimondo Carnera, with his entertaining and aggressive style, held 59 team titles from Danish national championships in the various fencing disciplines, and six Nordic titles. In his youth, Carnera was an Italian citizen and could therefore not compete in Danish individual championships but was eligible in team events. In 1942, he won his first individual Danish championship. He also represented Denmark at the Olympic Games in Helsingfors, in 1952.[12]

Fencing was a widespread and well-supported sports discipline in Italy, where the history of fencing has witnessed important developments. Much of the Italian community in Denmark was openly pro-Fascist, gathering at the Italian embassy, for example, to celebrate the 'March on Rome' in 1922. Raimondo Carnera was part of this Italian community and drew the support of his native countrymen at competitions in Denmark.[13]

Denmark's international fencing match against Germany shows how closely the occupation brought Danish and German sports together. The first international fencing competition against Germany, ever, took place in December 1940 with none of the famous Jewish fencers on the Danish team and, what is more, with Heydrich, notorious for war-time crimes against humanity, as present at the event.

Other sporting disciplines were also active. Most conspicuously, two Danish skiers took part in the Fifth International Week of Winter Sports in Garmisch-Partenkirchen, on the Austrian-German border, in February 1941, just as two other skiers competed in the student world championships in Kitzbühel, nearby, in the same month.[14] The Week of Winter Sports in Garmisch-Partenkirchen was the biggest sporting event in Germany since the outbreak of war, although they did not manage to secure French and Norwegian collaboration teams, which in itself demonstrates the success of the sporting boycott in Norway, normally so strongly represented in skiing. The German sports press regarded the event as proof of "the leading role played by the Axis powers, and its power of attraction in the midst of wartime." Visiting international sportspeople had their travel and accommodation costs met by the German organisers, and the Reich sports minister personally invited a number of diplomats and heads of sport from participating nations to attend, paid for by the ministry of propaganda, to promote how Germany was the leading European sporting nation.

Joseph Goebbels, however, held another view. He did not want the German population, who were beginning to suffer from a lack of shoes and proper winter clothing, to be force fed by the press with pictures of an Alpine extravaganza, not to mention what the men on the front would make of images of the apparently unconcerned Reichssportführer taking part in a jocular snowball fight, as happened the year

*This apparantly jovial gentleman in the snow is Reichssportführer Hans von Tschammer und Osten. The photograph was taken at the Fifth International Week of Winter Sports at Garmisch Partenkirchen in 1940.*

previously. Goebbels, therefore, took measures in March 1941 to ban the publication of text and images from elite sporting events that might be demoralising.[15]

In addition, the top Nazi leadership was allergic to German sporting defeat. There were no great surprises in the results of the Danish entrants, but Goebbels reacted strongly to a German defeat in ice hockey to occupied Czechoslovakia, on 10 January 1940, in Prague, causing Goebbels afterwards to halt sporting relations with the German Protectorate. On top of this came a defeat in football to neutral Sweden, furthermore on the day of Hitler's birthday, 20 April 1941.[16] The result was a toning down of reports about sporting relations in the German press.

# FOOTBALL WITH THE FOE

> There were unfortunate episodes that without exception were caused by irresponsible and morally defect elements among the crowd.
> Leo Frederiksen to Renthe-Fink 6 June 1941

## An international match in Hamburg

As the great sport of the general public, football was a top priority in collaborative sport for the German authorities. In the wake of the two Danish matches against Sweden in October, Germany at last had the chance of an international match against Denmark, to be held on Saturday 17 November 1940 at the Victoria Stadium in Hamburg. The frequency of international matches between the two countries throughout the 1930s had amounted to four in ten years. Over the initial occupation period, the two countries moved closer together in terms of sport, since a further match was played in the year following the match in Hamburg. An additional match, intended for the summer of 1941, never took place.

Two Danish players announced they were unable to attend, but not so that any direct political motive can be inferred. More noticeable, however, was that Alex Friedmann, a Jewish player from the club B1903, risked his skin and turned up, which the Germans apparently never noticed. Perhaps because the match was a team event, he cold blend in more easily among the numbers, or perhaps the German authorities did not wish to risk their first international match coming to nothing because of anti-Semitism.[1]

Gunnar Hansen was the Danish commentator in Hamburg for Danish radio broadcasting, and he underlined the continuity in collaborative sporting relations. "The match against Germany will be transmitted in the same way as previous international matches. At 3:20 pm, I will be turning on the microphone at Victoria Stadium … This will be the third international match between Germany and Denmark that I have broadcast."[2]

Their journey with Leo Frederiksen and the Vice-Chairman of DBU, Kristian Middelboe, at their head gave the squad a detailed picture of a country at war. Was it responsible to conduct young Danish players to a potential theatre of war to complete an international game of football?

The question becomes a relevant one when a closer look is taken of Gunnar Hansen's report in 1945, concerning the players' experiences on the tour. The players made it sufficiently clear that the journey had been "exciting and interesting", especially when reading a description from the Danish headquarters, set up in the fashionable Hotel Atlantic.

> The black-out curtains were carefully pulled to one side. Away off South, the sky was lit by bombing and anti-aircraft fire. Once in a while we could hear the flak crackling. The hard rhythm of the machine guns, and the thunderous thump of detonations played the background tune. Sometimes, there were sharp cracks from small explosions. None of the players were afraid. At least they didn't let themselves be effected by it.

During a lull in the bombing, Leo Frederiksen managed to get permission for the Danish squad to slip out of an air-raid shelter. They were making their way hastily to the hotel when "all hell broke loose above our heads." It was only on the following day that the team members realised "how reckless we had been." Their general attitude, however, was not so down as to keep them from a walk around the streets of Hamburg the following day. Outside the hotel, many Danish guest labourers stood waiting to greet the Danish players, some of them having travelled all the way from Kiel and, according to themselves, having bought tickets two weeks previously.[3]

Julius Larsen, a journalist, had also travelled to Hamburg. He got the impression that the British bombing was intended to disturb the Germany-Denmark game.

> They'd got the message in England. They wanted to demonstrate that Old England was still on her toes. It turned out to be the first air bombardment of Hamburg of the war, on the same evening and throughout the night that we arrived. Without question acceptable that the bombing should be done as a kind of propaganda. Propaganda for a country whose position might be in some doubt. Good, that they, the guests in Hamburg, could go back to their country and tell that a defence still lived on in Great Britain, and an attack, too.

As for the match, in the workers' and dockyard city of Hamburg that still retained groups fiercely critical of German developments, "the city that Hitler never crushed … It will never be forgotten, the sight of raised clenched hands, when the *Horst Wessel* was played after *Deutschland, Deutschland Über Alles*. Fists raised in the air, among the cheapest stands, with one common aim – a massive demonstration against a regime that had forced its way to power with lies and violence. Up on the podium, they screeched along with 'Über Alles' and also 'Die Hoch.'"[4]

*The Danish multiple ball-sport talent Knud Lundberg, who competed in a Danish international football match against Sweden on 20 June 1943, wrote in a reminiscence that "the Danish tradition that players stop still on the pitch during the national anthem – wherever they happen to be, with the ball at their feet or rolling off somewhere – is much more in accord with the meaning and atmosphere to a football match than the artificial 'march-in' formations that are used elsewhere in the world".*

Denmark, too, took a great interest in the match, the second half of which was broadcast on Danish radio. Gunnar Hansen had to stand on a beer crate to follow the match, which started according to tradition with the German players and German crowd giving the 'heil' salute during their national anthem. Around 2,000 Danish supporters had come to cheer on Denmark, with chants they had copied from the games against Sweden, in a sold-out stadium for 30,000. Around the stands, small Danish flags popped up, as Hansen lyrically put it, creating "flowers on a grass carpet."[5]

Denmark avoided a new Breslau catastrophe, but nonetheless lost 1-0. The Danish play was not good, and especially the first half was defined by strong German pressure, but without the desired results. The second half went better for the Danes, who had to watch the striker Helmuth Schön, who would later become national coach, score the only goal of the match in the 62nd minute, with a header into goal between six Danish defenders.[6]

## Austrian Wunder-teams

After the match between Germany and Denmark in Hamburg, collaborative football moved onto Danish ground, where the big question was whether everything would pass by as peacefully as it had in Hamburg. On the surface everything seemed calm. The spring of 1941 must be considered the most peaceful period of the occupation. A discrete form of protest, however, had begun to show itself as Danes started wearing the red, white and blue roundel of the British Royal Air Force.[7]

Organised resistance including sabotage was not the order of the day, and sporting relations, now they were underway, helped give the situation a gloss of normality. But the gloss did not last long.

The breakthrough for a large-scale meeting between the Danish sporting public and a German team came in the summer of 1941, with prospects of both exchanges at club level as well as a first football match against Germany to be held at a Danish venue. In June, the Copenhagen football association staged its 38th annual international football tournament at Idrætsparken in Copenhagen. What had drawn in the fans before were mostly "the English matches, such an incentive for our footballing standards", but now attention turned further South. The tournament committee kept the international flavour of the games by having Kurt Volkmann invite top teams from Austria, which – as a point of history – since its annexation by Germany was now called Ostmark, or the Eastern Borderland.[8] The match against the two clubs Austria Wien and Admira Wien turned out to have momentous consequences for Danish-German sports.

Austrian football was known for its light, elegant and improvised style, which had been established in the 1920s; the Austrian national side soon acquiring the epithet Wunderteam. In the same period – from 1926 – the clubs Austria and Admira turned professional. Austria won the Mitropa Cup in 1933, fought between two of the best sides from Vienna and teams from Czechoslovakia, Hungary and Italy.[9]

The invitations to the German-Austrian clubs came from a tournament committee, Stævnesammenslutningen, known as Stævnet for short, composed of representatives from the five major clubs in Copenhagen. The level of professionalism in a club like Admira became apparent during the initial negotiations, when the Danish organisers at first found it far too costly to bring the club to Denmark.[10]

## 'Heil' salutes from the opponents

On 28 May 1941, FK Austria played its first match against a select Danish team.[11] FK Austria lost soundly in front of 11,000 spectators, the 4-0 result being something of an anti-climax.[12] On 30 May, FK Austria played a return match for 15,000 spectators and this time won 1-0.

*The red, white and blue circles of the British Royal Air Force could be used as a silent protest against the occupying forces. The photograph is taken of a training session in the junior league. The German authorities had difficulty preventing such subtle forms of protest, which on the other hand requires no more inventiveness than for a boy to wear a hat in the middle of summer.*

The 'heil' salutes given by the Austrian players, however, had annoyed the Danish public and at certain points there had been scuffles.[13] The official magazine of the Wehrmacht noted the unrest in the Danish crowd with some irritation.[14] Publishing a photograph of the match with the headline "Viennese footballers in Copenhagen", it concluded that a number of the Danish spectators had unfortunately shown a "weak sense of sportsmanship". At the end of the match, when the FK Austria players gave "the German salute", a chorus of whistling started up – as the magazine explained – showing the Danish public's lack of discipline. What is not added, though, is that the spectators' demonstration had clear political intent.

As for the approaching match against Admira, a slightly threatening undercurrent can be detected in the tone of the Wehrmacht magazine, which hoped that similar episodes would not occur at the coming club match or at the approaching international game. When such episodes actually did occur, the magazine stopped covering German sporting relations with the Danes. As it turned out, there was every reason to be concerned about the reaction of the Danish public.

## Trouble on the terraces

The fire had been well-primed for Admira's match against a team selected by Stævnet. Admira, a top club, had last won the Austrian championships in 1936 and again in 1937. The team's jersey colours were the same as the Danish national team, red and white.[15] Over a seven-year period, Admira had played 21 games in Denmark and won the majority. The last match had been in 1936, actually won by the Danish side, but it had also been played on a pitch that "was covered in several inches of snow and slush". Now, after a five-year break, Admira was back.

In 1941, on the day commemorating the Danish Constitution, Grundlovsdag, 5 June, Admira played in Copenhagen, watched by a crowd of 12,500. For the team picked by Stævnet, the Jewish Alex Friedmann was playing, whose name was registered in the Nazi journal *Fædrelandet* neutrally alongside other Danish players.[16] During the match, Admira never managed to show the Copenhagen side its typical Viennese style, in which the ball passed along the ground, from man to man, with great precision. The pitch was both hard and uneven, which made the ball jump and change direction. Nevertheless, the Austrians still won 4-1 (including a goal in the very first minute) and could show "samples of the pure, intelligent and imaginative play that has always characterised the team".[17]

Admira's success on the pitch did nothing to improve the mood among Danish fans, who could regard the defeat as symbolic of the general superiority of the occupying power. The 'heil' given by the German spectators, mainly soldiers, to their team shortly before the match had also created unrest among young Danish fans, and "there were harsh remarks from both sides, and several of the German soldiers had their caps knocked aside." After the referee's final whistle, where "people streamed onto the pitch, it all went wrong. The Germans drew bayonets, while the Danish fans

*A shocking start to the match that marked the beginnings of Danish resistance, on the national Constitution Day, 5 June 1941. The centre forward for Admira, Wilhelm Hahnemann, scored in the first minute. A Danish defeat of 4-1 fed anger against German spectators present.*

brandished their beer bottles. The police presence was unable to stop the fighting. Before reinforcements arrived, four German soldiers and a half-dozen Danish fans had been sufficiently injured that they needed to be taken to hospital".[18]

At the same time as the disturbances on the pitch, struggles broke out between German soldiers[19] and Danes on the terraces, which in some cases developed into actual fighting.[20] When the German soldiers from the 'cheap' pitch-side stand tried to leave the stadium they did so in bunches, so that the Danish fans suddenly found they greatly outnumbered the Wehrmacht's soldiers. At the exits, the German soldiers became hedged in by groups of Danes, which led to a good number of standing brawls.[21]

The disturbances carried on outside the stadium, where around 50 soldiers gathered together in the middle of the huge crowd, to defend themselves as a unit. The situation was getting out of control. A Danish superintendent formed the police into lines and ordered "truncheons at the ready". They managed thereby to separate the Danes and the German soldiers, who quickly left. However, the Danish crowd still went "hesitantly forward", but the big attack had been deterred. A man who shouted at police "your turn will be coming soon" was arrested but the general use of batons was avoided. The situation could have developed into a pitched battle between Danes and German soldiers. Whatever the possible consequences, however, it was the impression of the police that if they had not intervened when they did, the German soldiers would most likely have taken matters in to their own hands "since they appeared to be extremely heated."[22]

Perhaps one contributing factor for the outbreak of violence at the Admira match had been that the Admira players gave the 'heil' salute both before and after the game, which made it abundantly clear that the Vienna team presented itself as a Nazi team, and that the Danish opponents were therefore playing against representatives for the occupying powers. The spectators could no longer ignore Austrian players appearing as active supporters of the Nazi regime and the idea of a greater Germany. Such an acknowledgement, however, must have already been made by hard-core fans amongst the Danish public quite some time before, since they would also have seen the two previous matches with Nazi salutes from the Austrian players. *Fædrelandet* was especially incensed at "Something so improper as to respond to a well-intentioned greeting from a sporting team by whistling."[23]

Two confidential reports, occasioned by Werner von Grundherr,[24] an official in the German foreign ministry with special responsibility for Scandinavia, suggest the relevant German representatives also recognised that the "German salute" had provoked strong reactions among the Danish public, both at the first match against FK Austria, on 30 May, as well as at the Admira match, on 5 June. Furthermore, the Nazi salute given at the Admira game took place on Grundlovsdag – the day commemorating the Danish Constitution and Danish representative democracy – where the current of national feeling ran high: a concurrence that may have helped to aggravate the situation. On top of this, there was the presence of uniformed German soldiers, who could not have passed unnoticed at a sporting event, not least when the soldiers returned the 'heil' salute from the Austrian players, both before and after the game. The German organisers must therefore share the responsibility for the situation boiling over, and it cannot be said that their handling of what should have been a friendly match against a 'Nordic brother nation' was particularly effective. But the potential propaganda effect of sport was the backbone of Nazi sports ideology, so it would have been hard to leave out the Nazi salute.

The events at Idrætsparken were taken extremely seriously by the Danish authorities. Three police reports were written, in which around 80 match supervisors, police officers, officials, committee representatives, referees and private individuals were interviewed. The questioning took a total of nine days to complete. According to the police commissioner's report,[25] written on the same day as the unrest, the match had been watched by many German Wehrmacht soldiers. In the "expensive pitchside" stand, a group of German Luftwaffe paratroopers sat, numbering around 100 men, who had arrived in several sealed tourist busses. In the "cheaper end" by the hockey pitches, small and large groups of German soldiers were gathered amidst an already tightly-packed crowd of standing spectators. The Wehrmacht's soldiers were conspicuous in their uniforms, their groups jumbled up amid the Danish fans. In addition to the match supervisors, there were 12 police officers on duty, to regulate the crowd flow and stay inside the ground during the match. Put bluntly, under a harsher contemporary footballing point-of-view, there was very little control over what would nowadays be called a high-risk game: without doubt because the Danish fans had always been well behaved.

Certainly, the German authorities were greatly shocked by the disturbances. There was much evidence at the time to suggest that the war would soon be over; and therefore that Denmark's task was to find its place within the new greater Germany. But was it not precisely this that was the situation's pivotal psychological point? For many Danish spectators, the overwhelming German presence became a suffocating reality. To have German superiority thrown so tangibly in their face, to see footballers from greater Germany, playing in (Danish) red and white, beating the capital city's select team at the Danish national stadium on a day to commemorate the national Constitution and, to top it all, to then see the players 'heil' at cheering uniformed representatives of the occupying power – this was all a very red rag to Denmark's wounded bull.

## Renthe-Fink steps in

The unrest led Renthe-Fink's to cancel the last Admira match, along with German participation in an All-Stars Race for professional cyclists at Roskilde, to be held two days later. He was infuriated at the Danish insubordination. In June 1941, Germany lowered the priority of sports, generally, but for other reasons.

The chairman of the Danish football association Leo Frederiksen now had to face the prospect that the whole arena of profitable sporting agreements would come crashing down. Leo Frederiksen was stunned by the unrest and afraid of German reaction, which until then had entailed their cancellation of the remaining Admira game. There was no trace from Leo Frederiksen that he held the German organisers in any way responsible for provoking the scenes of violence. On the day after the match, 6 June, he sent a letter to Renthe-Fink in which he expressed, on behalf of the Danish organising body, his deep "regret that the occurrence should lead to the cancellation of friendly sporting relations that had reigned between Danish and German football for more than a generation."[26]

Leo Frederiksen further regretted yesterday's "unfortunate episodes" that "without exception were caused by irresponsible and morally defect elements among the crowd." Frederiksen assured Renthe-Fink that the Danish organisers had taken every precaution but that it was impossible to avoid all undesirable incidents altogether.

## Departure of the Minister of Justice

Renth-Fink summoned Prime Minister Thorvald Stauning and the Minister for Foreign Affairs, Erik Scavenius, to a meeting on the day after the Admira match, on 7 June, to hand them his demand for the resignation of the Minister of Justice. In addition, there was a demand for a special police department to be established within the Ministry of Justice.[27]

The Minister of Justice, Harald Petersen had been a thorn in the side of the occupying powers because he refused to simply 'run errands' for the Germans. He showed great determination in face of German demands: such as his steadfastness in maintaining Danish prohibition against public meetings, which was an annoyance for the Danish Nazi Party; his pressing charges against Danish Nazis for violence against the police at the so-called spadeslag [battle of the spades] in the town of Haderslev in December 1940. The German authorities were especially angered that he supported an award to police officers of a financial payment and a medal, after that violent confrontation and, in the run up to the Admira match, Petersen's areas of responsibility had been increasingly eroded in accordance with German wishes.[28]

Renthe-Fink followed up his report from 7 June three days later with a confidential memo[29] in which he pointed out that cancelling the second Admira match had achieved the desired result. Nevertheless, he still believed it would be unwise to go ahead with the Denmark-Germany international game on 30 June, as the football union, DBU, had declared that the union would not be able to provide guarantees against new demonstrations.

The punishment for DBU's lack of control over Danish football fans came swiftly. For German interests, the aim was to hit other non-German sporting relations: "In the circumstances, we obviously cannot grant permission of entry to Swedish competitors in an international match between Sweden and Denmark, which was to take place already on 14 June, in Copenhagen." Renthe-Fink believed the denial of visas was more than a gentle hint for the Danes, but at the same time he emphasised that it would be a mistake to completely cut sporting ties between Germany and Denmark, and he therefore recommended against further reductions in collaborative sports. It was especially important to maintain a Danish presence at sporting events in Germany, since the cancelled international game had hit the Danish public hard enough. He also recommended, therefore, that a representative for the Reichssportführer, Tschammer, be sent to Copenhagen at the earliest opportunity to negotiate with the relevant Danish sporting organisations: which is what happened.

A week after the unrest, Renthe-Fink sent his concluding remarks about the occurrence to the German foreign ministry,[30] in which he outlined the chain of events and summarised the results of negotiations with both the Prime Minister and the Minister for Foreign Affairs. Harald Petersen's resignation had been conveyed to him personally by Scavenius, and Renthe-Fink could assert that all of his demands had been met.

It might seem strange that Renthe-Fink, who had formerly been so keen on collaborative sports, should now effectuate a temporary stop. A contributing reason may be that he had received signals regarding the scaling down of sporting relations because of the coming invasion of the Soviet Union, on 22 June 1941.

As a substitute for the cancelled international games, a match was instead arranged between Copenhagen and the provinces, at Idrætsparken. A match between Copenhagen and Jutland was held on Denmark's national day, Valdemarsdag, 15 June 1941, at which the King was present and "was cheered demonstratively: the King's presence being regarded as a gesture of sympathy for sport and to the city's sporting public."[31]

After the German invasion of the Soviet Union on 22 June 1941, Germany was in more need of its professional sportspeople for military service. The production of businesses and industries that had owned professional sports teams was directed more and more towards the war effort, which made the business of corporate branding through features such as cycling teams a superficial luxury that gave no decisive competitive advantage in the changeover from a market to a war-time economy.

As a consequence of anti-German activities and the opening of the Eastern front, it was the German authorities who now showed restraint towards sporting relations. Renthe-Fink had good reason for taking the football disturbances seriously. They were followed in the latter half of 1941 by a general increase in the will to protest, among Danes. The unrest at the Admira match had been a warning of an increasingly disobedient attitude among more defiant, anti-German, young Danish men. After the invasion of the Soviet Union, German soldiers were harassed more often, and the internment of Danish Communists on the day of the invasion led to other communist-inspired pioneers embarking on the first illegal activities. The Admira disturbances were never an expression of planned communist resistance, since in the beginning of June the Communists were still bound by the German-Soviet Non-Aggression Pact. Instead, they were a spontaneous popular protest.

A few months after the Austrian teams' visit, Castenschiold decided to throw in the towel. At a board meeting on 8 September 1941,[32] he announced that he would not stand for re-election as chairman at the annual committee meeting. He recommended his chair be succeeded by 63-year old Colonel Herbert Sander. Sander had had a fine career in fencing and he had organisational experience from the fencing and military sports association, as well as from the Danish National Olympic Committee.

The scaling down of larger Danish-German sports events held in Denmark, in particular footballing events, apparently had the desired effect. According to the Public Prosecutors' daily news report on the Danish-German clash,[33] no further instances of actual disturbance occurred in relation to sports during the rest of the occupation. But indirectly, a number of events over the succeeding period do indicate that a close working partnership with the occupying forces was no longer tolerated to the same degree as before. Denmark's adoption of the revived Anti-Comintern Pact on 25 November 1941 provoked protests and demonstrations against political cooperation, behind which were students connected with a resistance party, Danish Unity.[34]

Renthe-Fink was further proved right in his concerns about the reaction of the Danish sporting public. An example of less severity was a rowing regatta in Copenhagen, in 1942, where around two thousand people had gathered, at which a satirical anti-German song was improvised and sung aloud. Afterwards, those responsible were reported to the police, reprimanded, and banned from "reciting the song, henceforth".[35]

Moreover, despite the cooling down of collaborative sports, unrest could still be noted among the ranks of spectators. In an article for *Fædrelandet*, from July 1942, "Sport and Trouble", it was regretted that "young foreign sportsmen" no longer dared to watch sporting events. "Their clothing stood out amid the rest of the crowd; straight away you could see where they came from. And mean types don't like their country … or rather don't like the abilities of their leading men." Due to the risk of incidents, German soldiers now stayed away or else appeared in civilian clothing.[36] There were no Danish-German matches at that time, so it must be assumed that the presence of German soldiers as spectators refers to Danish or Danish-Swedish matches – a phenomenon that was then on its way back in. But it should be remembered that the Nazi regime placed great importance on the sporting education of young German men and German soldiers. So the wish among German soldiers to attend sports events, especially in an age before television, must doubtless have been great.

The German reaction to the Admira game across a range of sporting disciplines was to stop sending national teams to Denmark. This applied for the remainder of the occupation. The ambition that collaborative sports should illustrate favourable German-Danish relations could no longer be achieved in Denmark at a national-team level. The danger that a German presence would ignite Danish resentment in a show of demonstrations had become too great, and a series of agreed international matches between Denmark and Germany were thereby cancelled.

During the period from October to December 1941 – apart from international football matches – the spectacular international sports events in Germany were also limited because of the war against the Soviet Union. The pressures of military service, increased work hours, and poor nutrition began to tell on the opportunities for elite-level sports.[37]

It must therefore be concluded, in contrast to previous findings by Danish occupation studies, that it was not the student protests against the Anti-Comintern pact at the end of November 1941 that initiated collective disobedience towards the occupying forces. It was, instead, the disturbances surrounding the Admira game: an occurrence that also had a far broader social footing than the student protest.

It was the German authorities, then, and not the Danish sports authorities who toned down the interest in sporting relations, and what initially caused these relations to break was unrest from below, from agitating elements among the public and, as with the August revolt in 1943, it was unrest that emerged from below, on the whole, from Danish cities which led to a breakdown of former collaborative policies. The Danish sports authorities were not interested in a break, but in accomplishing a continuous collaboration at the highest levels. However, their sphere of influence was now so reduced that the question of international sporting relations was beyond their control.

## Meeting Hungary

Although there was a change in the political situation of sport, whereby German interests had depreciated collaboration after the Admira match, there still were those from athletics-association circles who continued to see political opportunities in Denmark's new European circumstances. It was for the time being not possible to implement agreements about sports events involving German participation but on the other hand the pro-German Copenhagen athletics association could hold an unofficial international match against Hungary, at Østerbro stadium, on 23 July 1941. After the occupation, these games did not receive the same negative reputation as did other sporting arrangements; supposedly because the opponents were not direct representatives of the occupying power, and perhaps because not everyone was aware that from November 1940 Hungary had joined the Axis powers. Organising a team was not without its problems for the Hungarian authorities, since Hungarian and Romanian forces were taking part in the invasion of the Soviet Union.[38]

# COLLABORATION WITH NORWAY

> For the Germans and their hangers-on, sports and especially football became a means for bringing society back to normal, for getting people to carry out habitual, everyday tasks as far as they could, and thereby grow accustomed to the new situation. Football had to be made safe, presented as an unbroken tradition, as a non-political activity.
> (On Norwegian football, Goksøyr, 2002, p. 56)

To understand the issues involved in participation in sporting tours of Norway, it is important to keep in mind that the Norwegian Government, under Vidkun Quisling, from the end of 1940 attempted to standardise all sport: though this did not give an organisation such as the Danish Athletics Federation reason to pause. From autumn 1940, the Danish federation was constantly producing plans for contact with Norway. For example, Johannes Bojesen Barsøe, the chairman of the Copenhagen athletics association and vice-chairman of the Danish Athletics Federation, spoke to *Fædrelandet* in October, saying that they would very much like to get collaboration with the Norwegians under way, although physical fitness among athletes at that time of year was never anything to write home about. But the 1941 season would soon begin and the Athletics Federation therefore would greatly wish "to contact them and make further arrangements."[1]

Their plan worked, too. On 28 September 1941, the Danish Athletics Federation took part in a Danish-Norwegian games against Norwegian sports collaborators at Oslo's large athletics stadium, Bislett, with its capacity for 25,000 spectators. The meeting against Norway was a blessing for the Danish Federation, at a time when Germany had opted out of collaborative sports due to the invasion of the Soviet Union.

After going underground, Olaf Helset, one of the two main leaders of Norwegian sport, dedicated himself whole-heartedly to mobilising the resistance movement – particularly within the field of sports, but also through the creation of a so-called Sporting Front, that took the initiative for a boycott amongst Norwegian sportspeople that lasted from November 1940 until the end of the occupation in 1945. An overwhelming majority of sports competitors and sports leaders declined to organise or take part in official competitions, and the new Norwegian federation football coach was forced to acknowledge that "the men who are still playing sports are not made of the right stuff and they're an impossible material to work with." Conversely, a phenomenon called illegal sports emerged, in which competitions took place in secret, where competitors practiced sports covertly in fringe locations or up in the mountains.[2]

The sports boycott became one of the biggest victories for the popular resistance in Norway. The starting gun for the strike was fired on 24 November 1940, in Tønsberg, where there were selection bouts for an international wrestling match against Finland. No wrestler would take part in the selections, and the Norwegian authorities never found any alternative way of putting together a team.[3]

## Changing attitudes

From 5 August 1940, the Danish sports federation, DIF, had been free to compete internationally, but how should DIF conduct itself in relation to Norwegian sports organisations that had no popular legitimacy?

In October 1940, Asbjørn Halvorsen, the secretary-general for the Football Association of Norway (NFF), came under German pressure to travel to Copenhagen to negotiate with DBU about a forthcoming international match. Per Finnerud, a Norwegian head of sport, also made the journey.[4] Halvorsen later became active in the Norwegian Sporting Front of resistance, and most likely he used this opportunity to inform Danish sporting circles of the true situation for Norwegian sports, warning against reaching an agreement for an international match with anyone but the legitimate representatives of NFF.[5] By all accounts, the DIF leadership would have been informed of the situation concerning Norwegian sport no later than by the end of 1940.

Despite democratic forces within Norwegian sport being against engaging in international sporting relations, DIF's defeatist attitude at the time meant that Danish sports associations could still organise Danish-Norwegian competitions. In this manner, there was nothing to stop a match in Copenhagen being arranged for a Norwegian women's handball team from Grefsen, who in December 1940 took part in an international games by the Sports Club for Women, Kvindelig Idrætsforening (KI); with the involvement of KI, Copenhagen women's gymnastics club, and the Jutland champions from Aarhus handball club.[6]

*Idrætsbladet* reported enthusiastically from the games and commended the organisers for "a spectacular entry march, excellent handball with loads of suspense, two quite beautiful gymnastics displays and a stylish finale." On top of this, the magazine pointed out that Laila Schou Nielsen played for Grefsen, which was the strongest women's handball team in Norway. Schou Nielsen was a multi-talented sportswoman, whose achievements included winning a gold medal in skiing at the 1936

Olympics when she was just 16 years old. Additionally, she was a skating star, she had won several Norwegian championships in tennis, and was now playing handball, which gave *Idrætsbladet* the opportunity to call her "the most talented sportswoman in the world". The magazine, however, considered that she was far better on skates than she was with a ball; Gunnar Hansen at the same time announcing that a radio interview with her would also be broadcast.[7]

The participation by the Norwegian women's handball team at the KI games became the occasion for a first official proposal being put forward at the DIF committee meeting for a reform of sporting relations to Norway. During the meeting, held on 30 January 1941, a report concerning the attendance of women's handball team was read out.[8]

Leo Frederiksen, in his capacity as DBU chairman, wished for clarification in regard to DIF's position on the Norwegian sports boycott, which had become pressing since he was to meet with representatives from the Nordic football association in Stockholm just two days later – a meeting that the Norwegians said they would not attend. The chairman of the rowing association, André Filtenborg, was in the same situation. Frederiksen underlined that they were in a precarious position, as Denmark openly acknowledged its sporting relations with Germany "who has a sporting governing body that now forces itself on Norway – on the other hand we have our old friends up there to consider." Frederiksen made no reference to comments by Asbjørn Halvorsen made during his October 1940 visit to Copenhagen, but said that "Sweden will not dwell in the past, but work in the present." André Filtenborg, however, did not believe that the Swedish organisers would cooperate with Norway under present conditions, since Swedish rowers had refused to take part. Holten Castenschiold, who was still chairman of DIF, until September 1941, concluded that emotionalism had to stand aside and therefore, in all correctness, they had to formally collaborate on an international plane; a position that the rest of the committee agreed with.

The situation before the federation committee meeting was such that the DIF leadership would not hinder member associations from conducting collaborative sports with Nazi sports organisations in Norway. But because of Leo Frederiksen's later contacts with Swedish heads of sport, he and Castenschiold had a strong sense that Sweden now adopted a negative stance on cooperation with Norwegian collaboration sports. With an assumption that Finland would follow suit, the Swedish and Danish sports federations against all expectations cancelled a planned meeting at the Nordic nations sports congress.[9]

The situation had suddenly altered and now DIF changed its decision, directly prompted by the Swedish stance. Before a subsequent board meeting on 3 March 1941,[10] Castenschiold had received solemn undertakings from a number of sports associations to support a rejection of collaboration with Norway. Involved were the associations for ball games, rowing, fencing and gymnastics. The tone from DIF had changed: "These aforementioned associations, in other words, will not let down our old sporting friends." Castenschiold sent out an appeal to avoid all collaboration with Norwegian sports in future, but at the same time noted that each association was still independent. However, Castenschiold's argumentation for ceasing sport with Norway shows just how flexible the slogan about keeping politics out of sports could be. A month previously, it would have been considered a political act to interfere in another country's internal sporting affairs through measures such as a boycott: now it was considered a political act to play against Norway.

> Everyone, as a private citizen, has a right to his political opinion, but he must remember that as a leader of a sporting organisation within DIF he is under an obligation to follow the line set by the Federation; namely the apolitical. It would be impossible, then, to join in fraternisation with Danish national socialist sports groups, which belong to political parties.

Castenschiold did not believe Norwegian sports were free but rather under Nazi control. The former Norwegian leadership considered the Norwegian federation to be dissolved, and they refused to cooperate with the new heads. As a consequence, the DIF chairman had refused to take part in a radio broadcast following an invitation by the Norwegian pro-Nazi Reichborn-Kjennerud, on the grounds that he could not possibly reach a decision before a Nordic conference had taken place. DIF's negotiating position was that "to cooperate with the present leadership is undesirable." "The old fellows of [Norwegian] sport" would consider it to be a hostile action.

The problem with this line of argumentation was that German sport, too, was entirely politicised: a point that the Nazi head of athletics Svend Jensen was not slow to underline. Why could they play against Germany and not the new Norway?

Castenschiold had ended up playing too many cards from his hand, and now found himself between conflicting positions. Since he would not exercise control centrally, he had also denied himself the facility of imposing sanctions against the Danish athletics association; so instead he opted to exercise moral pressure. Each association was free to do as it chose "but it will be interesting to see who maintain their liaisons."

There was no great support for Svend Jensen, however, among the remaining board members. Consequently, a number of association chairmen declared that they would cease cooperation with current Norwegian sports.[11]

In other words, continuing sporting relations with Norway was in reality optional – they just would not receive the moral support of DIF. And the responses were not slow in coming. On 29 March 1941, around three days after DIF's board meeting, Alfred Overgaard, treasurer of the Danish boxing association was quoted in *Fædrelandet* as saying he believed a national championships in May between Norway and Denmark was now settled.[12]

The Danish tennis association invited Norwegian tennis players to an open Danish championships, held in the late summer of 1941, but elicited a Norwegian rejection. In June 1942, however, the tennis association received an invitation from Norwegian sports circles, which in turn they declined due to the position taken by the leadership of DIF. The Norwegian invitation had been passed on via the athletics association.[13]

The idea that Danish and Norwegian sports competitors should be able to move more freely between the two countries came from the Danish head of athletics, Svend Jensen.[14] At the spring general meeting of the Copenhagen athletics association (KAF), in 1941, he proposed that they "should exchange sports competitors purely on the basis of a clearing account".

As already discussed, the boxers had never planned on following DIF's line, and here worries about levels of ability were of greatest concern, as they were already well into the season. Alfred Overgaard, though, believed that a Norwegian-Danish tournament should be undertaken.[15]

## Athletics games in Norway

DIF's refusal to implement an outright ban on sporting relations with Norway meant that an athletics association team, headed by their chairman Svend Jensen, and vice-chairman, E. Schnicker-Pedersen, a former chief librarian who on 8 January 1941 had become a member of the DNSAP,[16] could set out for Oslo, in September 1941.

Instead of the planned international competition, seven to eight Danish sportspeople had been invited to the Oslo games.[17] The Danish team eventually consisted of five members and was not especially strong. On Sunday, 28 September 1941, the games were finally held, which was not well-received by the Norwegian Sporting Front. According to a BBC broadcast to Denmark,[18] just before the start of the games, the Danish competitors were handed a communiqué from Sporting Front in which they were urged in the strongest terms to boycott the games in the final minutes:

> If you have the will and courage that becomes a fair sportsman and a patriotic Dane, then we leave it securely to you to decide the best way to avoid bringing disgrace upon yourself. You have perhaps come to Oslo through a misunderstanding, but you are not yet at the stadium. Remember that the contests today are not ladies' whist. What is done cannot be undone and a

day to give account of yourselves will come. Will you stand among those who bear the iron cross or among those who retain a clear conscience and honour towards their country and towards humanity.

The BBC broadcast ended by pointing out that sport was used as a political weapon by "the Nazi enemies of Denmark" and that sportspeople who wanted to help keep the reputation of Danish sport "can do this best by staying away from participation in sporting events of any kind involving Nazis of whatever type," which was also a blow to Danish-German collaborative sports. The Norwegian communiqué was published in the London periodical *Frit Danmark*, in November 1941.[19]

The political character of the games is underlined in that the winner of the 800 metre was Hans Spanheimer, a co-worker for the Nazi journal *Fædrelandet*, who won the "Cup for the best result" given by "Sports chief" Axel Heiberg Stang, against competition that included the best Norwegian present, Per Lie. The presentation of this cup, then, on a symbolic level, also bound the event to the Nazi new structuring of Norwegian sport. In an interview given to *Fritt Folk*, Svend Jensen said before the trip home that "Both the Norwegian Sports Federation organisation and its resurrection must stand today as a model that every true friend of sport can be proud of. It is nothing less than our own wishes that are realised today in the New Norway." The Norwegian team was so weak, however, that the games resulted in five Danish victories.[20]

The Danish press did not join the jubilation over Danish participation in the games. *Idrætsbladet*, *Politiken* and *Berlingske Tidende* used only a short Ritzau press bureau announcement, but *Socialdemokraten* chose to ignore the event completely, which may also have been because of the poor sporting quality.[21]

But after the athletics games at Bislett stadium, the collaboration with Norwegian sports came to a complete halt, with the exception of Turid Helland-Björnstad, a 15-year old Norwegian champion figure skater, who presented a figure skating show at the request of the Frederiksberg figure skating association, in January 1942. Helland-Björnstad came to attention when she entered a Norwegian championships and undertook a tour of Greater Germany, despite the Norwegian sports boycott. *Idrætsbladet* published a large photograph of "the Norwegian skating princess, who gave a display in national costume, hand-in-hand with a number of Danish champions, including Inger Weltzmann, Vibeke Goldberg and Per Cock-Clausen, who was one of the only two Danish figure skaters to compete in both the European and World championships, and reach the top levels of the international elite."[22] Per Cock-Clausen, according to himself, won the Nordic Competitions in figure skating, which were held in Helsingfors in 1941 for one time only during the occupation. Cock-Clausen gives no date for the competition, under his entry

*It caused some wonder among the executive committee of DIF that the Norwegian skating princess Turid Helland-Björnstad was allowed to present a figure-skating show at the request of the Danish Frederiksberg figure skating association, in January 1942. She is seen here in Norwegian national costume, together with Danish champions, including Inger Weltzmann, Vibeke Goldberg and Per Cock-Clausen, who was one of the few Danish figure skaters to reach the top levels of the international elite.*

in Dansk Sportsleksikon. Turid Helland-Björnstad is given as the winner of the women's competition.[23]

The appearance of Norwegian skaters on Danish ice caused consternation among the DIF committee who sent a referral to the chairman for the Danish skating association (DSU). Not much seems to have been gained from the meeting, however, as the minutes only record that the chairman 'replied': without more light being shed from the archives than that.[24] However, the minutes conceal a real difference of opinion between the leaderships of DSU and DIF. In all events, the scruples of DSU were not such that they had prevented the association from organising an ice-hockey match against a Norwegian team from Oslo's ice-skating association, which declined the invitation on several occasions; initially at the end of November 1941 and again in January 1942.[25]

The athletics association, however, was not about to be put off by the new breeze blowing through the DIF board, and in February 1942 Svend Jensen again tried to set up collaborative operations with Norwegian partners. Following a referral from the Norwegian federation, the idea was to organise an exchange agreement, whereby Danish athletes would be eligible to tour Norway, and Norwegian athletes be allowed to tour Denmark. The same idea was built on in July 1942, when Svend Jensen once more – this time by invitation – tried to send a troupe of sportspeople to Norway, representing a number of different sports disciplines.[26] The Danish associations politely declined his proposal. This collaborative initiative taken by the athletics association was never discussed, let alone condemned by either the DIF committee or its board, so its rejection seems to have come from the associations.

By such a process, and without being directly involved, DIF managed to avoid engaging with Norwegian collaboration sports.[27] And they held onto this strategy with some success. In August 1942, the athletics association received a visit from a Norwegian head of sport, whom they had sent on to DIF with the hope of securing permission for Danish sportspeople to travel to Oslo. At a DIF committee meeting, on 12 August 1942, the DIF chairman, now Colonel Herbert Sander, reiterated that "under no condition will DIF send athletes to Oslo. That is the responsibility of each sports association."[28]

Put bluntly, DIF did not have the will to forbid their member associations from collaborating in Norwegian sports. However, it appears in the beginning of 1942 that the DIF committee took note of the various Norwegian invitations to its member associations and advised them against accepting any offers.[29] At this point, it had become less costly to make a clear declaration in front of the occupying forces, since sporting relations in general were being diminished, and Germany now appeared to be having problems winning the war. But it seems that only Norwegian difficulties in putting together teams prevented further controversial 'Norway matches'. In January 1942, *Fædrelandet* could report on a planned Danish-Norwegian ice-hockey match, organised by the Copenhagen skating association at Peblingesøen. The event was postponed several times, to be finally cancelled and replaced by an international match between Sweden and Denmark. In the same month, the handball association of Copenhagen were invited to an inter-city championships in Berlin, which would include a Norwegian city team. The association had apparently accepted the invitation but the event was finally cancelled.[30]

The first clear signal DIF produced was to the Danish foreign ministry in March 1943, with respect to a visit to Denmark by a Norwegian head of football, to which Leo Frederiksen announced that he did not wish to receive any official approach.[31] At the time, because of German problems on the Eastern front, it seems that more forceful declarations of intent were having greater effect.

As argued by the current study, DIF accepted collaboration with boycotted Norwegian sports until it became clear that Sweden's stance was against collaboration. This meant that the sports boycott was broken when a Norwegian women's handball team, with Laila Schou Nielsen, the sports phenomenon, at their head, played in Denmark on 2 December 1940. Furthermore, the DIF decision to pursue a strategy of avoidance did not become an actual ban, since DIF would not challenge the German authorities by directly forbidding games involving Norway. Danish athletes could thereby travel to the games at Bislett stadium in Oslo, while the Norwegian skating princess Turid Helland-Björnstad could display her skating in Denmark. The scope for action commanded by the DIF leadership was not only narrowed according to German disposition but, because of the decentralisation of the decision-making process, it was also challenged by its own rebellious member associations.

Danish-Norwegian collaborative sports is so remarkable because the Norwegian boycott of international sports was highly effective. The best-known Norwegian sportspeople supported the boycott, with a few exceptions, which meant that plans for sporting relations involving Norway usually just ran out of steam as the Norwegian competitors declined to take part. The evidence suggests that a more comprehensive sporting collaboration with Norway was avoided, not solely by a negative attitude from the DIF leadership, but to a great degree by the Norwegian sports boycott.[32]

When considering Finland, it can also be stated that the poor condition of Finnish elite sports rather than any Danish hesitance was the reason that Danish-Finnish sporting relations were impeded, following the joint front by Germany and Finland against the Soviet Union, after the beginnings of the War of Continuation. Besides any purely sporting relevance, the situation for Finland gave opportunities for *Idrætsbladet* and Gunnar Hansen to convey the message of a common Nordic alliance; without necessarily clarifying whether supporting Finland also meant supporting the military ally that Finland sided with. A victory for Finland, whom Danes would naturally support, would also mean a victory for Germany.[33]

# RENEWED GERMAN CONTACT

## Trouble in the boxing ring

By the middle of September 1941, Hitler approved a resumption of the Reich's international sporting relations, and so up until and including January the following year collaborative sports between Denmark and Germany were once more up and running. The disturbances seen at the Admira match back in June 1941 meant that any propaganda value from international matches now had to be reaped in Germany, where the German public could be spurred on with entertainments, and by watching friendly cultural exchanges between the occupiers and the occupied. Hans Joachim Teichler, the prominent German sports historian, has found that Danish sports played against German teams, in football, handball, wrestling and boxing, were used as entertainments to soothe popular German fears over the beginning of the Winter war against the Soviet Union, from October to December 1941.[1]

In Denmark, games continued to be arranged with German participation, and in keeping with their earlier track record the sports association Sparta took an active role. At the large annual all-round games, four of Germany's best boxers took part, with a special commotion being made about a light heavyweight bout between Svend Aage Christensen and Rudi Pepper who at that point had only lost one fight in his entire career. Herbert Nürnberg, twice German European Champion, in 1937 and again in 1939, also made the trip to Copenhagen, but as he was in a class of his own it was not possible to find a suitable opponent. Instead, he took on the job of second.[2]

The games caused a few raised eyebrows among Danish authorities. The matches were to be held on 8 October 1941, but after the Admira disturbances four months earlier, there were still concerns that Danish spectators would again cause trouble for the occupying forces. A large number of police were therefore put on duty around Idrætshuset in Copenhagen, around 50 men, which must have been fairly conspicuous.[3]

The unease developed rapidly during the light heavyweight bout between the two all-time rivals, tough Rudi Pepper and the left-footer Svend Aage Christensen. Both the police and the boxing authorities must have been given a start when in the first two rounds the Danish fighter gave Pepper a battle right to the edge, and delivered so many counter punches that the public got wind of a sensation. Pepper's irritation increased in step with the number of points he fell behind by, and in the last round he launched a formidable offensive. The result was that Svend Aage Christensen went down twice from tremendous punches, on both occasions for the count of nine. Rudi Pepper was declared the winner, and for a moment there was "the buildup to some truly ugly feeling" since Svend Aage Christensen had delivered "an exceptionally fine performance over the first two rounds and for half of the final round."

But the tempers eventually subsided.

On the Danish team, there was only one real favourite. This was Viggo Frederiksen who was up against Ludwig Petri, whom Frederiksen had beaten once before. Petri, who was first in the ring "was welcomed with a huge cheer, which boded well for the course of the evening. But the cheer rose to hurricane force when Viggo Frederiksen climbed through the ropes." The Danish crowd, however, was in for a shock when the German, after landing a series of straight lefts, unleashed in a split second "a pre-planned and explosive right-hand hook" that sent the Dane to the floor. Frederiksen, too, was down for the count of nine and although he could not recover what he had lost "the Dane woke and stirred himself, and got back in a fight that had captured the public", which "gave rise to many bursts of applause and helped obscure the weak Danish effort of the earlier rounds."

In fact the tournament went so badly for Denmark that before the final heavyweight bout the Danish team had not won a single victory. For the finale, Carlo Nielsen fought Wilson Kohlbrecher, a "well-built and clean-fighting boxer", whom Nielsen beat on points after a very even fight, the judgement being described afterwards as questionable.

Cheered in this fashion, the Danish public was then treated to a new tournament a few days later. This was held on 19 October, involving the same German boxers, and once again Idrætshuset was sold out.[4]

It was clear that their annoyance about the poor Danish performance during the previous tournament still weighed on the Danish spectators, who conducted themselves with less control this time, perhaps encouraged, too, by a weakened police presence. Quite simply, the public demanded a Danish victory; their demand being pinned firmly onto the first Dane in the ring, Frands Zmuda, who was to meet Ludwig Petri. The Danish boxer had decided, presumably, to extract revenge for Petri's win over Viggo Frederiksen, and he attacked "almost unceasing" his German opponent. Petri – who took countless hard blows, according to the fight report – nevertheless scored most because of the exceptional quality of his counter attacks, but his win was not popular. Already, "tempers were flaring up again" after the first bout, and a "long-lasting chorus of whistling" broke out, which must have raised tensions inside the hall, given fears of a new Admira incident by the Danish and German authorities.

But the organisers were saved by the bell: or perhaps saved by the German team? Miraculously, Willy Jensen won the next bout against Carl Schmidt, which caused the Danish crowd to calm down a little. It was a "deserved but not a great victory", wrote *Idrætsbladet*, and considering the bad atmosphere it may be possible that the German boxer fell victim to a political game – perhaps along with the German heavyweight Wilhelm Kohlbrecher, at the previous tournament. It might be imagined that the German authorities were willing to surreptitiously step back, should the build up to an incident seem likely. Whatever the speculation, the tournament took a strange turn of events that simply did not match the usual German levels of fitness or the flair of their boxing. Schmidt seemed tired and lacking motivation, and he blatantly did not box a clean fight, making so many bad punches that he managed to incur a warning.[5]

Schmidt's frustrated, unclean technique becomes understandable if he had been given orders to lose: losing a fight could very well mean a one-way ticket to service on the front.

For this second tournament, the Danish organisers had been able to find an opponent for Herbert Nürnberg, the double European Champion. He won a predictable victory over Birger Petersen from a seaman's boxing club, Sømændenes Idrætsklub, but not with his usual superior style. *Idrætsbladet* believed his fitness level was poor and that he constantly tried to draw out the time. In the second round Nürnberg used "student boxing" that "is often used in long professional fights", but it is perhaps more plausible that this normally so supreme boxer had received orders not to use the Danish seaman as a punch bag.

The difficulty in matching the German opponents and at the same time avoiding a sound thrashing can be clearly seen in the fight between Rudi Pepper and Henry Lehmann, in which the Dane "grabbed on like a lobster" and fought so uncleanly that it was nearly "comic". The bout was obviously nothing to write home about, and in the last fight of the evening, an unenthusiastic Wilhelm Kohlbrecher, the German heavyweight, made sure of an anti-climax in a bout that "fell a little flat, after the proceeding fight." One can speculate whether Kohlbrecher was preoccupied with thoughts of his doubtful defeat in the previous tournament, and subsequently had difficulty in summoning enough enthusiasm. All in all, the second boxing tournament ended undramatically, and in that way exerted no influence over going ahead with the third Sparta event that month involving German competitors. These bouts were held on 26 October 1941 in Idrætshuset, in Copenhagen; organised together with the wrestling association, and with participation by two German and two Swedish wrestlers.[6]

The Danish home games all went off quietly, but altogether there was a palpable anxiety among the German and Danish organisers, especially over the first sporting tournament held on Danish ground since the resumption of sporting relations. A large police presence had a preventative effect, but at one point during Sparta's second boxing event there seemed to be an upsurge towards an incident; which shows the extent to which collaborative sports could be a double-edged sword.

# GAMES IN GERMANY

After September 1941, when the German authorities again permitted international sporting relations, a lively stream of activities resumed and a number of Danish teams as well as individual competitors travelled to Germany. The most important event was a game played by the Danish national football team on 16 November, in Dresden; but these footballers were not the first to compete on German soil. At the beginning of November, the Danish national handball team played an international match against Germany, as they had the year before, but this time in Hamburg. Not unexpectedly, the German team won easily, 13-8.[1] According to *Fædrelandet*, up to 10,000 spectators turned up to watch.[2]

## International football in Dresden

The handball match, however, could not compare to the international game in Dresden, which was given the highest priority by both Danish and German sports authorities. The game was to be a return match for the Hamburg game, in other words a replacement for the planned game at Idrætsparken June 1941 that had been cancelled by the German authorities. This would be the last international football match against Germany during the occupation.[3]

Although Alex Friedmann, a Jewish Danish player, had taken part in the Hamburg international and had also played against Sweden on 14 September 1941, he was not part of the squad for Dresden, perhaps because the positions of which country was most passionate about collaborative sports had been switched round, and now it was the German authorities who denied a visa to a Jewish competitor. Friedmann did not play in October 1941, against Sweden, either, but was nevertheless part of the team for the two international matches against Sweden held the following year.[4]

It was not only the Danish press that got excited. An article in Völkischer Beobachter guardedly cautioned against a well-oiled Danish machine, in the same way that the German dailies characterised the Danish squad having a team of extremely high quality. Furthermore, the sports writers for the German papers took a keen interest in the question of which players would be in the line-up.[5]

The Danish team played in a stadium filled to capacity in front of 50,000 spectators, which included groups of Danish workers who had travelled in from several German cities.[6] The match was to be played on a pitch that was frozen hard, in a biting cold wind, so the Danish players needed to have the studs on their boots cut down. The overall organisation of the match was clearly affected by Germany being at war. There were no corner flags and the stadium was not decked out for the occasion, with only four large flags: Germany, Denmark, Sweden and the flag of German Reich Sports. The flag of Sweden was doubtless included because of the Swedish referee, which gave the German authorities an opportunity to underline Nordic-Germanic unity.[7]

The Danish squad also came to play a role for German military propaganda. The Germans presented the event in a military context. The warm-up was provided by a match between two select teams, from the Luftwaffe and the local garrison in Dresden, which ended in a last-minute victory for the air force. When the 22 international players and the referee lined up in the middle of the pitch, greeted by "a lively cheer" from the crowd, a German military orchestra played King Christian and the two German war-time anthems, which means also the Nazi Horst Wessel.

*Spectators at a primitive stadium in Dresden, November 1941. To the front, most probably, are Danish workers in Germany, carrying the Danish flag, Dannebrog, in their hands. German soldiers can be seen among the crowd (seated figure, bottom right). The young men clinging to the trees suggest high levels of public interest.*

*An international match in Dresden. In the front row of the podium, third from the right, can be seen the powerful head of the Danish football associations, Leo Frederiksen, with hat in hand.*

For the first 20 minutes of the match, the Danes came under heavy attack, and the Danish defender Poul Hansen saved a shot from off the goal line delivered by the well-known German striker Edmund Conen. The Danish team were having trouble getting on top of their game, while the Germans were able to cut through, playing combinations almost as they wished. Perhaps because of the cold, the German spectators had become somewhat quiet. A Danish contingent in the opposite right corner could be heard chanting to one of the Danish forwards "Søbirk, Søbirk, with all your might, that's the stuff old Frits don't like". After a time, play became more even, but in the 38th minute, following a variety of misunderstandings and bad luck among the Danish defence, Hahnemann, the Austrian forward, managed to score.

The second half started off with the Danish players slightly disorientated, as the military orchestra continued playing at full force. It was likewise impossible to hear Ivan Eklind, the referee, blow his whistle when Hahnemann wasted a superb opportunity. But luck was on the Danish side. After 55 minutes, the German keeper made a dreadful error and dropped the ball at the feet of Kai Hansen, who resolutely pounded it into the net between two German defenders. During the remainder of the match, the defence on both sides fought hard. The German team had the most chances, but despite German pressure the match ended a draw.

There was an official post-match dinner held at the hotel, which brought the Danish squad and Danish diplomats together with the German political and military leaders in Dresden. Present were the City Mayor, his director, the president of the German football federation (DFB), Felix Linnemann, and from the Danish embassy Schøn, the embassy secretary, and Reimer, the ambassador. Speeches were given and the Danes received, "special mementoes of the match, various pictures of Dresden, a commemorative glazed tile and some books". On behalf of the Danes present, Leo Frederiksen gave a speech to the German leaders in which he emphasised that Germans could look forward to "an entirely different match", next year, when they would play in Copenhagen: a match, however, that would never take place.[8]

In the German press, the focus was naturally placed solely on the game, which they considered to be of high quality and whereby Danish players were praised in a number of sources. In the German special magazine Der Kicker, a Dr Nerz announced that the match draw resulted especially from the skilled efforts of the Danish goal keeper and the two Danish defenders, while the story on the game in the German journal Kampf stood out by its glorification in military prose of the German squad, at the same time believing the most brutal players of the match to be the Danes.

There were other places, too, where the Danish efforts were not especially appreciated but for quite different reasons. A summary of a BBC Denmark transmission from November 1941 is kept in the archives of the Danish foreign ministry and is testimony for an attack in strong terms on collaborative sports – particularly against the match in Dresden: saying that events such as these could present Danes as pro-German, when they dutifully and innocently let themselves be used by the Nazis. The Germans used the match for propaganda purposes and the Danish national team, therefore, should stay away from tournaments or matches against Nazis "of whatever shade".[9]

There were, nevertheless, serious concerns to be addressed leading up to the coming year's Nordic football congress in Stockholm, held in February 1942. The Danish Football Association was worried about the prospects of international matches being abandoned. As far as matches against Norway were concerned, there was nothing to be done and matches against Finland would likewise hardly be a prospect. But *Idrætsbladet* could still report that the congress would be attended by "a representative or deputation from the German football federation. Last year, as is known, Germany played against Finland, Sweden and Denmark, and they will presumably be taking the opportunity, where representatives from Norway are present, to line up agreements for German international matches with Scandinavian countries for the current year."

According to the Swedish press, Hungary, too, had entered negotiations with the Nordic countries with a view to organising a tour of Sweden, Denmark and Norway, with "international matches in the respective capital cities".[10] The Stockholm congress was eventually cancelled, so the Danish football association instead invited representatives from the football associations of Germany, Finland and Sweden to a conference in Copenhagen, on Sunday 15 March 1942, to "decide fixtures for that year's international matches between Denmark and the aforementioned countries". Finland had sent a telegram saying their association member E. Koskinen would be attending, which was especially well-received within DBU circles since "this message seems to indicate that DBU may well have its ambition fulfilled for an international match against the Finns, in Copenhagen." However, "because of circumstances" DBU needed to cancel the Copenhagen conference, but, in the words of Valdemar Laursen, a Danish international referee, "Hopefully, the cancellation of the coming conference will not hinder a new conference being convened as soon as possible."[11] The vice-chairman of DBU also travelled to Germany in May 1942 to negotiate yet another international match, but nothing availed from this approach either.[12]

Danish-German collaboration conducted around international matches continued on German soil with the Dresden game as its flagship. It was German reluctance that made the Dresden game the last international football match played against Germany during the occupation. In contrast, the leadership of the Danish football was in full swing with initiatives for international matches; but, as would become apparent, Danish representatives would soon be left with little room for manoeuvre in organising such events.

## The Danish war-time European champion
The on-the-spot reporter for *Idrætsbladet*, its editor, Magnus Simonsen, stayed in Germany after the Dresden game for Denmark's coming international boxing tournament, in less than a week's time, in Munich. At stake was a competition in which the Danish referee, Aage Krøll, would be participating. Krøll had also been active in Germany ten days before the tournament, when Germany met Italy in an international match, held in Breslau, as well as at a tournament in Stuttgart, where the Italian national team had met a select team of German boxers. From his close knowledge of German elite boxing, Krøll believed that the national Danish team could give the Germans an even fight.[13]

The Danish boxers were welcomed at an official reception.[14] Afterwards, they took part in German war propaganda by laying a wreath at a memorial for soldiers killed in the World War, and they were finally guests at a large reception at the city hall. At the tournament itself, on 22 November 1941, 5,000 spectators turned up at the Krone Circus buildings to a sold-out event. The German boxers had been in Munich for nearly a week, training for their bouts, and despite the war they all seemed to be fit for fight. The three judges were from Germany, Denmark and Sweden. The Swedish referee was Oscar Söderlund, the pro-German Swedish president of the International Boxing Association.

In contrast to the earlier fights in Copenhagen, the Danes were now up against a completely different kind of opposition that did not hesitate in the slightest. It was almost another 'Breslau catastrophe' but in boxing rather than football, and the tournament ended in total German victory. But for boxing enthusiasts, there were other developments that were worth reporting on in the Danish press.

In place of the cancelled European Championships, the Danish boxing association accepted an invitation to the so-called war-time European championships held at the Centennial Hall venue in Breslau, in January 1942. Eleven nations and around one hundred boxers fought in front of an audience of mostly Germans.[15] The event took place under the leadership of the chairman of the International Boxing Association, Oscar Söderlund, while the head of German boxing, Hans Hieronymus, managed to put on a war-time European championships that were every bit as colourful and grandiose as the usual European championships. Besides a contribution from Söderlund, there were speeches given at the opening ceremony by two top Nazi figures, the deputy for the Reichssportführer, Arnold Breitmeyer, and the Nazihead of occupied Silesia, Karl Hahnke, which in best propaganda mode covered the German war effort and the new order of European sport under German leadership.[16]

Denmark participated with two boxers and the 'activistic' head of boxing from the Sparta club, Georg Schmidt.[17] The heavyweight, Carl Nielsen, lost his first fight against his Italian opponent after what the Danes believed was a questionable verdict. On the other hand, Svend Aage Christensen, with his technical competence and wider repertoire, also from Sparta, could return home as the new light heavyweight war-time European champion. However, his victory is partially attributable to the weakened opposition at this point in the war. In fact, Denmark had failed to achieve European championship medals at the previous three European championships, and only took part in the world championships in Milan in 1937, in which only one of the five Danish boxers to compete won a single fight.[18]

The Danish camp was already aggrieved that Svend Aage Christensen had to meet Rudi Pepper in the semifinals, who not so many months earlier had won an easy victory on points at Idrætshuset, in which he had twice sent the Dane to the floor. But this time, apparently, Svend Aage Christensen had done his homework. In the first two rounds, Pepper opened up with a moderate tempo, while the Sparta boxers took a defensive position, replying with counter punches. In the third round, Svend Aage Christensen went more on the offensive, and in the end brought home a victory despite a warning for having bent over too low during the bout.[19] The result was the

*"Ceremonial opening of the wartime European championships ... Gauleiter and president-in-chief Hahnke at the welcoming reception." Such was the German propaganda text to this press photograph from Breslau in January 1942. Despite the hardships of the war, the propaganda value in sport clearly continued to have high priority.*

cause of a fierce chorus of whistling around the Centennial Hall. In the final, Svend Aage Christensen fought against Otto Profitlich, whom he beat on points. To put it mildly, the German press were unimpressed by Christensen,[20] who nevertheless received a handsome championship belt together with a bronze statuette of a boxer that, according to the Danish newspaper *Berlingske Tidende*, was Breslau's trophy of honour for excellent boxing. Was Christensen's dubious victory an expression of political appreciation for a small occupied country that sent competitors to Axis power games?[21]

What can be referred to with certainty is a 'war-time European championships' with low levels of competition. Apart from boxers from Axis-power nations, there were only Danish and Swedish competitors who achieved first-place results among the winning nations' boxers. In the national competitions, Germany came first, followed by Italy, Sweden and Hungary in a tied third place, and then Denmark and Spain. Sweden's K.G. Norén took the middleweight title.

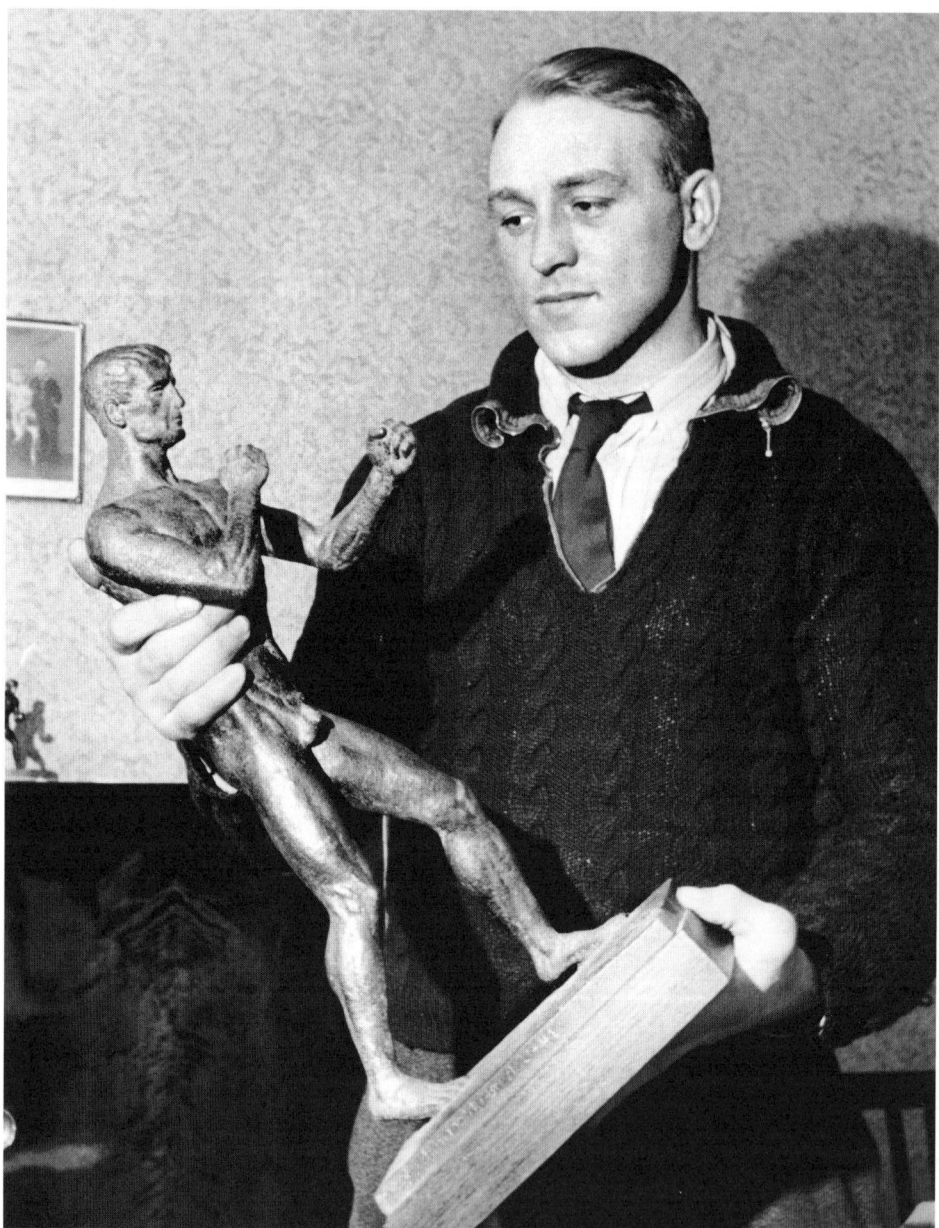

*The Wartime European Champion Svend Aage Christensen with his trophy. He had presumably no reservations against joining in the German so-called wartime European championships.*

As for the attitude of the boxing association, it is revealing that a Danish referee named Marius Sick, who had been interred by the Germans in October 1942, had the return of his licence refused by the Danish boxing association committee, because the boxing association did not wish to appear to be provocative. Later that year, however, Sick did manage to regain his licence but the association recommended to their clubs that he be used as little as possible.[22]

## A Jewish and a Communist wrestler

The two examples that the current study would now like to turn to deal with a problem that has not yet been treated. Nazi sports policy had grave consequences of course for the Nazis' declared public enemies among Jews and Communists, and in this respect it is possible to follow two national-team wrestlers, one Danish and one German, who both became entrapped by Nazi persecution.

Wrestlers from the Danish athletics union (DAU) continued to play an active role in collaborative sports with Germany at a national level. On 29 and 30 November 1941, a 'three-nations' international match was held between Germany, Denmark and Croatia, in Stuttgart. After the German invasion of Yugoslavia in April 1941, the German occupation forces set up Ante Pavelic's radical nationalists in a puppet government in Croatia, and under the wings of the German eagle Croatia annexed the remains of Bosnia-Herzegovina, committing wholesale mass murder of Serbs.

In the international wrestling matches, Germany beat Croatia 7-0, and won a 5-2 victory over Denmark, who beat Croatia with the same result. Gunnar Nielsen managed once more to beat the legendary but no-longer quite so young German star, Werner Seelenbinder, although this time only by a supreme effort. Matches were also won in bantamweight by Eigil Johansen and in lightweight by the Danish champion Robert Voigt from Sparta.

On 28 December 1941, the Danish club Dan held a competition with participation of, again, Werner Seelenbinder and the German weight-lifting champion Hans Clausen, who both won their events.[23] This would be the last time the Danish sports world saw Werner Seelenbinder. Seelenbinder provides an example of how German national competitors certainly did not have to be Nazis, as they were forced to give the 'heil' salute when the national anthem was played. Seelenbinder was a Communist and had won the Soviet Spartakiad in Moscow, in 1928, as the sole German workers' sportsman. In 1933, his local branch of KPD in Neukölln gave him the task of qualifying for international competitions in order to establish international contacts as part of the communist underground network. In 1937 and 1938, when he won bronze medals at the European championships, he took the opportunity to smuggle information and propaganda material into Germany. During the war, he formed a close alliance with a resistance group, built up around the figure of Robert Uhrig.

When the Uhrig group was exposed, Werner Seelenbinder was arrested on 4 August 1942 and executed in October 1944. After the war he was taken on as an icon by the 'anti-fascist workers' State', DDR, and a number of sports facilities were named after him – including the prestigious Werner Seelenbinder Hall in East Berlin, where arrangements such as party conferences were held by the East German Communist Party.[24]

It is not known whether Seelenbinder, during his visit to Denmark, tried to contact Danish communist circles, whose activities, though, had been mitigated up until 22 June 1941 by the German-Soviet Non-Aggression Pact.[25]

The occupation of Denmark also meant that Jewish wrestlers could no longer appear for the Danish national team in international events. Despite such limitations, the legendary lightweight wrestler Abraham Kurland, from the Jewish club Hakoah, made an enormous contribution to Danish wrestling during the first half of the occupation. He provided free coaching for a number of clubs – Sparta, Thor and C.I.K. – all at the risk that many of his competitors would become significantly better.

It is notable that Kurland did not take his place in the national wrestling competitions against Germany in November 1940. At that time, Denmark was under occupation and Kurland – who was an obvious candidate for the national team – had taken part in an international match against Norway, in Oslo, earlier in January that year. During the occupation, the Hakoah club magazine debated whether Kurland would be granted a travel visa to Sweden, in November 1941. The visa was not forthcoming, presumably because the German authorities prevented it. And it was not only in sporting circles that the refusal came to attention. In his diary, Vilhelm Bergstrøm, a journalist and author, noted

> There was talk about a bad affair in sport. There was supposed to be an international wrestling match between Denmark and Sweden. Naturally our notables, Abraham Kurland and Isak Paikin, should have been there. But there were difficulties in getting a travel permit from the German authorities. No-one wanted to know the two Jews. But when the wrestling association dropped their two best men, there were suddenly no more problems. It's made a lot of people in the sports world angry. They don't think the association should have dropped the two names; should have cancelled the match instead. The Swedish would definitely have understood us.[26]

Isak Paikin – who incidentally had moved from Hakoah to Dan perhaps so as not to signal so blatantly his Jewish background – and Kurland gained an opportunity to compete against Sweden at Idrætshuset in Copenhagen, on 12 December 1942, whereby the travel permit problem was avoided. With their two wins, Kurland and Paikin helped to limit the Danish defeat to 4-3 to Sweden, who typically were so strong in wrestling. Sports-Bladet wrote about the matches that "in the lightweight category, too, there's a good chance for Denmark, as Abraham Kurland still needs to be regarded amongst the European elite, even though he has fought only rarely against international opposition since the war." Kurland won, but only just, after his many coaching jobs had left his own training in the shade.[27]

The sports club Hakoah had been one of the strongest Danish wrestling clubs over the years up to the German occupation. In November 1941, to a sold-out house, the club won the team competitions above strong club teams such as Dan and Sparta, who were the main suppliers for the national team. From the lightweight to heavyweight classes, the Hakoah champion club team members were K. Leizerowitz, Michael Kurland, Jacob Leizerowitz, Abraham Kurland and Isak Paikin. At Hakoah's own competitions in December 1941, Abraham Kurland was able to celebrate his victory number 700 in front of a capacity crowd at Borgernes Hus, in Copenhagen. Abraham Kurland also won the Copenhagen city championships in January 1942 and 1943.[28]

DIF accepted their sporting relations with the occupying powers even though it meant that Jewish-Danish wrestlers were excluded from taking part on equal terms with their sporting colleagues at international events. The situation surrounding Abraham Kurland, especially, was not only a political admission but also a major loss to sport. As long as the top leadership of DIF wished for continued good relations with the occupying forces and that Danish sports should avoid reprisals, their room for political manoeuvre was so diminished that they could not even protect their own members. The Danish sports world cheered its war-time European boxing champion, but made no great deal out of the lost opportunity for a Danish victory from one of the greatest Danish sportsmen ever, Jewish Abraham Kurland. In practice, DIF thereby gave an admission to the Nazi racial policy.

# THE LAST COLLABORATION

## Matches against Italy and Hungary

As it had become too dangerous to arrange international matches played in Denmark against the occupying forces, DIF needed to turn its attentions to other Axis powers. The Danish tennis federation (DTF) therefore organised an international match against Italy at the indoor tennis courts of the ball-sports club B.93, at Østerbro in Copenhagen, for 30 and 31 November 1941. There was much anxiety over whether the Danish players would be able to compete, since at the last international match in KB-Hallen in 1939 Italy had won all nine matches of the tournament. And in the middle of the War, Italy was still one of Europe's strongest tennis nations, having the top two supreme men's singles players at their head: Giovanni Cucelli and Francesco Romanoni. Danish hopes were founded on the Italian team's lack of experience at indoor tennis. The Danes had only recently lost a tennis tournament to Sweden, but then so had the Italians. Denmark lost the tournament 6-0, and a short time afterwards lost again to Sweden, 5-0.[1]

Although sporting relations with Germany were grinding to a halt, there were still opportunities for representatives from Axis-alliance countries to compete in Denmark. In March 1942, Denmark's largest tennis club, Hellerup Idrætsklub (HIK), reached an agreement with the Croatian tennis players Pallada and Mitic to play exhibition matches at the HIK indoor courts at Hartmannsvej, in Copenhagen. The tennis hall had a capacity of up to 2,000 and was often used for international matches. Every evening, three matches would be played, in which the Croatians would compete against HIK's best players, which included Helge Plougmann, Aage Seier Hansen, Per Thielsen and Jannik Ipsen.[2]

The two Croatian players also entered the Danish Open tennis championships in April 1942, and took a large share of the cake, when they ran off with gold medals in both the men's singles and men's doubles competitions.[3] In the same way as the previous year, when German players had dominated men's tennis, the two Croatians also appeared as Danish national champions in the annual report of DIF.[4] A German tennis star, Hilde Sperling, who happened to be married to a Dane, was a Danish triple national champion by winning the women's singles as well as the women's and mixed doubles.[5]

Sperling was born Hilde Krahwinkel, in 1908, and was "the European Continent's greatest active lady tennis player and ranks high among the world elite. She won a whole parcel of European championships, several times the French and German, and has played in finals at Wimbledon, both at singles and mixed doubles."[6]

For DIF, it was a problem when individuals from either Axis-alliance countries or from the occupying powers became Danish national champions in sports such as tennis. This would immediately prompt associations along the lines of mixed German and Danish national identities, which could be reminiscent of Nazi impressions of a unified Germanic people. The Federation decided therefore, on 4 May 1942, that only naturalised Danish sportspeople could become Danish national champions and only at championships held in Denmark.[7] The decision did not stop foreign nationals from taking part, but if they were to win, the national champion title would go to the best-placed Dane.

As late as 20 November 1942, a Danish national handball team played against Hungary in Copenhagen, and lost narrowly by 13-12. In this way, the activistic Danish handball association hold the questionable honour of playing the last national match against a team from the Axis powers during the occupation. On the front cover of *Idrætsbladet*, the text and images showed "When Hungary won the international handball match in the very last seconds".[8]

The Danish team had led three to four minutes before the final whistle from Åke Thorsen, the Swedish referee. Nevertheless, *Idrætsbladet* chose to see the positive side of the situation, since it had been "an especially brilliant game. Certainly, it had been a tough match, as the Hungarian didn't mind so much as to what methods they used to stop the Danish attack. But there was tension and excitement in the game, so field handball has surely gained a lot of new supporters since Wednesday."[9]

## Germany backs out

Over the last half-year of 1941, it became increasingly difficult for Danish teams to play international teams on Danish ground. For example, the Danish swimming association had applications for travel permits turned down on three occasions, for international matches against Sweden. Within the association, the feeling was that the refusals were a response to declined invitations to German competitions when the parents of Danish swimmers had withheld permission. Meanwhile, the association found no problems in competing against Germans but it would not send off a second-rank team.[10]

*Fædrelandet* squarely placed the blame on the swimming association's chairman Niels Bruun Jagd, and in their January number 1942[11] the magazine criticised Jagd for not being able to get the Danish swimmers to cooperate. The swimming association had been invited to an international competition in Germany, but in an interview Jagd explained that he was not especially keen to "send our people out, in these times" but he would happily have an international event here at home, especially against Sweden. He left the question of an international competition against Germany up to the swimmers themselves: whether "they are allowed time off, and that sort of thing …" The international event was later cancelled, for which *Fædrelandet* held Jagd personally responsible.[12] Jagd also resigned as chairman in 1942.

In the New Year's number of *Idrætsbladet*, there was a retrospective evaluation of 1941, without over-due focus on the many Danish sporting defeats in Germany. The magazine stuck to its usual line of reporting results, seen very much through Danish glasses.[13] If a comparison was made with the previous year, then activities abroad were certainly reduced: a situation that was not about to improve. According to *Fædrelandet*, the Reichssportführer, von Tschammer, had issued orders around January 1942 that sporting relations with teams that were at a distance of 50 kilometres or more would be put on hold until further notice. On those grounds, an intercity tournament in Berlin was cancelled, to which the Copenhagen handball association had been invited.[14]

Very gradually, the war effort began to take its toll on the sports-loving German nation. In 1939, German teams took part in 106 different sporting events, competing against 19 countries; the level falling in the first year of the war to around half; and in 1942 German teams taking part in 51 events against just 9 other countries.[15] The remaining Axis-alliance countries were also becoming too involved in the war to be able to spare much time for sporting relations with Denmark, apart from the one handball match against Hungary in November 1942.

Germany was so involved in war action that sporting activities began to seem an unnecessary luxury. The flagging interest of the occupying power was expressed in a communication to the collected Danish sports associations, from 24 January 1942, in which Sander wrote that DIF and the German legation had agreed to limit the extent of Danish-German sporting relations because of "the current difficult situation that reigns". Collaborative sports should be restricted to matches in which DIF had a special interest "in seeing Danish colours represented".[16] Put briefly, more control over collaborative sports was needed so the German authorities would not feel provoked by activities such as a lively traffic in sport between Denmark and Sweden.

The new agreement between the DIF leadership and the occupying power imposed hard limits on the freedoms of individual associations and clubs in terms of the collaborative sports that DIF now had greater control over. But only a short period afterwards, the situation turned sour when the executive committee of DIF learnt in February 1942 that the skating association of Copenhagen, Københavns Skøjteunion, had invited a Swedish skating club, Göta, without the knowledge of DIF.[17]

As a result it was decided that a suggestion be made to the ministry in charge that all applications concerning international relations should be put before DIF "so that in reality it is DIF that makes a decision."[18] In contrast to the earlier situation, it was now DIF who regulated levels of collaboration. They needed to prioritise requests for entry and exit visas, which had become limited due to fading German interest in sporting relations. The goods needed to be divided fairly. As it turned out, though, Danish sportspeople gained plenty of opportunities to compete against their Swedish counterparts, perhaps because the German authorities had lost interest in sport as a medium for politics. They were busy, instead, trying not to lose the world war.

There were limits, then, on what could be achieved. In February 1942, a team of Danish cyclists and ballplayers from the club Cyclisten travelled to Germany and in December 1942 Sparta invited a German and a Swedish team of boxers to take part in a tournament, in January the following year. The German boxers would come "from Hamburg – from the Luftwaffe, where Sparta had visited earlier."[19] The events were cancelled, however, but not from a lack of enthusiasm from Danish quarters.

The last Danish-German event was organised by the Danish shooting association, set for September 1942, comprising a shooting match held on the home ground of each team, whereby scores would be exchanged via telephone; in other words, the German shootists not being physically present.[20] The events passed off unnoticed, however, by the Danish press and even *Idrætsbladet*.

The chairman of the shooting association, Ove Bjørn, had laid plans during the occupation for four shooting matches against Germany, of which only the first in September 1942 actually took place. In an article from April 1942, published in the illegal *De Frie Danske*, Ove Bjørn was attacked for using the shooting association as "a propaganda object for the German Wehrmacht" and for having tried to organise "friendly shooting matches in Berlin" since 1940, all of which, however, had come to nothing because of factors such as the competitors' "pronounced aversion to take part in such manifestations of a Danish-German spirit of friendship." *De Frie Danske* encouraged shooting association members, as soon as possible to "liquidate this pest".[21] Ove Bjørn resigned as chairman in 1944.[22]

Collaborative amateur sports were now approaching their end. The Germans were busy elsewhere, and their sporting relations both with foreign countries and internally within Germany were grinding to a halt. As will be shown in the next chapter – this was extremely important for the professional Danish sportspeople who were working in Germany.

Altogether, it can be stated regarding sporting relations that it was most certainly not Danish enthusiasm that was in short supply, but rather that Germans withdrew of their own accord, because of difficulties on the battle field.

## Professionals say farewell

The primary professional sportspeople involved were cyclists and boxers, as already discussed in this study.

On Christmas day 1941, the Danish boxer Hans Holdt fought Carl Busz in Busz's home city, Strasbourg. Holdt lost an otherwise even fight. There were also defeats for two other Danish professional boxers who were fighting at around the same time in Leipzig. Henry Nielsen lost badly to Gustav Eder, and Valdemar Krontoft was knocked out in the second round by Kurt Bernhardt.[23] *Idrætsbladet* was very positive about Hans Holdt, and the magazine published a large illustrated interview with him, for his 38th birthday in January 1942. There were other boxers involved, too. Carl Andersen, the most successful Danish professional boxer during the war, had found work in January 1942 in Germany in the hope that he could use this as a platform for boxing tours around Germany. In May 1942, sports journalist Gunnar Hansen could report that Andersen and Henry Nielsen, fronted by a promoter, Bjørn Thalbitzer, would take part in a tournament in Milan, on Sunday 10 May, in which Andersen would fight the excellent welterweight Peire, while Nielsen would go up against Mussina, who was ranked on the newly established Italian-German boxing federation list as the European champion. *Idrætsbladet* wrote afterwards that both Danes lost before a crowd of 7,000, which "can't really come as any surprise" because although they were "both physically fit" "they had to fight after a 54-hour journey, and for most of the trip they'd had to sit on each other's laps."[24]

The Italian promoter and the public were nevertheless offered new bouts, on the spot. The promoter thought that there were a great many fights in Italy but that travel was a big problem. The Danish boxers had to insist on flying, otherwise the relative strengths between boxers would be unfair. The promoter stayed on in Italy while the two Danish boxers returned home "as it was far too expensive for us to stay down there."[25]

However, criticism of the Danish boxers came from Swedish sources. The critique was founded solely on sporting reasons, though, because what the Danes had done in Milan was "such a disparaging performance that it will damage the entire Nordic reputation."[26]

The individual boxers especially had trouble accepting that the golden days of Danish-German tournaments were over.

Hans Drescher, a professional Danish boxer, on Saturday 27 June 1942, achieved "a fine victory" in Hamburg by knocking out the German Fritz Reppert – Reppert being unlucky enough to hit the canvass with his chin. The fight was part of a tournament, the main attraction at which was Adolf Heuser, defending his German heavyweight title against the challenger, Walter Neusel.[27]

In September 1942, Hans Drescher met the European champion, Jupp Besselmann, in Leipzig and brought off the expected Danish defeat. *Idrætsbladet* wrote on its front cover that Drescher was "the public's darling, because of his excellent technical boxing. He was well composed, energetic, and time-and-again stopped the European champion's heavy attacks with his fast one-two combinations." The German papers praised Drescher's "inventiveness, his elegant and entertaining boxing".[28]

But it was not only boxers who persisted in their efforts. In May 1942, an announcement came from Berlin that Frode Sørensen, a Danish road race cycle rider, who had turned professional, "this splendid fellow now slightly on in years" had won the Berlin Tour on Monday 11 May, which was passed on in a report to which *Idrætsbladet* had exclusive rights. In blazing sunshine, Sørensen won a sure and deserved victory in front of a large crowd, with estimates of around 50,000 people having lined the 75-kilometre route in northern Berlin. The field comprised 39 riders. Originally far more had registered but "the demands of war precede those of sport, and many well-known riders were unable to attend."[29]

Frode Sørensen, together with Knud Jacobsen and Christian Christensen, were on the road again in June 1942, travelling South for professional races. Frode Sørensen, in a report to Gunnar Hansen, said they had competed in seven cities, including Saarbrücken and in Luxemburg, and "had been among the top ten each time". Gunnar Hansen explained that the Danish riders would be competing again in Germany in July 1942, since certain results could now be expected as they "were better accustomed to the conditions and they had learnt, in the short street races, that they couldn't use the same high gears as they did in Danish rural road racing."[30]

The results were also impressive. Frode Sørensen may only have come in at number three in the sprint race, but he had gathered enough points along the way to win on aggregate. Later that summer – in August 1942 – a Danish team took second place in a race called 'Round Breslau City Hall', comprised of 40 laps of 2 kilometres. The Danish results were not so dazzling, and was partly the result of "the odd course, which wound its way round Breslau's city hall, over asphalt, cobbles, and unfortunately also over tram lines." *Idrætsbladet* assured its readers, however, that although the Danish riders did not win they were extremely popular.[31]

But it was not only in road and street racing that the Danish riders were active. Track racing, too, received an extra boost when Willy Falck Hansen and Mogens Danholt won the track race Preis der Reichshauptstadt, held in Deutschlandhalle in Berlin, in the middle of November 1941.[32]

The Danish pair were thereby much sought after and it can be expected that they would have earned well. Falck Hansen and Mogens Danholt continued throughout the winter of 1941-42, taking part in events such as the six-day races in Berlin; and again, in June 1942, Danholt travelling to Berlin for competitions.[33]

Willy Falck Hansen did not seem to have any intention of stopping his international career. Despite his downward performance curve, he was invited along with Hans Chr. Nielsen to a grand prix in Hannover, in August 1942, among a star-studded field with the likes of Arie van Vliet, who had beaten the Dane two months earlier, and the former many-times Belgium world champion Jef Scherens, as well as the German stars Jean Schorn and Tony Merken.[34]

He also applied to the German embassy for permission to travel to France, where he would race on French tracks, to get in form for his 20-year jubilee season as a rider, in spring 1943. A contributing factor in his motivation to come to France would doubtless have been that he wished to see his home and property that he had promptly left when the Germans invaded that country.[35]

Professional cycling and boxing continued to witness sporting relations with Germany long after amateur sports had ceased. But because of the war, the summer of 1942 finally became the last date for those international competitions.

## From international to national sports

The continuation of the war was becoming increasingly difficult for Germany. In the beginning of 1941, Germany had to send the *Afrika Korps* to North Africa to support the Italians with their difficulties against British forces, and in December 1941 the world war took another serious turn for Germany due to the Japanese attack on Pearl Harbor and Germany's subsequent declaration of war against USA.

After 1942, international matches against Germany officially came to an end, despite Germany having taken part in 51 international matches that year. It suggests that Denmark was still held on ice because of mutinous Danish spectators. Sweden competed in three official events against Germany in 1942, culminating in an international football match on 20 September, at the Olympia Stadium in Berlin. The Swedish team managed to beat Germany 3-2 in a packed stadium, causing Goebbels to henceforth forbid such events in the capital on the grounds that the crowd became depressed, since winning at international football meant more to them than the army taking whatever town it happened to take on the East front.[36]

Instead of Danish collaborative sports with Germany, 16 international competitions against Sweden were held, throughout 1942. The results that year were not encouraging, as Denmark lost nine of those matches. Worst of all were the two defeats in Denmark's national sport, football: initially by 0-3 at Idrætsparken, where the Danish striker Paul Hansen began by scoring in his own goal, then afterwards in Stockholm by 1-2 after a depressing Danish performance.[37]

Throughout 1943, it was likewise only Sweden left on the Danish international calendar, resulting in no less than 15 international matches. The atmosphere was buoyed slightly when Denmark found its feet on the football pitch, and on 20 June, in brilliant style, and with a fine debut game by the famous Danish multitalent in ball sport Knud Lundberg, they won the only international that year by 3-2, in front of 40,000 spectators at Idrætsparken.[38]

The wave of anthem-singing euphoria, combined with a reduction in opportunities for other entertainments and diversions generally, meant that support for sports increased. The football association in fact closed the year 1941 in an improved state, with an increase in spectator figures at Idrætsparken of 71,000 above a previous year's figure of 425,000. That year, the match against Sweden and the two controversial Austrian matches had given a good yield in the cashbox, and although several other matches had been cancelled because of the Admira incident, DBU had resorted to other sources of income. Instead of the cancelled internationals, matches between football unions were played, such as Jutland against Sealand, and the capital against the provinces, which could attract 31,500 spectators. Furthermore, 23,000 spectators turned up in June to a local Danish championship final between the clubs Frem and Fremad Amager, which Frem won 4-2.

All in all, as matches against both Sweden and Axis-alliance countries became impossible, sports increasingly turned its attention towards events between select teams from Copenhagen played against the rest of Denmark. Developments during the occupation resulted in a stronger focus on internal Danish sporting collaboration where, instead of the fascination for competition against international teams, a tension was built up in the rivalry between the capital and the provinces.[39]

In July 1944, athletics competitions were held between Copenhagen and the capital's island home, Sealand, while in November of the same year gymnastics competitions were arranged between Copenhagen and the provinces. Football continued to be the big popular outdoor public sport, while boxing followed by handball were the most popular indoor sports.[40]

In the period in Denmark beginning with the German action against Danish police on 19 September 1944 until shortly after the liberation, namely 13 May 1945, in which period Danish policing was not possible, DIF introduced its own security service that helped match officials keep the crowd quiet "so that the matches could be carried out in peace." A good many well-known sportspeople took part in this service. Whether the service also helped to divert anti-German demonstrations that might lead to a clampdown on sport cannot be documented.[41]

# OTHER CULTURAL COLLABORATION

To understand the particular role that sporting collaborative relations played in Danish cultural collaboration, comparisons can be drawn to other collaborative activities in the cultural fields.

In the summer of 1940, the German authorities embarked upon fundamental cultural propaganda. The aim was to win Danes over to the Nazi project, which was undertaken through the German propaganda 'friendship' organisation for the region, Nordische Gesellschaft, who organised exhibitions, concerts and other cultural events. Even the German chamber of commerce exerted itself in this area. Items were sent such as German films and weekly reviews for the cinema, and the Wehrmacht was only too happy to contribute with parades and live military music.

There was only one problem with this kind of cultural propaganda, however, and that was – in contrast to sport – its one-way communication never being met with much enthusiasm or active response from the Danish people.

Furthermore, cultural policy towards Denmark was weakened because the German authorities were involved in internal power struggles, resulting, in part, in the German foreign ministry trying to prevent Nordische Gesellschaft in their attempts to win over Danish culturally conservative groups to the German point of view.

To make the Danish-German front more tractable, and get a genuine collaboration underway, the Danish foreign ministry formed a Danish-German society, the Dansk-Tysk Forening, on 24 June 1940. The society worked together with Nordische Verbindungsstelle, which was financed by the German ministry of propaganda. The idea was to ensure contact between the occupying forces and the Danish cultural elite. For the occupying authorities, the society was a nest from which to hatch a pro-German leading circle in Denmark. The aim was never achieved, however, as the approximately 1,400 members were not quite prepared to take on the role. With the exception of the mainland town Aarhus, the Danish-German society never managed to gain prominence in the provinces.[1]

The Dansk-Tysk Forening, Dansk-Europæisk Selskab, Nordische Gesellschaft and Nordische Verbindungsstelle, together with German institutions in Copenhagen, became the collective centre for appeals to the Danish cultural elite, and that only with limited success. German-oriented radio talks, too, were no great success, since neither the foreign ministry nor the German authorities could get prominent figures to create an understanding between the two represented peoples.[2]

Beyond these activities, attention was turned to a number of established Danish cultural institutions. The Royal Danish Theatre had toured internationally only very rarely in the 1930s, so it is much more notable that Danish ballet and theatre troupes visited Germany on a total of four occasions from 1937 to 1939. Towards the end of the 1930s – due to the impact of increasing self-censorship of criticism towards Nazi Germany in the Danish media – there was only subdued protest against these guest performances. The time was over when a writer like the famous Kjeld Abell, in the January catalogue from the artists' union Grønningen, could explicitly warn against participation by Danish artists in the 'artists' Olympiad', which was a special feature of the Berlin 1936 Olympics. The theatre publication Forum, for example, stopped using articles that were critical of Germany, such as accounts of attempts by German Jewish theatre people to escape the Aryanised Reich. The tour invitations came from Germany and were strongly encouraged by the Danish ministry of education, who spotted an easy way to build up goodwill with the Nazi authorities through such guest performances.

In contrast to their sporting counterparts, the Royal Danish Theatre – with a few exceptions – had not actively gone in for cultural exchange with their larger southern neighbours throughout the 1930s, and a certain resistance can even be detected against such events. In 1938, a section chief of the ministry of education, Cai Hegermann-Lindencrone, took over the position of theatre director and he was forced to allow the last of the guest performances to go on, performed in Berlin, in May 1939. However, he refused another invitation later that year, without hesitation, on the grounds that the theatre could not perform in a country at war. The most important feature when making comparisons with sport, is that Hegermann-Lindencrone consistently rejected invitations for Danish guest productions in Germany, during the occupation, whenever the opportunity arose, and in a way that was never especially diplomatic. This attitude was reflected among the artists and players. At a Copenhagen guest performance of a work by the Nazi cult author Heinrich George, in May 1941, the Danish actress Bodil Ipsen and several others refused point blank to attend a luncheon, organised by the Royal Danish Theatre and the foreign and education ministries.[3] This historical comparison would not be complete, however, if it were not emphasised that Danish theatre was never exposed to the same onslaught from the Nazi authorities as sport had been; doubtless because sport appealed to a 'mass public' to a far greater degree.

For the German authorities, propaganda was of utmost importance. It meant that mass media such as film and public sports were areas of special interest. In the world of film, though, the German authorities met with strong Danish resistance. Heavy German pressure had been applied to Danish cinema owners to show more German films and to have the German weekly reviews shown more frequently as part of the cinema programme. Despite this, the net results for 19 Copenhagen cinemas in 1941 show that American and Danish films took up 30 % of the collected Copenhagen film market, while German films, much to the regret of the Wehrmacht, comprised only 13 %.

Although the German authorities eventually managed to increase the screenings of German films and the frequency of the German weekly reviews, either through economic incitements or through direct enforcement, it did not lead to any great enthusiasm among the Danish public. On the contrary, on several occasions disturbances were seen at the weekly reviews, as well as demonstrative applause when features such as American films began. There were German successes in influencing film culture, however, when Danes flocked in large numbers to see German films such as Veit Harlan's Die Goldene Stadt (1942).[4]

Over the course of the occupation, it became increasingly obvious that young Danes were more interested in American jazz and swing music than in German films and literature, which led to the summary bombings or destruction of relevant Danish entertainment spots, instigated by German Nazi stooge groups such as Schalburgkorpset.[5]

The Danish public proved to be not very receptive to Nazi propaganda, whether it came served in Nazi periodicals or at outdoor concerts, which incidentally were a contributing factor to the sudden enthusiasm for Danish communal singing in venues around the country.[6] The Danish cinema owners were put under enormous pressure with reprisals taken by the occupying forces, but many German films and reviews of the week were simply too propagandist for Danish tastes. Much indicates, then, that the Danish sports leadership could have commanded a greater share of the decision making – in a way managed by organisers such as the cinema owners – if they had been willing to accept a measure of conflict with the occupying forces along the way and accept exposure to reprisals.

With the continuity of sport's internal forms, where the rules and the play on the pitch were themselves left untouched, sport had a much stronger grasp on the public, despite its being framed with 'heil' salutes and swastikas, and with the presence of German soldiers among the crowd. Sport became the sole area of Danish culture in which Danish-German collaboration for a period experienced a breakthrough to the delight of crowds both in Denmark and Germany. Through the images in books of athletes and their spontaneous bodily collaboration, it can be seen at a grass roots level how sport offered a unique opportunity for the occupiers and the occupied to meet over common emotional experiences. But, often, the pictures of Danish and German athletes in close contact were clearly stage managed with one eye on propaganda goals.

# SPORT IN 'NEUROPA'

## The new order of European sport

> 1) Sport serves the health of the people, production, military readiness and helps calm the populace. It is therefore crucial for our military enterprise that the pursuit of sport is continued during the war.
>
> 2) Sport also benefits relations between peoples, not least in regard to the consolidation of New Europe. It is therefore important that international sporting relations be continued during the war.
> The German Reichssportführer, June 1942[1]

The military progress of the Axis powers in the first half of the war encouraged German and Italian heads of sport to imagine a new dawn, and they went a long way forward in planning the 'New European' organisation of sports policies. These plans give us a source for evaluating how Danish sport would have been structured in the greater German empire after a German victory.

Following the occupation of Belgium, the Olympic administration in Bruxelles came under German control and plans were made to move the administration to Berlin, which would become the new European metropolis, renamed the World Capital Germania. The German 'foreign minister of sport' and administrator of German sport, Carl Diem, believed that the Olympic Games should be preserved almost intact, both in form and content, and he argued that a permanent stadium with room for 200,000 spectators should be built in Berlin for exactly this purpose.

In 1940, Diem also defended the idea that 'higher' and 'lower races' should be allowed to compete against each other at the Olympics because "in the long term, we can only preserve the superior race's master role when it is supported by health and physical prowess." Since 'natural people' were in need of the 'higher spirituality" of civilisation, they would be expected by and large to lose the competition in spite of their apparent physical fitness. Accordingly, the entire propagandist power of German sport was to be continued and strengthened, following the Berlin Olympics: "We will have an international games because we will show the world what we can achieve." Women, however, would be given no access to the new Olympics, which would be solely for the praise of individual men's performances.[2]

The German authorities had further ideas, too, about how to hold the Olympic games after a German victory. According to Hitler's chief architect, Albert Speer, the Führer intended that the Olympics would be held on a regular basis in a new planned, gigantic Deutsches Stadion, in Nürnberg, with room for 405,000 spectators. There were no hints about whether such proposed games would continue the sporting principles of the previous games,[3] and it is impossible to imagine that Hitler – without being pressed by international opinion, as he had been in 1936 – would have accepted black or non-Aryan athletes beating his 'blonde' Germans, let alone entering the competitions.

The new order for sports was begun at a number of places throughout Europe, as the Nazis gradually took over power directly or else set up their puppet regimes. The new order for French sport was given a positive reception by *Idrætsbladet*. Under the title "Football crisis in France", Gunnar Henriksen wrote about Jean Borotra, a French tennis star, who had been named national commissioner for sports and education under the Marshal Petain Government in 1940, and that "after France's capitulation, he was given the task of recreating national sporting life." *Idrætsbladet* approved the withdrawal of Jules Rimaud as the chairman of the French football association, presumably because he "had difficulties in adapting himself to the new sports regime, which placed sport under State control."[4]

Denmark also had a place in these plans. When Herbert Sander was on holiday, in July 1942, Leo Frederiksen, as the acting chairman, received a German "confidential inquiry" about whether DIF would accept an invitation to come to Berlin at the end of the month. The occasion – the details of which were unknown to the DIF leadership at the time – was that the Reichssportführer, Tschammer, had plans to assemble the European sports federations under one pan-European federation, with its headquarters in Berlin and with himself as president. Presumably, the position of general secretary had been ear-marked for Carl Diem. In the first phase, Tschammer's goal was the most comprehensive participation from German occupied countries as possible, as well as the as-yet neutral countries together naturally with European Axis alliance countries.[5]

All the evidence suggests that the new European federation would be run on the principle of Führer leadership, which means led by a president with absolute powers, which was also the conclusion drawn by the Swedish historian Olof Holmäng. The preparations more than intimate that the Nazi plans would be achieved by threats and coercion. Such was a communication by Carl Diem, on 17 October 1940, to the German ambassador in Paris, that the irregular precedence in international sports administration in France had to stop, forthwith. He referred more specifically to two French Jewish heads of sport.[6]

A meeting in Berlin, in 1941, shows that nothing was being left to chance. Agreements had already been reached that Tschammer would take on the position of president, while the two vice-president positions would go to Italy and Hungary. Italy and Germany had a further agreement about how the two countries would divide the chairmanships for the various sports federations between them. The new order of European sports would thereby be governed by the Axis alliance, with Italy and particularly Germany having absolute power.[7]

To get plans under way, Tschammer proposed a European sports conference to be held alongside the world skiing championships, at Garmisch-Partenkirchen, in February 1942. Participation in the world championships meant those relevant countries automatically qualified to take part in the conference. Tschammer's aim was to gather all the occupied and neutral European countries, so that the new order for European sport could achieve as high a degree of legitimacy as possible. Tschammer managed to obtain positive replies from just about every occupied and neutral country, including Denmark, from where the Danish Nazi Party, the DNSAP, promised to send a delegate,[8] which might be an indication that DIF's refusal to participate would be the signal for others to take over.

Preparations were well underway by the New Year, when a pre-conference event on 27 December was cancelled. In the last moments, Goebbels had persuaded Hitler to call off the winter sports competitions for 1941/42, thereby cancelling the conference as well, due to the winter crisis caused by the German military campaign in the East. Nevertheless, Tschammer did not abandon his undertaking and, after further obstacles, finally fixed a date for a European sports conference for 20-28 October 1942, in Munich.[9] It was this conference that was behind the initiative to invite DIF to Berlin in July for an exploratory meeting.

## The new European Sports Federation

The response by DIF was to tread water. Leo Frederiksen together with DIF's chairman Sander decided to inform the German embassy that the end of July 1942 was not a date when they could travel to Germany.[10] For DIF, the problem was saying 'yes' to a sports federation that did not have Sweden as a member might sever Danish-Swedish sporting relations; as likewise would a 'no' to a federation of which Sweden was a member. DIF, therefore, desperately needed to know Sweden's position on all this before giving Tschammer a reply. That DIF declined the invitation did not go down well, the German embassy informing that the embassy would then have to make the invitation official.

At the same time, the German organisers put pressure on DIF through the Danish foreign ministry. Intriguingly, these exchanges took place at a time when the Germans had long since lost interest in establishing a greater European economic sphere. Throughout the summer of 1940, under the impact of German victories, the Danish foreign ministry had pursued an activistic policy intended to build up goodwill with the German authorities, but their enthusiasm cooled off over the following autumn as a consequence of determined British military resistance. During spring 1941, Germany achieved renewed military advances, which encouraged the Danish foreign ministry – in concord with Danish business and industry organisations, including the trade council for the workers' movement, Arbejderbevægelsens Erhvervsråd – to begin cooperating towards a new European economic order.[11] Following the German invasion of the Soviet Union, however, the situation again became more volatile and foreign policy measures more hesitant.

On 18 July 1942, Gebhard Seelos, a German diplomat, suddenly appeared at the Danish foreign ministry and announced that the Reichssportführer, Tschammer, had invited the chairman of DIF to preparatory discussions prior to the sports conference, which Sander had turned down. Seelos now requested the foreign ministry's "assistance in ensuring that Colonel Sander under whatever circumstance attend the initial discussions with Herr Tschammer und Osten at the beginning of August." Seelos was also asked by the ministry whether the neutral countries Switzerland and Sweden had been invited, too, but Seelos was 'unaware of further details of the meeting'.

One week later, the foreign ministry received a 'verbal note'[12] from the Reichssportführer, in which Sander again was invited to Berlin for preparatory negotiations and to participate in a sporting gala at the Olympia Stadium in Berlin, on 2 August.[13]

The foreign ministry's involvement increased the pressure on DIF. Herbert Sander cut his holiday short and went along to the ministry. A series of negotiations subsequently took place, the content of which is not provided by the source materials. In his résumé, Sander indicated that the foreign ministry very much wanted the issue to proceed unhindered, and even offered to pay travel costs. As a consequence, DIF felt obliged to change position. In a letter dated 29 July 1942 sent to the Reichssportführer, via the foreign ministry, the answer came that it would be "an honour" for Herbert Sander to attend.[14]

The official German invitation came a shortly afterwards. On 4 August 1942, the DIF chairman received a telegram from the Reichssportführer describing the purpose of the conference to create a European sports federation. The conference would be held at the end of October and Sander was requested to reserve this period. Because of the conference, Tschammer also wished for a preparatory meeting with Sander in Berlin, in September, a time that Sander had previously indicated was suitable.

On 12 August 1942, the matter was brought before the DIF executive committee[15] where it was agreed that DIF would not reach a decision before the matter had been discussed by the joint committee for the national sports federations of the Nordic region, De Nordiske Rigsidrætsforbunds Fælleskomité.[16] On the same day, Sander wrote to Tschammer that a relevant meeting had already been arranged with

Sweden, and that they first needed to await this meeting's conclusions.[17] For DIF, it was crucial that they continue their profitable and legitimate working partnership with their Swedish sister nation, and Sander would therefore try to coordinate lines between the two Nordic federations.

The occupying power reacted promptly to this communication. A few days afterwards, Leo Frederiksen received an invitation from the German embassy for lunch with Gebhard Seelos on 25 August, where he and Sander might be informed about the earlier meeting in Berlin, held 31 July, where DIF had not been represented, in which the various sports 'Führer' from Bulgaria, Finland, Italy, Croatia, Holland, Norway, Romania, Slovakia, Hungary and Spain had called on Tschammer to set up a European sports federation. The chief aim of the luncheon was to pin down a date for Sander's trip to Berlin, which was settled as 9-11 September 1942. Sander asked that his vice-chairman, Leo Frederiksen,[18] be allowed to attend, too – a clear sign of Sander's dependence on his vice-chairman's experience and reputation in conducting the important footballing collaboration with the occupying power. The German representatives agreed to the request and to meeting the travel costs.

On the same day, the Swedish sports federation reported that it was prepared to bring the date of its next committee meeting forward but only to 19 September 1942.[19] It was therefore not possible to confer with the Nordic joint committee before the trip to Germany: perhaps because the Swedish representatives did not want to take on the responsibility of Danish sports policy in regard of the Nazis.

## The meeting in Berlin

At the following executive committee meeting of DIF, on 4 September 1942,[20] Sander outlined what would be DIF's position at the coming meeting in Berlin. The federation should maintain its solidarity with Sweden and resist coercion to collaborate with those countries "we at present do not collaborate with" (meaning Norway).

Five days later,[21] Sander and Leo Frederiksen met with Tschammer, the Reichssportführer, in Berlin, together with the leader of an athletics department from the Nazi sports federation, SS-Obersturmbannführer Dr Arthur Jensch – a man notable for his efforts to have Czech heads of sport exhibit a spirit of 'loyal collaboration' towards Germany, in an otherwise brutally occupied country.[22] According to Sander, the meeting took place in a relaxed, almost convivial atmosphere. The Reichssportführer described the personal nature of the project and that he had waited three years for its fruition, the time for which was now. Europe was in need of one joint federation, in the same manner as the pan-American and African federations. The current international associations for each sporting discipline should be encouraged to continue their work while those which in reality would no longer exist would be replaced by the European federation. After the war, a final new order would be established. Tschammer had an apparent understanding for Denmark's current need to adopt a waiting position and he reassured the two Danish representatives that this would not exclude Denmark from sporting relations with those countries who joined the new federation.

The message must have been a relief to the Danish representatives. Sander and Frederiksen replied that "in principle, Denmark has nothing against the creation of a pan-European federation" or else against sporting collaboration, as such, but that DIF at that time could not reach a decision regarding membership. The matter had first to be dealt with by the joint committee for the Nordic national sports federations, and then presented to the DIF board. The Danes expressed their appreciation for the sports Führer's understanding of DIF's difficult situation, since the Danish federation was obliged to take heed of the general opinion of the people of Denmark. In reply to Tschammer's intention that disputes between national federations would be settled by arbitration, Sander and Frederiksen said, according to their own minutes, that DIF would not intervene in an internal Norwegian dispute and for that reason DIF currently preferred to remain outside the new federation.

Tschammer seemingly approved. That the matter was "an embarrassment" for DIF was something he would respect without discussion. And even if DIF chose to remain outside of the coming joint enterprise he would provide DIF with the opportunity to take part in the conference as 'guests'.

Shortly before Sander and Frederiksen's journey home, they were presented with a draft proposal for the statutes of the European Sports Federation. The proposal had been preserved, and what it intends is that the new European federation should have unlimited powers over the various separate European sport federations and that their 'congress' would meet every four years. In such manner, it was up to the president to call board meetings at his convenience: although a board meeting could be called following a request from three of the board members.[23]

Tschammer's promise that DIF would not be excluded from sporting relations with member countries, however, was contrary to the wording of the statutes in the proposal. In paragraph 3, it was stated that only member federations would be acknowledged, and that this excluded "sporting relations with any non-member federations", while paragraph 25 stated that "without the approval of the [new European] federation, any member sports federations or their associations may not conduct sporting relations with federations or associations that are not members."

As will be shown, in the coming sections, Sander realised the ramifications that were crucial for DIF. If participation in sporting relations necessitated membership of the new European federation, then in future DIF would not be able to compete against Germany or other Axis power nations such as Hungary. DIF's Achilles' heel, however, was if Sweden joined the new federation, in which case their vital partnership with Sweden would also collapse.

## Boxing in New Europe

It is possible to follow how the particular Danish sports associations tried to make best use of their opportunities, in the midst of Italian-German attempts to achieve hegemony over European sport. Because attempts were also made to introduce 'new organisation' within specific sporting disciplines, in so far as the initial starting point was the Nazis' joint European federation.[24]

Within Danish sporting circles, it was the thoroughly activistic boxing association, especially, that swung into action. In the beginning of July 1942, the former chairman of the boxing association, Henrik Meincke, a barrister, attended an extraordinary congress of the international amateur boxing federation (FIBA) in Rome, where there were representatives from nearly every country in German-dominated Europe, including Norwegian collaborator sports.

According to the author and journalist Vilhelm Bergstrøm, Meincke was "somewhat shady".[25] He had been the boxing-team leader at the Olympics in 1936 and had also been a referee at an international boxing competition between Finland and Germany in Pressau, on 8 February 1940. The congress was held at the end of a three-nations competition between Italy, Germany and Hungary, which Meincke watched and reported on, after his trip home. Meincke, who commanded a number of languages, was no longer a member of the Danish boxing association's leadership, but *Idrætsbladet* guessed that he would again be made chairman, on his return, as the board had dwindled to only its treasurer, Alfred Overgaard, and secretary, Alfred Christensen. The three remaining board members had otherwise withdrawn.[26]

Henrik Meincke actively participated in Rome on behalf of Italian-German attempts to gain full power over European sport. At the FIBA boxing congress, a professional international boxing federation was inaugurated (APPE), as an attempt to oust the international boxing union (IBU), which can be seen in the German decision to immediately withdraw from IBU. The president of APPE was Vittorio Mussolini, son of the Italian dictator, while the vice-president was German W. Metzner. The creation of APPE also gave rise to considerations of whether to amalgamate the amateur and professional boxing associations. Among the recognised European boxing champions, there were only German and Italian boxers, apart from a single French competitor, in welterweight.[27] It was agreed that only boxers belonging to the new federation could fight against each other, and all-in-all fifteen countries signed up to the new federation, including Norway and Sweden.

Meanwhile, in FIBA, a new general secretary was voted in, Hans Hieronymus, the German national coach, well-known to Danish boxing, while Meincke was voted onto the executive committee. There were other changes, too, with Axis-alliance countries taking the lion's share of the administrative positions. The chairman of the executive committee, however, continued to be Oscar Söderlund, from Sweden, but he was entirely submissive towards German and Italian aspirations for power, and had himself been an official organiser of the so-called war-time European championships, held in Breslau, in January 1942. As a sign of the new distribution of power, it was decided that the new board, under the Finnish leadership of Victor Smed, should revise its statutes, and that the European championships for 1943 should be moved to Italy, and to Finland for 1944.[28]

On his return home, Henrik Meincke believed that "the congress was definitely concerned with useful and practical things, whose effects will soon be seen." He was thinking of measures such as the decision that the international boxing federation would pay travel expenses to heads of boxing when required. This would mean that the Danish boxing association would be able to invite "for example, an Italian referee, but only need to pay for his travel from the Danish border to Copenhagen, as well as his keep." On what for the world of sport was an unusual planned amalgamation of professional and amateur sport, Meincke said that "it had been agreed on by most countries, although Romania and Denmark have made conditions. Nevertheless, I believe a coalition will become a reality. For the amateurs, it will mean that we won't risk situations like a large professional tournament happening right next to a national competition."[29]

Meincke's comments to the Nazi newspaper *Fædrelandet* show that the Italian organisers placed great emphasis on gaining support for the new order from other countries, organising promotional events such as a trip to the impressive Fascist sports centre Foro Mussolini. "We were given an enormous reception by the Italians ... it was almost too much with all the banquets and the excursions to the most beautiful sports facilities near the city. Vittorio Mussolini, it's him who's the president of the Italian boxing federation, had worked out the programme himself and he and his aides being the perfect hosts ... It was a real comfort that the police, all throughout the trip, provided us with transport whenever we needed."[30]

Besides being thoroughly pampered by the Italian hosts and being invited onto the executive committee, Henrik Meincke had also achieved another concrete result from his trip. An agreement was reached for Denmark to take part in an international tournament against Hungary, in October 1942, "if we wish." "Moreover, the plan is that we fight an international against Sweden in November and against Germany in February 1943."

When Meincke came home he realised that the association secretary Alfred Overgaard had taken over the chairmanship, but this did not cause any immediate change of course. Because in September 1942, it was announced that the boxing association had agreed to an international tournament against Germany, on 14 February 1943.[31]

## A miraculous save

Herbert Sander and Leo Frederiksen were now in a position to travel to Sweden and negotiate a joint position between Denmark and its sister nation. If the Swedish representatives signed up to the new order, Denmark's only remaining opportunity to take part in international sporting relations would be to follow suit.

Before the meeting of the joint committee for the Nordic national sports federations, Sander and Frederiksen had gained the impression that the Swedish attitude was positive toward the new European federation. Leading up to the trip to Stockholm, Frederiksen had heard rumours that the German head of sport Carl Diem had discussed plans for the new federation with Prince Gustav Adolf of Sweden, in Stockholm, who was supposed to have discussed it later with the Swedish Government.[32] He had also heard that Sweden would send observers to the congress.[33]

There were indications that Sweden did in fact wish to join a European sports organisation along with the Germans. The International Amateur Athletics Federation (IAAF) had its main offices in Sweden, and Siegfried Edström, the federation president, was Swedish, too. On 19 August 1942, the newspaper Kristeligt Dagblad published an article from the Ritzau bureau under the title "International Sports Federation Blown Apart". Great Britain and USA were supposedly intent on creating a purely "Anglo-American Federation" all brought on because in spring 1942 Edström had introduced a number of replacements to the European committee of IAAF: including Dr Carl Ritter von Halt, an SA officer and influential German sports-policy maker, who was given the job of chairman on condition that the powerful general-secretary post went to Carl Diem. According to the article, this was the actual reason behind the British and American break.[34]

For the joint Nordic committee meeting in September 1942, Herbert Sander and Leo Frederiksen met with representatives for the Swedish federation. The Nazi-oriented Norwegian federation had not been invited and representatives from war-torn Finland had been prevented from attending in the final moments. The meeting took place behind closed doors, and the public were told nothing about the actual nature of the negotiations.[35]

By way of introduction, Sander gave an account of "the heavy pressure they had been subject to from both the German embassy and the Danish foreign ministry," and he referred to the negotiations in Berlin. As a starting point, Sander explained that DIF had no specific objection to a European federation and a subsequent membership hereto, but that they wished to discuss the matter with the joint committee before reaching a decision. There is much to imply, therefore, that Sander, based on his belief that the Swedish negotiators would agree to Tschammer's sports federation, was willing to agree on Denmark taking part.

A somewhat surprising answer came back. No official invitation to the Munich conference had been received by the Swedish federation. They were, however, entirely

*In 1942, the Swedish national sports association was not interested in taking part in a European youth association on the grounds that, as a neutral country such as Switzerland, Sweden would have an important role to play in the rebuilding of international sporting relations after the war. Two years earlier, the situation had been different. The photograph shows an international athletics games held on 7 and 8 September 1940, between Germany, Finland and the winners Sweden. Before the games, the German and Swedish teams marched in to honour the German wartime invalided soldiers who had received special seats in the stands. The photograph shows this event.*

aware of these plans since the two leading German heads of sport, Carl Diem and Ritter von Halt, had presented their case to them in Stockholm. The Swedish national sports federation had decided that under the present circumstances they would not join the new European sports federation and neither would they send observers to Munich. The Swedish federation had also coordinated their position with the sports authorities in Switzerland. The chairman of the Swedish executive committee, Bo Eklund, in Berlin for an international football match between Germany and Sweden, had taken the opportunity to clarify their position for the Reichssportführer that the Swedish federation were not interested in receiving an invitation.

During the succeeding exchange of views, it was agreed that behind the creation of a European sports federation lay a political intent, which was "part of a collective action" of which a European Youth Federation[36] was another. The Swedish representatives defended their and the Swiss decision by pointing out that it was important that free neutral countries remain after the war, who could organise the rebuilding of international sporting life. That the Swedish federation also decided not to send observers to Munich was because the Swedish public would be unable to distinguish the observers from genuine representatives in a situation where they had no control over press coverage.

Sander and Frederiksen sought cover under the shield of neutrality. They expressed a wish for a joint announcement on the matter, which the Swedish negotiators said they could not agree to, having inadequate authority, since the Swedish federation had received no official invitation. The meeting therefore ended without any joint position and, as is apparent, there was not much direct support for the Danes from their Swedish sporting colleagues. For Sweden, the issue was a delicate one, and they would rather remain neutral than take a common stand with DIF against a German superpower.

In advance of a follow-up executive committee meeting of DIF, Sander wrote down his impressions of a new European sports federation, which presumably formed the background to his statements at the meeting. In his report, Sander completely adopted the Swedish position, reusing the arguments of the Swedish negotiators: that after the war neutral countries would be needed for the restoration of international sport. In respect to the question of observers, DIF should not send any since the public would be unable to tell the difference between them and genuine representatives. Sander's complete dependence on whatever position the Swedish took can be illustrated in his belief that the matter should be taken up again should the Swedish federation eventually change its opinion.[37]

But there were others to take notice of, too. At the meeting, Frederiksen and Sander were unsure of how the board would deal with the situation, or how the matter would appear to the Danish public. Both the chairman and vice-chairman gave the opinion that, at the coming board meeting, they "should avoid discussing the question, since opinions expressed over the board would doubtless be recorded in the minutes. The most fortunate outcome would be if immediately there was a motion to take the chairman's report into consideration and thereafter to empower the executive committee to continue working along the same lines." Furthermore, it was agreed that the board would be obliged to treat the matter "in strictest confidence" and not to report back to individual associations until the decision was official.[38]

To put it bluntly, this meant putting the lid on. At the board meeting on 28 December, Sander reported on the negotiations in Germany and emphasised "one thing is a written undertaking" and another was Tschammer's promise that did not concur with the German draft proposal. Sander was clearly shaken in discovering the disagreement between promises that Denmark, without cost, could remain outside the European federation, and the written document stating that only member countries would be allowed to compete against each other.[39]

In consequence, Professor Knud Secher, an ordinary board member, took the floor. His contribution seemed to be coordinated with Sander and Frederiksen's wishes for the meeting. Secher believed that the matter was a difficult one to be discussed in the current assembly and that it would be best if the executive committee were allowed to reach its own conclusion, since the matter was not "without political character". He proposed, therefore, that the board accepted the report for further consideration without discussion, which was subsequently unanimously agreed on. The executive committee, then, had its scope for political action widened considerably, and the board managed to keep the matter secret.[40]

In his reply to Tschammer, Herbert Sander deferred membership of a European sports federation to a later point in time. He repeated that DIF "in principle" had nothing against the idea of a federation and membership of such, but because of present conditions "a change too soon in the current structures in the country would work to the contrary." DIF therefore recommended the Reichssportführer not to invite DIF to the meeting in Munich – neither as co-founder nor as a guest.[41]

Presumably it was not without some trepidation that Sander awaited the Reichssportführer's reaction, but it was a long time coming. At an executive committee meeting on 29 October 1942,[42] Sander reported that according to the press the Munich meeting had been postponed. They were still unwilling for the whole business to come to public attention, so the committee decided not to mention the matter to the meeting of the association representatives, unless directly asked.[43] Their tactic of secrecy continued to work. The extent to which both plans for a European sports federation and DIF's negotiations were public knowledge was extremely limited. The only thing *Fædrelandet* reported on them was a very short bulletin from Reuters press bureau stating that Leo Frederiksen and Sander were on a visit to Tschammer in Berlin.[44]

But there was good reason that DIF did not receive a written reply. The sports conference in Munich set for 10 October 1942 had already been postponed by the German foreign ministry because of war conditions. Tschammer believed, up until that date, that it would go ahead, but eventually the idea of a conference was definitively dropped – again on the recommendation of the German foreign ministry.

All this was partly a result of the expected victory at Stalingrad going into slow motion. On top of this, there was an opinion, espoused especially by Goebbels, that Germans under increasing military pressure losing international matches against neutral countries would prove something of a problem for the morale of the German people. The time was therefore not a choice one for new organisational creations in the field of sport.

The course of the war, however, was hardly the only reason for the postponement.

Involved, too, was an all-too-common power struggle within the Nazi State apparatus, in this case between Tschammer, the minister of propaganda, Goebbels, and the German foreign ministry. Another factor that ill-disposed the Nazi top leadership to new sporting plans was that Baldur von Schirach, the German Nazi youth Führer, had in the middle of September 1942 with a ceremonial flourish let himself be elected as the Führer for European youth, at an 'operatically staged' conference in Vienna.[45]

As an almost symbolic image of the fate of German sporting imperialism, the steadily worsening situation in Stalingrad towards the end of 1942 followed the deteriorating physical condition of Reichssportführer von Tschammer, which had never been that good to start with. He died, disillusioned, on 25 March 1943, from a heart attack that he did nothing to fight against, only 55 years old. Goebbels held a State funeral, demanded by Hitler. *Idrætsbladet* received the news with sorrow, since "first and foremost it was he who had organised the Olympic Games in Berlin and made it such a huge success; while the Kraft durch Freude [Strength through Joy] movement had also been one of his ideas. Germany had lost a very talented man and a valuable force in the service of sport."

Before then – earlier in March 1943 – in the wake of Germany's comprehensive difficulties in the World War, signs of an increased self-awareness began to emerge from DIF. Leo Frederiksen, for example, as mentioned earlier, flatly refused to meet with representatives from the Nazi-oriented Norwegian football association, who had come to Copenhagen to negotiate with the Danish football association.

The chain of events shows that again it was the working relationship to Sweden that was decisive for the development of Danish sport during the occupation – both because competition against the 'arch-rivals', Sweden, had great importance for the Danish public, but also because the Swedish matches provided a 'fig-leaf' for potentially morally embarrassing sporting relations with Germany. It was with great probability the reserved Swedish position on Tschammer's European sports federation that saved Denmark from entering the federation and thereby risking having to compete against Norwegian collaboration sports.

In light of the threat of having to join the European federation, DIF's room for manoeuvre had never before been so small, during the occupation. Joining the federation would have meant, on an organisational level, that Denmark would have to give up the fiction of neutrality in relation to international sporting relations, providing a final demonstration of the cocktail of sport and politics. Luckily for DIF, the plans fell apart, but the sphere of influence commanded by the DIF leadership had also become limited, in that Danish sport would now have to operate in a highly restricted area, as international sporting cooperation was slowly coming to a complete halt.

Finally, the internationally renowned gymnastics innovator Niels Bukh was under way with plans for a new structuring of Danish youth culture. There is no doubt that Bukh did not entertain ambitions that Denmark should become a German puppet State. His vision was rather one in which Danes, under relevant pressure from outside, would realise that a corporative society and a strong spirit of unity centred around a charismatic leader would prove the best opportunity for Denmark to manage so many of its own internal affairs itself, in a new Europe under German leadership. To these ends, he developed plans for a strongly centralised federation involving the whole of Danish youth culture, together with a labour service,[46] all rounded off with a 'festival for peace' when the Germans eventually won the war. Through political negotiation with German Nazi leaders in Denmark and Germany, Bukh showed the large scope within which he could operate, unrestricted as he was by either political parties or boards, as 'merely' the head of a Danish sport academy.[47]

# TURN OF THE TIDES

## Battles over sports orienteering

With DIF on the outside of a European sports federation, it found itself in a much freer position to make its opinions felt by the Nazi-influenced athletics leadership that had broken DIF's boycott of Norwegian Nazi sports. There were numerous points of disagreement between the DIF leadership and the people involved in athletics, and one of the most important struggles that took place was over the sports discipline of orienteering, along with its offshoot "terrænsport".[1] The reason this struggle was important was that orienteering and its military value could be misused by the Nazi leadership of the athletics association.

The real battle, then, was over orienteering and was fought over questions of whether particular orienteering events should go ahead, and fought over the general organisation of the sport.

In the beginning there was a degree of tolerance. The Danish skiing association had held its second open orienteering race in November 1941, in Grib Forest in North Sealand, in partnership with the athletics association of Copenhagen (KAF), and at that point it had not bothered the skiing association to be collaborating with the Nazi-oriented athletics leadership. They were concerned about promoting the sport and, under the title "KAF strikes a blow for orienteering", Gunnar Stenholm, one of the heads of the skiing association, could report that athletics circles in Copenhagen had begun to work directly on attracting more public attention to orienteering. Stenholm's association saw this as a positive step and they wished to cooperate, so that as many as possible "could get used to reading maps and using a compass, which, after all, is extremely important."[2]

But the unanimity did not last, and during spring 1942, DIF developed a wish to gain influence over orienteering. On 18 May 1942, the federation reached a board agreement – on behalf of the skiing association – to set up a committee to "investigate whether it be opportune to establish a unified organisation of orienteering under the auspices of DIF." The committee comprised the chairman of DIF, Herbert Sander, who personally wanted to stay in touch with developments, together with two other representatives, from the skiing association and from the athletics and rowing association. According to Sander, the representatives seemed to be close to reaching a positive result, when "suddenly, due to an irreconcilable position from one person, it all fell apart." Presumably, Sander was indicating that the athletics association wanted orienteering to be organised by them, which the remaining committee members resisted. What occurred was a complete break. In the press, both the skiing association and the athletics association insisted that orienteering now belonged to them.³

DIF were obliged to act. At a meeting on 28 September 1942, the federation decided to place orienteering under the administration of the skiing association, which then changed its name to the Danish Skiing and Orienteering Association (DSOF). However, it looked as though "the athletics association is very dissatisfied with the arrangement and, in comments to the newspapers *Nationaltidende* and *Berlingske Tidende*, Svend Jensen, the chairman of the Danish athletics association [DAF] makes it perfectly clear that DAF intends to hold Danish championships – or equivalent championships … There is a huge demand for this sport that only a few years ago was so unnoticed."⁴

And they were as good as their word. Shortly afterwards, the Danish athletics association organised its "first open orienteering race" at a Sealand forest location, Jægersborg Hegn, which according to *Idrætsbladet* was a great success – the winner of the B-Class race, Ole Dorph-Jensen, later becoming the Danish champion at 400-metres hurdles. The skiing association was not about to take this lying down, and therefore organised an open 'Cup Race' at Grib Forest, which was also a great success.⁵ All-in-all, the sport was certainly undergoing a period of growth.

The skiing association's event was followed up by a DIF-recognised Danish championship at Tisvilde Hegn in North Sealand, in November 1942. Doubtless as a sports-political gesture, Colonel Sander turned up as a race official, of which *Idrætsbladet* published a picture. Orienteering, however, never became a big sport during the occupation, even though it experienced a growing tendency.⁶

The fall out from 'the battle for orienteering' may have led to the chairman of the athletics association, Johannes Bojesen Barsøe, resigning from his post at the end of October 1942. In any circumstance, the conflict must have made it clear to him how isolated the athletics association was in relation to DIF. In a resignation speech, Barsøe said "he could not resist commenting on the approved decision by DIF to place this sporting discipline under the skiing association." The approval seemed to Barsøe to be illogical, since orienteering certainly did not take place on skis.⁷

But it was hardly criticism of the chairman's position on sporting relations with the occupying powers that made him resign. Dissatisfaction with Bojesen Barsøe at the representatives' meeting of the Copenhagen athletics associations in 1942 was not founded on his personal disposition towards so-called 'German games' but, seen in several signs, that he was involved in a typical power struggle for the chairmanship. Gundersen, a board member, for example, was accused of having designs on the chairmanship at a board meeting on 30 September 1941; a claim Gundersen denied.

During the occupation, criticism of Bojesen Barsøe was aimed at everything *but* his collaborative work with the Germans. At the representatives meeting in October 1942, he surprised everyone by not standing for re-election to the chairmanship. In regard to his withdrawal, *Idrætsbladet* ran a whole-page interview with him, entitled "Sports leader's worst opponent is the small-time man":

> With his powerful, sturdy figure and his large broad head, he is the personification of calm and strength, a man on whom the many attacks he has been exposed to over the years have left little mark. Perhaps, this year, he could have turned back the tide at the recent KAF representatives meeting but chose to withdraw without opposing the opposition that wanted to bring him down.

Instead, Ancher Jensen from the Ben Hur athletics club was made chairman, but according to *Fædrelandet* Bojesen Barsøe was willing to put himself forward for the chairmanship even as late as February 1943.[8]

In the Danish illegal press, there was criticism of Barsøe's Nazi sympathies in an article entitled "Nazis inside Danish athletics", published in Frit Danmark, at the late date of July 1943. Somewhat belatedly, *Frit Danmark* identified two leading men inside the Danish athletics association of whom readers should beware. One was Svend Jensen, who "until this year has been chairman of the Danish Athletics Association, who, among other things, participated in the Nazi march to the landsoldaten memorial." The other was Bojesen Barsøe. At a meeting with "the Nazi consultant doctor Charles Hindborg", he presented "an extensive written account of how Danish sport was to be reorganised 'when we take over power in 14 days' time'. Nevertheless, B.B. still tries to convince his fellows that he is a good Danish man."[9]

Altogether, events did not work out so well in athletics for the two pro-German chairmen. Svend Jensen, too, as chairman for the Danish athletics association became more and more unpopular, and a number of board members believed that his continual argumentativeness brought the association into disrepute. The first complaints about the chairman's disposition came out at a DAF representatives meeting in April 1942, where among other things the tour to Oslo was criticised. Svend Jensen defended himself, but a majority called for a secret ballot, for or against the chairman, which resulted in his withdrawal.

At the same time, there was no-one who would take over the chairmanship, which resulted in Svend Jensen remaining in his chairman position until the next representatives' meeting in March 1943, with a majority against him.[10] At this point he chose to resign, purportedly because of a lack of available time,[11] but surely also prompted by an increasing realisation that Germany would never be able to win the war, and that the Danish people, at the March election in 1943, held onto their old political parties and turned sharply against Nazi ideology and the Danish Nazi Party.

All in all, the scaling down of collaborative sporting relations with Germany, and that the creation of a German-dominated European sports federation had been abandoned, clearly meant that DIF was less bound to follow the German lead. This situation gave heads of DIF a greater room for manoeuvre in internal national politics, which came out as an opportunity for a political point to be made against the Nazi-oriented leadership of the athletics association, who were denied sports orienteering and its military potential.

## The situation at club level

With the changing conditions of the war and the increasingly realistic possibility of a German defeat, signs were also apparent, within sports, of a somewhat cooler attitude towards the Germans. In July 1943, a German general and one of his secretaries had signed up to a Copenhagen sports club, Hellerup Idrætsklub (HIK), to play tennis, but after they had played there for a few days their memberships were annulled; the club committee fearing unrest and demonstrations. The general accepted the club's decision, but was dissatisfied when his entry and subscription payments were not returned, and therefore complained to a high-placed official at the German embassy, Dr Friedrich Stalmann, who reported the incident to the Danish foreign ministry. The chairman of HIK was thereafter called to a meeting at the foreign ministry where he expressed regrets at the turn of events but stood by his decision. He pointed out that the general and the secretary had registered themselves as belonging to the Wehrmacht: members of the German diplomatic staff, conversely, could become members of the sports club without problems.

Stalmann's superior was then brought into the proceedings: Paul Kanstein, a German SS Brigade Officer, right-hand man to the new German main political leader in Denmark, Werner Best, and a political moderate. He and Stalmann, along with F. Hvass from the Danish foreign ministry, reached an agreement that personnel from the Wehrmacht should not seek membership of private clubs in Denmark. Kanstein, however, could recount that earlier he had played at the Hellerup club without any problem.[12] The times had apparently changed – at least they had if you came from the military wing of the occupying power.

After the end of Danish-German competitions, though, there were still a number of German members in the various Danish sports associations. The Danish county representative for North West Jutland, M. Jørgensen, explained in a report from spring 1943 that "handball still has many German players in both town and rural district councils; and the same is true for badminton, but to a great extent this is hampered by the very restricted local conditions. In boxing, which has a very large public, the numbers of Germans are few."[13]

In November 1943, then, in North West Jutland alone, Germans were participating in associations for handball, badminton and boxing. Most probably, this situation also applied in many other areas throughout the country, and just as probably representatives from the other regional counties were keeping quiet. At the same time, there were other collaborative signs. In the beginning of 1943, for example, a football match was held between Danish and German teams, in which Thisted town sports club played two matches against the German Wehrmacht after the winter season 1942-43.[14]

There is much to suggest that sport at Danish club level was not particularly politicised, and that it would not lead to threats or protest when Nazi-minded people happened to be members of sports associations, during the war. One example– partly the result of favourable experiences from a cycle tour of Germany – is of two brothers who joined the Danish Nazi Party as early as 1940, one of them volunteering for service on the Eastern front. The brothers' political affiliations did not prevent them from becoming popular members of the Lyngby Cycle Club and the Lyngby ball club, where one of the brothers, Karl Aage Jensen, was a prized striker for the champions league team, from 1940 to 1945. However, it is unclear how much their club mates knew about the brothers' political enthusiasm.[15]

There are other examples from other sports. The gymnastics and swimming club Hermes, in 1941, had a new trainer for its men's gymnastics first team. He was a captain and was regarded as having sympathies for Nazism, but nevertheless he remained trainer even during the later years of the occupation, where he managed to lead his team to victory in the Danish championships. He also attracted the attention of the Danish resistance movement, and after the liberation he was interned and then put before a military court.[16]

The example from Hermes shows how the wind had changed. True to form, the club magazine published a picture of the trainer and his victorious team, in May 1944. In the members' gazette from April 1945, there was a laconic remark that "Hermes has to do without its coach … who's been hindered in putting together a team," while the club's anniversary book from 1949 states that the trainer "in terms of gymnastics, was a remarkable replacement" but he "never managed in the same way to gather club members around him." He now became such an embarrassment to the club that, entirely without precedent, he was cut out of a group photograph of the victorious 1944 team in a section that dealt with "German Tyranny".[17]

Several Germans were active as trainers in Denmark. The professional trainer for Skjold, a Copenhagen rowing club, was Ulrik Jaensch – who was also head of the rowing association's coaching course from 1940 to 1943 – who withdrew from Danish sport in May 1943. As the comment in *Idrætsbladet* put it,

> Ulrik Jaensch, who in recent years has taken the red shirts from Langelinje [in Copenhagen] to the top of Danish rowing, will be leaving the country next month. This will be a great disappointment for the men from Skjold who just this year managed to achieve particularly fine results. The club has a long list of crews, and under Jaensch's leadership they have all been training hard. The loss of Jaensch as a guiding force will be tough to deal with, even though the crews are so far advanced in their efforts that they can surely continue the good work with the help of amateur trainers.[18]

The winds changed: but they changed – as the example from Hermes also shows – slowly.

## The loss of Ragnhild Hveger

In a sporting nation like Denmark where there has not continually been a track record of top results, there was no one above or to even match the Danish swimming girls.

Denmark, for example, had several good boxers and cycle riders. There was Abraham Kurland, a world-class wrestler (whose opportunities became limited, though), and on the football front Denmark had a good national team as well as a tradition for creating good players – testified to by a bronze medal in the Olympics in 1948 and the subsequent flight to professional football, to countries like Italy. The swimming girls, on the other hand, were quite something else in the public imagination. At the same time both Ragnhild Hveger and Jenny Kammersgaard had very close links to Germany, and it is for this reason that a closer look needs to be paid to how they got on as the course of the war slowly changed, and the Nazis acquired other priorities than pursuing sports.

In December 1941, Ragnhild Hveger was again on tour in the Third Reich. Her trip involved a broad range of contacts, comprising a large programme of cultural events that made it possible for her to give the impression of a harmonious and attractive all-German theatre.

> It was a fabulous trip – and it's so nice to travel once in a while ... In Vienna, I swam at a hall that had room for 3,000 spectators, and I was given a beautiful crystal bowl. We went to 'The Prater' [park in Vienna] and to dinner at

the Danish embassy, and we spent time with Danish workers. Their leader ... was a very big help.[19]

As described previously in this study, because of the course of the war, great efforts were gone to on the part of the hosts whenever international guests were visiting, and in Vienna Ragnhild Hveger together with her instructress Kirel Nørregaard and an Austrian girlfriend were able to visit the unique Belvedere Palace. Hveger also spent a good deal of time at the Olympic facilities at Garmisch Partenkirchen and in Linz, taking part in a competition at the Parkbad pool, where "we also [met] Danes – there were two engineers and an architect from Odense."

Ragnhild Hveger also performed in Munich. At a newly opened pool, Nordbad, she swam 100 metres freestyle, 100 metres back stroke and 400 metres crawl on the same evening. Afterwards she could recount that she had received lots of new invitations. Ragnhild Hveger also spoke with a Dr Brewitz from the international swimming union, who unfortunately could not help her with her missing five diplomas and plaquettes for her world records, as "the union's money is all in London with the treasurer." During her tour, Hveger again tried to contact Jenny Kammersgaard but she was not "at her former address in Charlottenburg". They spoke with her teacher and were told that Jenny was doing well and that she was coming home to Denmark at Christmas.

After a period without touring performances, Ragnhild Hveger ran into problems in Helsingør, in April 1942. According to the leading sports journalist Gunnar Hansen, she had been made unemployed because of restructuring at the tourist bureau in Helsingør, her latest work place. It is not entirely logical for a tourist office to get rid of an internationally renowned swimmer without good reason, given that she could easily create extra favour with international and especially German visitors. It is therefore conceivable that because of her fondness for Germany Hveger may have acquired a certain discredit among sections of the Helsingør populace, where rumour had it that she and her parents were Nazis.[20] In any case, it then appeared that she had in mind to leave Helsingør swimming club in favour of either the Women's Sports Association (which ended up being the case), where her instructress for many of her international tours, Kiril Nørregaard, was trainer, or to Sparta, where she knew a number of other swimmers.[21]

But Ragnhild was still at the top of her sport, in April 1942, setting her last world record (no. 44!) at the pool in Frederiksberg Svømmehal – although this time in the not-so sought-after distance of 500 yards. Hveger did not seem especially nervous, as "she stood chatting to a couple of girlfriends when the starter said 'take your marks', whereupon the speaker asked her to pay more attention, and Ragnhild Hveger took the request with a big smile."[22]

More and more swimming events, however, were starting to be cancelled. A 'ladies international' between Denmark and Germany in Brandenburg/Havel planned for the month before was cancelled by the German swimming association; the same occurring with a swimming tour in December 1942.

On the home front, things were also going wrong. The annual swimming match between Copenhagen and the provinces, in the beginning of 1943, was cancelled, among other reasons because Hveger was no longer available for the provinces team following her change of club.[23]

Ragnhild Hveger's downward spiralling form, and her capricious turns of mind when it came to performing, led to something of a crisis in Danish swimming. At the swimming tournament for Aarhus gymnastics association (AGF) in February 1942, the public turnout was so disappointing that *Idrætsbladet* was forced to acknowledge that "A Ragnhild Hveger picture has to be on the poster at the swimming pool is the usual opinion, not least among the public."[24] Her last tournament in Denmark took place in the pool at Frederiksberg Svømmehal, mid-March 1943. Here, in the team relay event, she suffered an ignominious defeat by the new comet from Aarhus, Fritze Nathansen, whom she raced against over the final stretch.[25] As a special irony, Fritze Nathansen was Jewish.

At the same time, though, *Idrætsbladet* hoped that Fritze Nathansen's "final battle against Ragnhild can create a new hectic atmosphere around swimming tournaments."[26] There is nothing better in sport than a successful come-back: even in war time.

But Ragnhild Hveger, who in the first hard years of the occupation had managed to inspire Danes with a sense of self-confidence and hope through her victories and world records, was no longer on their side. In March 1943, she was hired as swimming instructor, in Kiel, and remained in Germany until the end of the war. In the North German press service, Pressedienst Nord, Hveger's transfer to German sport was reported under the heading "Ragnhild Hveger becomes swimming instructor in Germany". "From among countless international offers, she has decided to accept an offer to become a swimming instructor in Germany. She has often competed in Germany and for many years has had close friendly relations with German sport." Her record at 400-metres crawl in 1940 was especially emphasised; "an achievement that brought her to the very top of elite-class swimming."[27] It is a telling indictment of Hveger's sympathies, however, that she chose to settle south of the German-Danish border at so late a point in the war, a decision that did not go unnoticed. The London-based magazine *Frit Danmark*, in July 1943, registered her move, mentioning that at this point Hveger had become "very unpopular in Denmark because of her Nazi friends."

The important question however is the degree to which the Danish public knew about her political frame of mind? There was still a need for her as a symbol of a dynamic, forward-looking, victorious Dane.²⁸

Ragnhild Hveger's transition to German swimming was not directly commented on by the Danish sporting press. *Idrætsbladet* came up with a very brief statement, in April 1943, that Birthe Ove-Petersen, together with Eva Arndt and Elvi Svendsen, were now the only three left from the golden age of Danish swimming from 1937 to 1939. The magazine refused to accept her decision and in May of the same year wrote in a leading article "it is too soon to write farewell notices for the girl with 44 world records and a fantastic international reputation."²⁹

Both for Danish swimming and for Danish national pride, the loss of Hveger, symbol of the hardy Danish woman who could beat the world, was severe. When there was no longer a chance of a new Danish world record, the public stayed away. The effects could be felt in the cash box. In 1943, a swimming tournament was again held, and the Copenhagen swimming union (KSU) had "almost certainly expected a full house … given that they could more or less promise the public a new world record, but the visitor numbers were no more than could only just cover expenses." *Sports-Bladet* wrote that the good weather and Hveger's absence kept the public away, just as a rather peculiar world-record attempt in the extremely rare discipline of women's 4 x 400 yards could hardly make things better. The 4 x 400-yard women's relay actually achieved a new record but according to one report there was no great round of applause.³⁰

Although Ragnhild Hveger was now gone, she still very much haunted the stage from the wings. There was a desperate hope that a new Danish star of the same calibre could be conjured forth, one who could beat her records. One of these contenders was Karen Margrethe Harup, who also managed to beat several records. She swam 200-metres crawl in 2:42.3, which "was only a second from Ragnhild's Danish record" and it was also likely, at a tournament in Østerbro Svømmehal, on 19 May 1943, that a new record would be written out to her in the 400-metres back stroke. In this discipline, "Ragnhild Hveger has a world record that 'hangs in the wind', just as the 200 metres is in danger, if Karen Margrethe Harup seriously decides to take up back stroke. And we believe she should, given that training in back stroke would not impede her speed in breast stroke."³¹

At an international swimming competition against Sweden in Helsingør, in August 1943, the competitors tried to shake off Hveger's shadow. The Danish team managed to beat Sweden – but "it does not matter that we must do without Ragnhild Hveger, because in Fritze Nathansen we have a front crawl swimmer who at any rate is significantly better than the Swedish ladies."³²

It did not go much better with swimming in 1944. But there were hopes for a new men's swimming star as a replacement for Hveger – perhaps most of all because the women swimmers could not maintain the very high standards. The word about Erik Christophersen, in December 1943, was that "For the first time in many, many years, it is a man's name and not a woman's that comes to the fore when the year's swimming achievements are reviewed." Neither did it help Danish women's swimming that the legendary breast stroke swimmer, Inge Sørensen, also retired from competitive swimming in January 1945.[33]

## Kammersgaard's comeback

There were also Danish swimming stars outside the swimming pool, and after Jenny Kammersgaard came home from Germany she distinguished herself again as a long-distance swimmer in Denmark. Nevertheless, it was a case of continuity in terms of her relationship to Nazi circles. There is no doubt that the 'charm campaign' waged by the German authorities had contributed to weakening her 'spiritual immune system' in the face of the enemy.

It was not the best political company Jenny Kammersgaard sought after she left Berlin in May 1942, and she quickly came to the attention of the Danish resistance. According to a central index that the resistance movement set up covering Danish Nazis and Nazi sympathisers, she had "for a time been on courses at the Reichsportfeld in Berlin. Has received congratulatory telegrams from Hitler … has had relations with a man by the name of Hansen in an SS officer's uniform, and is German-minded."[34] From 1 December 1942 until 1 March 1943, she also worked as an office assistant at a German aviation base in Aalborg, that originally had been a small offensive airbase but which eventually was extended on a large scale to be part of the Germans invasion defences of North Jutland. Afterwards, according to her own testimony, she became a seamstress in Copenhagen.[35]

Jenny Kammersgaard carried on a private correspondence with her manager, called 'Hagensborg', whom she had become acquainted with through another woman swimmer.

Her relationship to Hagensborg lasted from 1942 or 1943 until 1944 when he moved to Sweden, where Kammersgaard also stayed for ten months between 1944 and 1945. She was entirely aware that Hagensborg was "an interpreter for the Germans, as he had first been a naval guard, but she did not sever relations with him for this reason." Hagensborg organised two swims for her in the summer of 1943 that had to take place in fresh water because of mines in the open sea. Her long-distance swimming of the Gudenå river, especially, from Ry to Ans, of around 75 kilometres in just under 23 hours struck a chord, as the longest fresh-water distance so far swum in Europe.[36]

For Jenny Kammersgaard, the fall from being a cosseted swimming star to becoming an ordinary worker was a bitter pill to swallow. Perhaps it exasperated her most that she never managed to get herself established as a swimming instructor at one of the Copenhagen swimming venues.

When she disappeared for 43 hours in June 1944 swimming from Skodsborg to Humlebæk, in Sealand, the press began to write her obituary, hinting at suicide. The current had carried her over to Helsingborg, towards the Kullen coast, but she was found and brought back to the Gilleleje beach hotel on the Sealand north coast by the Gestapo.[37]

## August revolt and athletics

Over the summer of 1943, Danes began to talk about the collapse of the Axis alliance, and many believed that the war was entering its final phase. This led to an increase in resistance actions against the occupying forces, and acts of provocation descended into more or less organised street fights involving large numbers.[38] Under these conditions, the large gatherings that came about with sports could prove to be particularly dangerous for German attempts to keep the peace.

At the same time, acts of sabotage began to escalate, much to the growing irritation of the Wehrmacht, who placed guards at key sites such as dockyards. One consequence was that a number of workers went on strike over the course of August, and the strikes eventually spread to several cities in the provinces; well-orchestrated by the Danish Communist party. The strike led to unrest in the North-Jutland city of Aalborg, on 23 August, which also spread to other large towns in North Jutland. In Funen, and its main city Odense, the situation turned rough when throughout the last half of August there was general unrest, street fighting, assaults and strikes. On 28 August, the German leader in Denmark Werner Best delivered an ultimatum to the Danish minister of foreign affairs, Scavenius, in which a list of demands were presented, including the death penalty for sabotage and the declaration of a state of emergency. When the Danish Government refused, the German military Commander-in-Chief, General von Hanneken, placed Denmark onto a state-of-emergency footing, on 29 August, announcing that the Government was now dissolved and that the German Army had taken over supreme command. From that day on, Denmark came under the administration of a so-called *departementchefstyre*, which meant government through the heads of the various governmental departments, under the leadership of the Permanent Secretary in the Ministry of Foreign Affairs of Denmark, Nils Svenningsen.[39]

In Copenhagen, the business of sabotage was getting under way. Most attention was gained when Forum, the old winter-pitch and hall, was hit on the morning of 24 August 1943. The Germans had taken over Forum as a military billet, and the explosion took place half a day before they moved in. The boom of the explosion could be heard over the whole city and the destruction was extremely thorough: "the glass roof was smashed and the walls collapsed, so that only the metal framework was left standing." So many people turned out to look that the police had to put up barricades, which meant that in the evening crowds could gather outside the sectioned-off area to sing national songs. As compensation for Forum, the Germans took over somewhat brutally the Idrætshuset facility in Østerbro, which had otherwise been the scene of a good many Danish-German sports matches, during the first year of the war. In the evening, the Copenhagen crowd then gathered in front of Idrætshuset to sing *The International*, so presumably the Communists had taken a hand in the proceedings.[40]

The August revolt took place at the same time as an international athletics competition between Sweden and Denmark, held in Stockholm between 28 and 29 August. It was intended that the competition should be heard on radio by sports fans in Denmark, broadcast by the ubiquitous Gunnar Hansen. The match against Sweden, a strong athletics nation, gave rise to a good deal of Danish national feeling at the stadium. Niels Holst-Sørensen won the 800-meter race, setting a new Danish record, and he was the anchor man during Denmark's sensational win over Sweden at the 4 by 400-metre relay race, which also brought the team the gold medal of the Danish newspaper B.T. As Gunnar Hansen put it,

> For the first time in many years, the Swedish got a taste of their own mortality ... like a bunch of school kids we all gathered round Niels Holst-Sørensen and Gunnar Bergsten after their gigantic performances at 800 meters, and with pride in our hearts and our eyes welling up we followed them when the public demanded a lap of honour around the flag-filled stadium.[41]

On the Saturday of the competition, after covering the 800-meter race, Gunnar Hansen complained about the break in transmission for the exciting needle match in the 10-kilometer race, where the hardened, experienced Danish runner Harry Siefert tried to challenge the Swedish favourite, and who looked as though he might improve on the Danish 10-kilometre record. At that point, no one at the stadium knew about the events taking place in Denmark, nor that all telephone communications between Sweden and Denmark had been broken in the wake of Prime Minister Scavenius being handed demands for the country to be put under a military state of emergency.

On Sunday morning, Danes in Stockholm could read about developments back home on every news bill-board announcement. Radio connections were re-established, but despite this the transmission was taken off the air due to the seriousness of the situation.[42] A few journalists turned up at the national team's hotel, where

> The gravity of the situation effected everyone. Anxieties were everywhere. We agreed, when the international games resumed in the afternoon, that we'd adopt a calm, composed manner. Of course we could be pleased if we achieved fine results – but, conditions being what they were, there was no

reason for getting over-excited, nor for showing off any great jubilation. It was only through sport that we'd stand up tall.

National sentiments were turned up full volume. The crowd sang

> *Der er et yndigt land*, the Danish national anthem. Gun Robertsson, the actor, read a poem by Hjalmar Gullberg, *Hälsning til Danmark* [Salute to Denmark]. In the inner circle, both teams stood in line … The stadium was as quiet as a church. Never will the Danes who were present that day forget the buildup to the final competitions.[43]

It was an ironic twist of fate that the most activistic Danish sporting association – with its former Nazi leadership – became (after its leadership change), through no will of its own, the association most closely associated with a national manifestation directed against Germany, because of a coincidence in timing between the August revolt and an international games.

The athletics games in Stockholm at the end of August 1943 acquired a special air of pathos since Denmark, at the same time, was placed under direct German administration. The occasion was ripe for a fierce and angst-ridden sense of unification around ideas of Denmark and Nordic identity, which in the post-war years could be interpreted as a coupling between Danish sport and an anti-German, liberational, national position, a coupling later fronted by the athlete Niels Holst-Sørensen, who was also an officer in the Danish military. According to Holst-Sørensen, though, it was not sport but the military that led him into German opposition.[44] After August 1943 and the introduction of government through departmental offices, international sporting events against Sweden also came to an end, as the German authorities in general would no longer accept the issuing of visas.

Furthermore, in January 1943, the German authorities decided to halt all sporting relations between Germany and other nations. And in the same year, on 2 February, Germany participated for the last time in an international match, while national inter-German sporting events continued well into 1944.[45] But at the same time as more and more German athletes were killed or injured, the Third Reich slowly moved towards a state of total mobilisation, in which sporting events made less and less sense.

# JEWISH PERSECUTION

Denmark's sports federation, DIF, was willing to practise competitive sports with Germany. But could the organisation also accept without protest that German authorities persecuted DIF members, who had to flee for their lives, leaving behind them broken sporting associations?

One of the results of the August revolt was that the Nazi 'final solution' in formal terms came to Denmark – between 1 and 2 October 1943, the roundup of Jews in Denmark was put into operation. It is probable that the German plenipotentiary Werner Best allowed his Naval counsellor G.W. Duckwitz to leak information so that around 7,000 Jews were able to escape to Sweden. Despite this, around 480 Jewish people fell into the hands of the Gestapo,[1] making it the most severe action committed against Danish citizens during the German occupation.

The chairman of the Danish youth organisation, Dansk Ungdomssamvirke, (DU) Hal Koch, was arrested on 29 August, but his organisation reacted, undaunted, by setting up a petition in protest against the persecution of Jews:

> In recognition of the injustices committed against a group of Danish fellow citizens in recent days, in absolute contradiction of Danish and Nordic conceptions of law, we the undersigned heads and chairmen of Danish youth organisations express our deepest condemnation of what has happened.

The protest petition was delivered somewhat late to Werner Best, on 7 October.[2] The document was signed by members from all of the various Danish youth organisations, and also by the handball association and the women's sports association. Among the signees not affiliated to DU was the Danish-Nordic youth association and the hikers' and ramblers' association Dansk Vandrelaug.[3]

The dilemma facing DIF in relation to the persecution of Jews in Denmark was that the organisation was particularly vulnerable to attack by the German authorities. If the Germans in command got wind of anti-German sentiments among the broad, collective crowd of sporting people, it might well lead to serious limitations being imposed on the internal autonomy and ways of functioning in Danish sport. Sport's special vulnerability can be seen in the way that the state of emergency from 29 August automatically led to a prohibition against all sporting activities. DIF, with assistance from the Danish police, very quickly managed to get the ban against training lifted, and indoor spectator sports, too, started up again after 9 October, but outdoor sporting events had to take place without spectators until the end of November, which in the opinion of DIF leader Herbert Sander precipitated large financial losses. For the area of greater Copenhagen (and apart from one small break) the prohibition against sports lasted until February 1944.[4] Knud Lundberg, a national-level football, handball and basketball player, reflected on how it was to compete without a crowd.

> It was a peculiar feeling to run round Idrætsparken where normally every lucky move would be applauded and where you were *always* called up on the moves that went wrong. Over that period, you couldn't hear a sound apart from the advice shouted by other players.[5]

Herbert Sander learnt about the petition protest on behalf of Jews in Denmark at a very late date, 5 October.[6] In principle, therefore, DIF did have time to add its signatures. The committee chairman for DDSGI, I. Skeltved-Madsen, made a telephone inquiry on behalf of his association chairman Niels Arnth-Jensen into whether DIF had received a referral from Dansk Ungdomssamvirke regarding the petition in response to the events surrounding 1 October. Sander replied that DIF had not received any referral, that they did not have any working partnership with DU and that it would be an "engagement with political activities" to do so. In response, Skeltved-Madsen said that DDSGI were in agreement. His organisation was also very reluctant to sign "as it would be the same as signing their own death warrant." He was nevertheless pleased that the two organisations took the same position as DDGSI hardly wished to stand alone on the issue.

That Sander would do anything not to provoke the occupying forces at that point might have been due to the lingering effects of the state of emergency, which lasted until 6 October, and involved a prohibition against public gatherings, including gatherings for sporting events. In October, when the protest on behalf of Jews in Denmark was taking shape, Sander was struggling to have restrictions relaxed: he and Leo Frederiksen were doubtless afraid the occupying forces would be less willing to negotiate with a sports federation that adopted a confrontational position.

Herbert Sander, however, was never allowed to let the matter die off in silence. On 9 October, DIF received a letter from K.E. Enrum,[7] a veterinary surgeon, who wrote saying that he had heard a number of associations and centrally-placed individuals had signed a protest to Werner Best, condemning the persecution of Jews. This protest involved not only the King but also the Danish Commander-in-Chief, national organisations such as the employers' association, the combined labour movement organisations, together with a section of national organisations from nearly every youth association in Denmark. To his amazement, the signature of DIF was missing, and Enrum asked "Is this really true? Has DIF refused to take part in such a protest?"

The question was a little difficult to answer frankly. C. Vincent, the secretary for DIF made a not too successful attempt a few days later when he wrote "The question referred to in your previous communication is quite unknown to the Danish sports federation." This prompted Enrum to write a personal letter to Sander,[8] in which he most earnestly asked Sander to sign the protest petition. Enrum had learnt from the committee organising the protest that they had passed by DIF because the federation, according to the committee, had always been so afraid of political involvement. Enrum had replied that the persecution of Jews was not a matter of politics but one of decency, to which the DU committee had conceded with "regrets and many apologies". To close, Enrum sharpened his tone towards DIF. It was of "paramount importance that all the youth of Denmark join the protest. And we can well dispense with those who do not share our opinion."

Sander was in doubt over how to deal with the matter, and wrote a confidential letter to his vice-chairman, Leo Frederiksen.[9] A clear sign of his dependence on Frederiksen is seen in the way Sander asked his vice-chairman, a barrister, for his "sporting and juridical opinion". Afterwards, Sander put forward his own position that if the highest authorities in the country had already protested, then a spread of other protests would "only weaken the 'wall of silence', and be not only superficial but possibly directly damaging." Furthermore, with the King as their protector, DIF was already gathered behind the King's protest, and "we owe due notice to the King."

Leo Frederiksen[10] agreed and believed the crucial point was that nothing would be gained by the protest, and nothing would be changed by a DIF signature. The protest was therefore superficial and meaningless. Frederiksen however, did not believe that it would damage their relations to the German authorities in Denmark. Nevertheless, he considered the issue before them to be "so important that the question of how to treat it demands the very greatest seriousness and level-headedness," in which case the King's protest must prevail as the protest of the Danish people. Any separate interference was simply "untimely officiousness".

Herbet Sander thereafter replied to Enrum that DIF placed the matter with DDSGI.[11] The reason that DIF had never received a referral from the committee, he explained, was because DIF constantly strove to steer clear of "the moment's strongly-politicised youth associations". Enrum, unsurprisingly, did not share the opinion.[12]

The DIF executive committee were first oriented on 21 October 1943,[13] and decided to accept the decision, taking it 'for further consideration'. The board, however, were never informed. Perhaps members were worried that DIF's isolationist position might become known to the general public. The episode is also a good example of how much room for internal manoeuvre the leadership of DIF had. The chairman and vice-chairman reached an important decision without first conferring with the executive committee, and without any involvement of the board at all.

In fact, DIF was much more effected by the action taken against Jews than the correspondence would suggest. One context in which the politics of the top leadership of DIF becomes conspicuous is when one of its member clubs, because of the action, suddenly ceased to exist. Hakoah had grown during the occupation into the largest Jewish sporting association in the Nordic region, with 374 members during the period 1942 to 1943,[14] but now the members had to either escape the country or go underground. Today, encountering the Hakoah club magazine in the archives, the situation becomes clear when the magazine stops at no. 15, in September 1943, and only begins again in 1946.[15] Other Jewish sportspeople were forced into similar decisions: for example Alex Friedmann, the Danish national-team football player from the club B1903, also escaped to Sweden.

In Sweden, the evacuated Hakoah members were given space, sports equipment and sports clothes for their own use, and under club names such as 'The Jewish Sports Association of Göteborg' and 'The Danish Clubs' Sporting Assembly' they practised wrestling, handball and football. Abraham Kurland's younger brother, Simon Kurland, has very positive memories of his time in Sweden, where the wrestlers prospered, many of them becoming well-known in Sweden.[16]

Jewish sportspeople also played an active role in sports organisation, in Sweden. The former national-team player, Leo Dannin, became head of a Danish sports office that organised events such as two football tours throughout Sweden in the summer of 1944.

On the birthday of Christian X, the Danish King, on 26 September 1944, the sports office organised a large banner parade at the stadium in Stockholm as the opening of a games, amply filled by the appearance of a Danish football team.[17]

## Towards liberation

Changes along a whole front in sports took place at that period. In September 1943, Magnus Simonsen was replaced by Carl Ettrup as the editor of *Idrætsbladet*. It happened after Gunnar Hansen, who had been co-editor from 1940 to 42, also left the magazine. It is tempting to think that perhaps Magnus Simonsen, in the middle of the state of emergency, the prohibition against sports and the collapse of the Danish policy of cooperation, believed it was high time he left a sports magazine that had been the most enthusiastic mouthpiece of all for collaboration with Germany in the field of sport.[18]

The state of emergency lasted from 29 August until 6 October 1943, providing a full stop to international sporting relations. Nevertheless, the tennis association managed to take part in an international match against Sweden in Stockholm, in January 1944.[19] But with this match, all sporting interaction across the national border ended, until the liberation. It is noticeable that Danish sport, as compared with other examples of social exchange, was active both very early and very late in its contacts with Sweden during the occupation.

Everyday life did not get easier for sportspeople over the remaining two years of the occupation. From 1943, sabotage actions and Nazi counter-sabotage, such as *schalburgtage*[20], got underway and to a great extent both hit the large, expensive sports facilities, including those the Germans had commandeered. The destruction hit, as on 23 March 1943, when Stadionhallen sports facility in Aarhus was targeted. The fire "was without doubt deliberate, since the hall contained a large amount of German beds." This episode resulted in the German powers enforcing a "ban on all entertainments, together with curfew between 19:00 and 05:00" in Aarhus.[21] In June 1943, Sundbyhallen facility that had been taken over by the Germans was burnt in a sabotage action, while Aarhushallen was hit in October 1944. Sports rowing, in particular, its boat houses and equipment was hardest hit in attacks directed against Danske Studenters Roklub, and clubs like Skjold, Glimt and Silkeborg, all damaged in the *schalburgtage*.

On 11 June 1944, KB-Hallen sports venue in Copenhagen was blown up in an act of *schalburgtage*. The building was used as a dancehall for jazz and swing enthusiasts, with their American-style 'relaxed' attitude, their "giant sweaters, large-check jackets, white sports socks, thick-soled shoes and their ration-quality-priced underwear", in contrast to the straight-backed, sporting, military Nazi ideal, widespread not least in sporting circles.[22] All-in-all, a form of cultural resistance developed among the American-oriented Danish youth, to which there are no parallels in the world of sport, despite the English and American sources that inspired modern sports.[23]

There was also a drain on the numbers of sports competitors after 23 August 1943. Even before the August revolt, the process had started. It must have been painful for a military man such as Colonel Sander when the Danish military sports federation (DMI) had to shut down, with its 22 member associations and 1,050 active members, in the wake of a German attack on barracks in Copenhagen, 29 August 1943. General Castenschiold had been chairman of the federation from 1918 to 1922; Herbert Sander from 1929 to 1932.[24] On top of this, there was the Jewish flight to Sweden in October, as well as the internment of Danish police, resulting in the closure of their sports clubs, in September 1944.

There were obstacles on a practical level, too. Sports clothes were difficult to manufacture and in March 1944 a ban was placed on the production of certain types of sportswear. Travel had become more difficult because of sabotage actions, and on 24 July 1944 a ban was implemented on taxi journeys of over 40 kilometres,

*It is unclear how many sports people were arrested for 'behaviour that was disloyal to the nation', after the liberation, but what is known is that 16 sports competitors and heads of sport came under the spotlight of the resistance. There were others, however, such as athletics phenomenon Svend Aage Thomsen, who had joined the side of the resistance. Here, Thomsen is seen in the middle on service in the Danish Brigade during the summer of liberation.*

which despite protests was not lifted for the benefit of DIF. Denmark was grinding to a halt, while it raged beyond its borders, and with the so-called "peoples' strike" in the summer of 1944 a state of emergency was again declared in many areas, with a curfew and bans against sporting activities – such as the period 26 June to 9 July, in response to a general strike staged across greater Copenhagen. On top of this, there was the insecurity of getting to and from sports facilities after dark, in a period without state policing from 19 September 1944 onwards.[25]

At the same time increasing numbers of sportspeople became involved with the resistance movement.[26] Many members of the Danish students' rowing club (DSR) were members of the Danish resistance, some of them sacrificing their lives: but in no sense can it be said that these clubs coordinated the resistance efforts of individuals.[27]

There is one example, though, of an entire football team taking part in illegal activities, in the last months of the war. Tønder sports association, or rather its football team, won promotion to the middle division. The team were not members of DIF. Their trainer, Finn Kristiansen, was a teacher of English and gymnastics at the State school in Tønder, and he more or less managed to get everyone connected to him involved in resistance work. A great opportunity was presented in that three of the players worked for the Danish State Railway (DSB), and had special permission to be out after curfew. The team handed out illegal literature, carried out railway sabotage and hid weapons – including in the attic of the sports-hall's changing rooms. One of the group's members explained,

> All of this sounds so dramatic, but I don't remember us feeling any great fear in taking part in the resistance. It was simply something that had to be done, and it cemented our relationships even more as a football team.[28]

It is quite clear DIF feared that supporting the protest on behalf of Jews might place the federation in a bad light with the occupying forces. DIF would do anything in the world to avoid seeming to challenge the German authorities at a time when the organisation struggled for their source of economic wealth, in the form of spectator crowds, to be again permitted by the Germans, who were nervous about anti-German feelings among large bodies of people. Throughout the final year of the occupation, then, cultural resistance to German domination became more widespread, but the defiance seen within dance and youth cultures was not seen on the sports field. As far as the press were concerned, German sport simply disappeared from the pages, which became increasingly absorbed in a renaissance in English sports. Gunnar Hansen had long since left *Idrætsbladet*, which of all the sporting periodicals had cheered on Danish-German collaborative sports. Examples can be found of whole teams involving themselves in the struggle for liberation, but in the ranks of DIF resistance took place among individual sportspeople and not at club level.

# NEW ALLIANCES

## Friend or Foe?

After the liberation on 5 May 1945, it became crucial that DIF shake the mental images of Danish-German collaboration from its memory as quickly as possible. Through hastily-organised matches against Denmark's English liberators and against Nordic sister nations, the signals of Danish sport were thereby changed.

However, liberation did not mean that the tribulations of Danish sport were over. Many sports facilities, such as Idrætshuset in Copenhagen, were taken over either as military hospitals or as internment centres for German refugees. Besides, there continued to be severe shortages of resources and materials, leading to measures such as early closing times and limitations on travel between the various parts of the country. Because of the danger of typhus infection spreading from refugees, swimming in many places such as Copenhagen and its surrounding districts was restricted, hitting swimming pools and halls particularly hard. On the other hand, DIF could delight in "the intoxication of liberation and the celebrations for our allied friends."[1]

For DIF, it was important that traditional sporting relations with Norway and Sweden were re-established. The first big breakthrough came on 24 June 1945, and then on 1 July in Idrætsparken, when Denmark played against Sweden, initially in Stockholm at Råsunda, then in Copenhagen. At the match at Idrætsparken, 40,000 spectators were able to cheer the Danish King, placed besides Leo Frederiksen, who in the words of *Idrætsbladet* "expressed his admiration for the King's firm stance during the first years of the occupation." The match at Råsunda was the first official international match in the world, after the end of the war in Europe. It was "staged as a tribute to the Danish people and as a celebration of the reunification of Nordic sport." Before the match, the Danish public were encouraged to learn the words to the Swedish national anthem, which came across superbly on radio, broadcast in both countries. The two other international matches against Sweden held in 1945 were also coloured by a sense of reunion. In the match at Råsunda, the Swedish public cheered the Danish players, on a signal from their cheer leader.[2]

Despite the rekindling of a Nordic sense of unity achieved after the liberation, it was Sweden who now became the 'evil' arch rivals. It was only in badminton and in a single field handball match out of two that Denmark beat Sweden. In football, the Swedish national team was impolite enough to beat Denmark 2-1 and 4-3, in

June and July 1945, and before the year was out Danish humiliation was complete with yet another defeat at 4-1, on 30 September. On top of this there were international defeats to Sweden in tennis, athletics, weight lifting, archery, wrestling, boxing and golf. The Swedish also won an international swimming competition, in which the Danish loss of Ragnhild Hveger and Inge Sørensen could be felt, not least because both had moved to Sweden as trainers, together with another Danish champion swimmer, Lilli Andersen, who had been employed by the Swedish swimming association, Svenska Simmförbundet, since 1938, training Swedish elite women swimmers in Stockholm. But mostly, the loss of Denmark's international ace, Ragnhild Hveger, became more noticeable now that international competition was reawakened.

## Games against the English

The first international football match against British players after the liberation was held at the main stadium in Aarhus, on 15 May 1945, between a Danish saboteur-team and some of Montgomery's soldiers, in front of 12,000 spectators. For Aarhus, the match was a great draw for the crowds, but there was also a good deal of activity lower down the spectrum. Tønder's sporting association, which during the occupation had nurtured an entire team of saboteurs, played in that summer of liberation against a detachment of English soldiers stationed at Niebüll, south of the Danish-German border. The Danish players had no passports, but the problem was solved by the British who drove them to Niebüll in military vehicles. After the game, the players relaxed together, Danes and British soldiers sitting side by side, drinking beer, while the Danes brought eggs for the British who had chocolate and cigarettes to give in return.[3]

During the occupation, sport had become an important symbol for attempts to maintain cultural relations between Denmark and Germany. After the liberation, the Danish sports authorities used sport as a means to demonstrate solidarity between Danes and their British liberators. To put it briefly, sport was once again being used as an arena to demonstrate that soldiers from a foreign power were welcome on Danish soil.

With his firm grip on the value of public communication, Leo Frederiksen gave an opening speech, when on 16 May 1945 a team of British paratroopers played in Idrætsparken against a Danish saboteur team in front of a 21,000-strong crowd. Leo Frederiksen said "We are grateful, glad and proud of the efforts you and your organisations have made for the liberation of Denmark." The two Danish teams were composed of members from the sabotage groups Holger Danske and Bopa, who won 2-1. There were no known sportsmen among them, but rather an artist, the sculptor Knud Nellemose, who was captain of the saboteur team. On the gate, a total of DKK 30,000 was taken, which went to Norwegian children in need.[4]

*A journalist, Vilhelm Bergstrøm, at the Danish newspaper Politiken was surprised when his colleague, the most celebrated Danish sport journalist of all times Gunnar Hansen was arrested by the Germans, in 1944, since Bergstrøm "had always thought that he [Hansen] was on the other side". And there is a great distance between being arrested and being in the resistance. Nevertheless, Gunnar Hansen allowed himself to be represented as a resistance man. The careful stage management here is unmistakable.*

On Saturday of the Whitsun Holidays at Idrætsparken, in 1945, "games against the English" really got underway, with entry music from a British military band, followed by a regular inter-Danish match between ØB and Køge. The international game was between a resistance group, Korps Aagesen, led by Count Valdemar, who played against a team of British marines. The Danish team included the former national-team player Ernst Nielsson, the 'old giant' from B1903. The result of the match remains uncertain.[5]

It was not only stationed British soldiers who turned up to play at Idrætsparken. A match was quickly organised between a number of internationally well-known professional British football players and, through negotiations with the British Army in Germany, the Danish league was able to arrange further games. Under the headline "The English are coming", *Sports-Bladet* could enthusiastically report that a select team of British professionals would play at Idrætsparken against a select Danish team on 10 July 1945. Happily, it was forgotten that the last international professional team that had played at Idrætsparken had been the 'heil'-saluting Admira team from Vienna.

The British team was almost regarded as a goodwill or an all-star team, and they had previously played in Paris, Bruxelles and Rotterdam, and in an international match against France at Wembley. There were many well-known former national-team players in the squad from Scotland, England and Wales, including Eddie Hapgood from Arsenal. But what they had in common was that they were all still in military service, and were led in by an amateur player, also an officer, Bernhard Joy, also from Arsenal. A British military orchestra was booked to play and 4,000 tickets were sold in advance alone to British fans in Denmark. The political symbolic value of the event was taken seriously at the very highest level, evidenced by the presence among the spectators of the British chief-commanding officer, General Dewing. The current British ambassador, A.W.G. Randell was also expected to turn up.

As a symbol of the joint Danish-British struggle against Germany, half of the proceeds from the game were to go to the widows of fallen British soldiers, while the other half would go to the widows and bereaved families of Danish resistance people.[6]

In contrast, at the 1936 Olympics in Berlin and during the first years of the war and the occupation, it had been Germany with its many eminent athletes who had amazed the Danish public and who had been cheered as the model of fair play and technical skill. Now it was the turn of the British.

> It is not news that English sportspeople are welcome guests in Denmark. It is not the war that has created a special liking for British sportsmen. That is something we have always had. Whether it was football players, boxers, or

*No more football with the foe. Friends were onto the pitch, and on 10 July 1945 a British team played against a select Danish team at Idrætsparken, Copenhagen, where the guests won 2-1. Two months later Great Britain and Denmark played again in a particularly brutal match where the friendly relations had noticeably cooled: the Danes winning 6-1. In the photograph, Eddie Hapgood and Bernard Joy can be seen coming onto the pitch. To the left stand General Dewing and Commander Adams.*

players from whatever sporting discipline who came here, we always knew that if the sport was English then it was good, it was fair, and it was exactly as it should be. Nothing about winning at any price for these fellows from Great Britain: never a small dirty trick to gain the advantage. They fight, but they fight fair. It's because the English are like this and have always been like this that Idrætsparken was filled to the very last seat, despite growing prices, despite knowing that it was something of a holiday team that the British were fielding, and despite knowing that the Danish team on paper left much to be desired.

The match itself was "an experience", and although the British only had "enough wind for the first half" they won 2-1, over a well-functioning Danish side. The British showed "how football should be played. They pushed the ball forward, along the ground, with precise, decisive passing. Rarely was the ball seen in the air. And with that precision, emanating from their game, the passing also became very quick. The Danes were a surprise, however – brilliantly following the game. It was as if the English play was infectious. They tried to copy the English, at which they were often very successful. The match confirmed once more that if the Danish game is to be raised then we need the English over here, to watch them and to learn."

Both Walther Christensen, from the Danish club Frem, and Carl Aage Præst, who during the 1950s and 1960s was to enjoy a golden period in Italian professional football, were praised by *Sports-Bladet* as having something of "the English style about them".

The last time the Stævnesammenslutningen league of major clubs in Copenhagen had been given new lease of life from abroad was in their matches against greater-German teams from Austria and against Admira, in the summer of 1941. In the late summer of 1945, a team of league players was given the chance of travelling to Germany for a revenge match against the British, on 19 September. The Danish players were flown over bombed-out Germany to Hanover, where they would meet a British military team that in many positions was the same team they had played against at Idrætsparken some months before. Again, the Danish football association and Leo Frederiksen went along with the mixture of sport and politics, all for a good cause. German spectators were refused access to the game.[7]

Three bombs had fallen on the pitch. The damage had been repaired, but the stands still bore the marks of the terrible battle. After the national anthems were played for the 3,000 allied soldiers, the commander-in-chief of the British airforce in Germany, Sir Sholto Douglas, came onto the pitch and greeted the two teams. The match ended a 0-0 draw, despite the British advantage, and afterwards there was a reception dinner at the British officers' mess.

Danish sports in the intoxication following the liberation was once again opening itself to a comprehensive politicisation: seen in the way the victors stepped onto the field at local club level, too – in November 1945, an American military orchestra, for example, playing a football match against Handelsstandens Boldklub.[8]

Much has been written about how the broad fever of liberation ran through Danish society. For football, this meant a return match at Idrætsparken, at the end of September 1945. The daily routine had begun again and the whole-heartedness of the affection between Danes and the British disappeared in a match that the Danes won 6-1. The game had been played rough. Perhaps it had not been so amusing for the British team to be swept off the field by a small nation sheltered from the ravages of war and whose players could train to top fitness levels while the British footballers lost both their friends and their stars in a struggle that had brought about Denmark's liberation. If the reports are to be believed, it was solely due to political ramifications behind the game – that this was a friendly match between liberators and the liberated – that no player was sent off. The match was "unfortunately not the success we expected. On top of which, there were many unfortunate episodes. The English stepped over the line. They felt badly treated by the Danish players whom they considered weren't playing by the rules, badly treated by the referee, Valdemar Lauersen, who didn't seem to be just, and badly treated by the Danish crowd who whistled them off the pitch." Valdemar Lauersen, who had refereed other games such as those between Germany and Sweden, was now on the pitch serving a new cause.

According to *Sports-Bladet*, Whittingham, the British centre forward had provoked the crowd by crashing his elbow into the face of Oscar Jørgensen.

> Whittingham deserved to be whistled off in the way he was at half time, but it should have stopped there. In the second half, if not he then the other English players should have been showed fair play, which they didn't get from the incessant shouts from the crowd. What did the crowd achieve? Only the ruin of the game. Whilst the first half had been brilliant, there was simply no proper play in the second half. The English were irritated, played hard and often became violent, which has nothing to do with football. Lauersen was involved in a couple of episodes in which he certainly could have given British players their marching orders, the way they carried on, but naturally that would be the last thing he'd want.[9]

But the state of British football slowly returned to its old form and, where the Danish sports sections had previously reported on German sporting victories, German sports lay in ruins, leaving Danish columns to once again fill with reports but on British football. In October 1945, *Sports-Bladet* could report under the headline "Football in England – Chelsea's sensational victory" that "the English are now attending football matches in almost the same numbers as they did before the war. In spite of the rain, Saturday's big game was watched by 681,000 people compared to the 56,000 who saw the international between England and Wales."[10]

Throughout 1946, a number of British club teams travelled to Denmark, but only managed to win two out of nine games. In addition, a team from the Royal Air Force turned up for a match that ended in a 1-1 draw. For the first time, the legendary technician Stanley Matthews played in Denmark. In the same year, the Danish football association hired a British trainer, J.D. Butler.[11] All in all, within a five year period a significant shift can be registered within Danish sports from matches against German soldiers for example from Luftwaffe to matches against British soldiers for example from Royal Air Force.

In the summer of 1946, a team of Danish athletes were sent to the Inter-Allied Games or 'Olympics' in Berlin, and in August, on the invitation of the Dutch military, a football match was held between Danish and Dutch military teams at the Olympic stadium in Amsterdam. For two national-team players, Ivan Jensen and Karl Aage Hansen, it was a shock to travel by bus through the devastation in Germany. "We sat quiet for a moment, completely quiet. It was the same depressing sight everywhere. Piles of ruins next to piles of ruins. Everything lay untouched. The Germans did nothing. They shuffled around, drooping, like in a trance." It was no longer German military music that reached the ears of the Danish public but American popular music from the American club in Amsterdam: "It was a real American club, just like we know it from the films. A big show and laughter, howling and noisy people … full tilt the whole night."[12] These were new times.

Whereas Danish sports journalists during the first years of the war reported on competitions between Axis powers such as Italy and Germany, it was now clashes between Allied powers that were foremost in their minds. In November 1945, the Dynamo club football team from the Soviet Union came to London for a tour of Great Britain. This sporting exchange also had political motives, not least from the Soviet side, in softening the growing animosity between the two former allies: clearly seen in a comment from the Dynamo striker who on landing in London (according to the Danish press) "threw his arms out wide in an embrace and said 'here we are, and maybe with our sport we can create a better friendship than the politicians'."[13]

A stir was caused in the first game when, in front of a crowd of 78,000 at Stanford Bridge, Dynamo managed to draw 3-3 with the home team, after Chelsea had led 2-0. The English public were completely thrilled by the Russians, who showed themselves to be "brilliant football players, excellent technicians, sure in their ball work and very quick." The enthusiasm grew even more when Dynamo pulled off "a sensation" in front of 40,000 spectators, in beating Cardiff City by a massive 10-1. For the next match, Dynamo were to play Arsenal, and the English side began acquiring players from other top teams as "several of Arsenal's best players were on service in Germany." Nevertheless, in their final game in London, Dynamo still managed to beat a reinforced Arsenal side with Bernhard Joy as striker, by 4-3. The match, however, was marred both for the players and the public by poor visibility because of thick fog.[14]

## Norwegian partisans

The first sporting competitions against Norway were rather awkward, as Danish teams had not managed to completely avoid playing against Norwegian collaborator-sports organisations during the occupation. And doubtless, the Danish interaction would have been more extensive had the Norwegian boycott not been so effective. There was also a Danish reluctance to humiliate the Norwegians with a well-trained Danish team, which would only highlight that the Norwegians had been under far greater pressure through their resistance and their boycott. Voices were therefore heard in public, in Denmark, leading up to an international football match on 26 August 1945, asking the Danish players to moderate their game.

At the match, Idrætsparken's own band played, and both the Danish King and Queen greeted the players before the game – the referee was Swedish, of course, for the greater good of Nordic brotherhood. *Sports-Bladet* quoted the King saying to the Norwegian striker Øivind Holmsen, "It is wonderful to see you all again." "It was a great occasion for the Norwegians, but we need a new conductor for our band. The music was not at its best."

For DIF, and not least the football association chairman, Leo Frederiksen, it was apparently so important to demonstrate the correct national attitude that they entirely forgot about their precept of not mixing sport with politics. A display had therefore been arranged in honour of Danish and Norwegian resistance fighters. In such a manner, DIF was able to associate Norwegian and Danish resistance to the wide umbrella of sport. *Sports-Bladet*, however, thought that "the Danish resistance people shambled along while the Norwegians marched." For *Sports-Bladet*, the event was little concerned with winning.

> The result of the international game is of little importance. First and foremost, the day is an occasion for reunion ... The impressive sports strike mounted by the sporting youth of Norway during the German occupation is well known. But, naturally, sportsmen cannot lay idle for six years without performance levels falling.[15]

Perhaps the Danish players had listened to the pleas of the press, because they won 'only' 4-2, after an energetic Norwegian team actually threatened the moderately-achieved Danish victory. Afterwards, the Danish team was criticised for its weak play.[16] At the follow-up match in Oslo, the gloves were off, and the Danes beat the Norwegian team by 5-1. Denmark brought home wins in tennis and boxing, too, but as *Sports-Bladet* wrote "Norwegian sports should of course have the required time to get back on its feet, and in the meantime we simply refuse to discuss results of Danish-Norwegian international matches. International competitions with Norway are only concerned with re-establishing mutual cooperation."[17]

On the athletics track, it was clear that for Danish sports fans the Swedish runner Gunder Hägg had taken over the prize position from the German star Rudolf Harbig who had died on the front in 1944. Sheltered from the waste that the war made of international sporting youth, Hägg had been able to achieve no less than 14 world records. As a final example of how circumstances were now reversed, Hägg turned up in Copenhagen shortly after the liberation of Denmark, to compete in a Danish-

Swedish games on 8 June 1945 organised by the athletics association of Copenhagen (KAF), the association that with its former pro-Nazi leadership excelled in earlier years at Danish-German games, and even on one occasion at mounting a games against a Norwegian collaboration team. *Sports-Bladet* praised Hägg as "unconditionally, the world's greatest sporting name", a claim justified by his successful tour of USA in 1943. But if a closer look is taken at both the verbal descriptions and visual presentation, it can be seen that the Swedish runner acquired the symbolic value Harbig once had as a male aesthetic sporting icon. No other runner in the world had "the style, the rhythm and the tempo of Gunder Hägg. There is a beauty, effectiveness and lightness about his running that can do nothing but amaze the crowds."[18] Despite the usual difficulties with the arch-rival Sweden, it was becoming obvious that the nations who had either fought a brutal war or been brutally occupied were badly positioned in terms of sport. This was an important factor in Denmark's football triumphs of 1948, with an 8-0 win over Poland, its bronze medal at the Olympics in London, and its export of Danish football players to Spain, France and most of all Italy.

As is apparent, DIF succeeded through its comprehensive games activities to clarify new patterns of cooperation with England and the Nordic countries. On top of which, DIF now permitted unrestricted politicisation, with marches on the pitch by resistance fighters, sabotage-team matches, English military bands, the exclusion of German spectators, and Danish competitions against foreign soldiers – but English ones this time. Football thereby provided an important symbolic contribution to Denmark's habilitation into Allied circles.

# A 'JURIDICAL PURGE'?

On 4 May 1945, German forces in Holland, North-West Germany and Denmark capitulated, followed by total capitulation on all fronts on 7 May.

Precisely how many sportspeople were arrested after the war is hard to say, but at least 16 heads of sport and competitors were being watched by the resistance movement, and a number were interned.[1]

The top leadership of DIF very successfully avoided arousing public interest for a purge within Danish sport. By making affiliations to the Nazi party or Nazi ideology the corner stone of the Danish sports world's own cleansing operations, attention was drawn away from sporting relations and collaborative sports with Germans. In this way, a protest in *Idrætsbladet* by a Danish sportsleader that had originally called for an investigation of the sporting relations with Germany did not need to be addressed. Danish-German collaboration on the sports field was thereby not raised as a problem, at the same time as DIF came down hard and consistently on Nazis in the sportsworld, despite membership of the Nazi party not being in itself illegal according to the Criminal Law Amendment Act of 1 June 1945.

The leadership of DIF did little to hinder "a night of the long knives" in sporting ranks, and the DIF top again succeeded in decentralising the decision-making process about expulsion to individual member associations, whereby the central leadership was freed from assuming direct responsibility, and whereby the juridical purge, the *retsopgør* of Danish sport had a less potent, less unified tone and instead could be carried out fragmentally and more or less in silence.[2]

During the occupation, the dogma of DIF about a non-political role for sport had been used as an explanation for collaborative undertakings with the occupying power, and for DIF's rejection of the anti-Nazi organisation Dansk Ungdomssamvirke. Now, people were being expelled from Danish sports whose only infringement was membership of the Nazi party. They were being punished, therefore, for their political convictions, and not for having brought about damage to Danish sport. In this way, DIF again lost its grip on its declared non-political policy, and its clash with members of either a Nazi disposition or who were members of the Nazi party – who had done nothing punishable by law or brought sport into discredit through their actions – went directly against the principles of the Danish Constitution about freedom of expression and freedom of association.

The successful avoidance of a juridical purge into DIF's own activities paradoxically went together with a notion, increasing throughout the occupation, that the pursuit of national sentiment meant the protection of Danish democracy and unconditional independence. DIF may well have played football with the foe, but now various national and royal frameworks (such as DIF) were regarded as guarantors for positions of Danish sovereignty – even though the coupling between a strong sovereign nation and democracy had not always been an obvious one. On the contrary, it had been the Danish anti-parliamentarian right wing who had blown air into an inflated idea of nationalism during the 1930s: and on this point, too, times had now changed.

Denmark's two big swimming stars, Ragnhild Hveger and Jenny Kammersgaard, did not fare well under the Danish *retsopgør*. It was a great blow to morale for the Danish sporting world when Hveger, the country's international star, was arrested by the resistance movement.[3] The reasons given were that she "worked for the Germans", because the resistance had intercepted a communication from the North-German press bureau, from 30 June 1943, that she was to be employed as a swimming coach in Germany.[4] For Hveger, the liberation marked a family tragedy, in that both her father and her brother were interned.[5] In 1952, however, Hveger succeeded in making a comeback onto the Danish national swimming team, at the Olympics in Helsingfors, though not without great obstacles and heavy disputes.

In 1966, Hveger's name entered swimming's Hall of Fame, in Fort Lauderdale, USA, and since then in the Hall of Fame for Danish sport, established in 1992. In 1996, Hveger was named by DIF as the Danish sportswoman of the century.

Jenny Kammersgaard's relations to dubious political circles did not end with the war. She maintained her relations with her pro-German manager, 'Hagensborg', who in the meantime had been jailed at Sundholm, in Amager, Copenhagen. Through a solicitor, she contacted him, to reinstate him as her manager,[6] and on 1 September 1945 both parties signed a contract for a five-year period, assuring Hagensborg the rights to organise swimming events on her behalf for 25 % of the net profits.[7]

In April 1946, however, the 30-year old, German speaking 'Hagensborg' was accused of having allowed himself to be hired into German naval affairs, for having performed service as a uniformed, armed guard at locations including Lynetten docks in Copenhagen, and in spring 1943 for having informed the Germans that "the supervisors of an internment camp at St. Grunnet and those British citizens interned there had contravened regulations that were the condition for Danish command and supervision."

To finish off, he had been taken on as a translator by the German security police from July 1944 at Horserødlejren, a prison at Horserød, in North Sealand, used for internment. At his trial, Jenny Kammersgaard provided testimony "in high praise" of Hagensborg, who despite the changes in climate towards leniency was convicted and sentenced to five years in prison, and declared "for all time unworthy of common trust." After the court's decision, Jenny Kammersgaard made a request for bail, if the convicted could remain free from prison, but "this matter can of course be given no such consideration."[8]

But this was not the last occasion on which Kammersgaard's name is found associated to controversy.

In the aftermath of the breakup of the Third Reich, German and Baltic war criminals tried to escape prosecution. One option was to cross the Øresund into neutral Sweden, and from there return to the Baltic countries or back to Germany, or even for certain German criminals to flee the Continent altogether and escape to South America.[9]

On the night of 20 August 1947, the Danish police stopped a truck carrying six Estonian refugees from a camp, after a tip-off from an individual at Humlebæk who noticed "that a boat had entered the Sletten harbour shortly before, which he believed plied illegal traffic to Sweden."[10] In the boat was the captain, Mogens Otzen Gadeberg, and his girlfriend Jenny Kammersgaard, who was also arrested and remanded in custody for 10 days. They both admitted to previously having transported refugees but without the police being able to uncover what nationalities were involved.

To the police, Jenny Kammersgaard admitted that the six Estonian refugees had obtained her and her partner's name and their joint address in Copenhagen "through other refugees in the camp". All six came from the Allied refugee camp on Artillerivej, in Copenhagen.[11] A fisherman, who had taken part in illegal transportation during the occupation, on behalf of Dansk-Svensk Flygtningetjeneste, for the resistance, told the police that Kammersgaard's involvement was probably to provide the refugees with an alibi, namely long-distance swimming.[12]

The Danish court found Jenny Kammersgaard and her partner guilty of "taking money to provide services to persons who were present in the country as Allied refugees, to assist them in leaving the country without passport control and without valid travel documentation." The case concerned three completed transportations in July 1947, involving a total of 20 refugees, together with three aborted attempts in July and August 1947 to sail a total of 11 refugees to Sweden.[13]

After several years' residence in Germany, Kammersgaard had some difficulty in steering clear of political problems, and even after the liberation she did not quite manage to move out of the shadow of the Third Reich. After the refugee episode from 1947, however, a change in signals did occur, when in 1950 and 1951 she swam the English Channel.[14]

In the post-war period a long tradition developed within Danish sport for disguising the role sport played during the occupation, a tradition that began directly after the war. That the disguise was carried off so astonishingly well is due partly to the assumed divide between sport and politics that created a barrier against any critical investigation into the sports policies and politics of DIF.

In contrast, shortly after the liberation, the DIF leadership presented sport as a defence against the enemy. According to this myth, sport had been quietly preparing the way for a day of reckoning. In a self-image current within sporting circles, collaboration with the occupying forces had only occurred under duress. Furthermore, after the liberation there were only extremely rare indications of acknowledgements within Danish sport of the propagandist and racist foundations of Nazi sport – which was why it was possible to take discrete pride in the relatively few Danish victories over Germany during the war; not least Svend Aage Christensen's light heavyweight title in the so-called war-time European championships from January 1942. So the idea of whether even to compete against a politicised opponent was therefore never questioned, not concerning the period leading up to the Second World War, nor after the War's outbreak and the occupation of Denmark on 9 April 1940 when football was played with the foe.

*This picture of "little captivating Inge", who after her bronze medal at the Berlin Olympics of 1936 didn't give the 'heil' salute at the award ceremony, was used again and again after the war, and indeed has become an icon for Danish perceptions of national resistance to Nazi propaganda.*

*The Danish sports federation (DIF) celebrated its fiftieth anniversary on 14 February 1946 at the KB-hallen sports venue. At the same time, DIF published a book on 'Danish sport throughout fifty years', in which the federation presented its authoritative version of the story of sport during the occupation, and the role in that story played by DIF.*

Sport proved difficult to criticise, a result that owed much to the growth of sport into a large popular well-loved movement, coupled to that community-singing spirit in Denmark whereby sport was regarded increasingly as a manifestation of anti-German feeling and therefore of a democratic Danish identity.

# REVOLT FROM BELOW – CONCLUSION

> A piece of Danish sporting history – international matches during the occupation – have been hotly discussed. That they have, and only the fewest can judge the question. It is still far too early to talk about the details of Danish sport's position during the years of occupation, but in its large strokes this important episode in sporting history can now be told.
> (DBU chairman Leo Frederiksen's response to critics, 17 May 1945, *Idrætsbladet*)

> It is a good thing that straight backs were found among the leadership of DIF, led first and foremost by 'the old General' H. Castenschiold and his clever, fearless comrade Leo Frederiksen. Because when the Germans came to Denmark, there was no end to Tschammer's belief in how wonderful times would be for the sporting youth of Denmark together with Hitler's youth. But Leo – The Lion – was a master at finding all sorts of excuses to not taking part in collaborative events, and in the setting up of this and that, not least a European sports federation for every occupied country.
> (Idorn 1971, p. 207: interview with the sports journalist Julius Larsen)

Danish research into collaboration policy during the occupation until now has focussed especially on opinion makers and leaders in sports and economics. The current study, however, has aimed to uncover Danish-German relations at grass-roots level and among ordinary people. Collaborative activities were not the filtered-down results of efforts by the top political circles to achieve goodwill with the occupying forces, encapsulated in initiatives such as the Danish-German association, but rather, in the field of sport, were an expression of an independent interest shown by the Danish organisers and public for preserving relations with Germany.

Of all the arenas for cultural-political collaboration with Denmark, the German authorities came close to pulling off a major coup through sport. The institutional frames were in place well before the occupation, both on formal and informal levels. In contrast to other German initiatives, sporting collaboration was directed towards the masses and could thereby influence broad opinion. In the area of cinema, too, the German powers had a number of successes. But in contrast to relations with the leadership of Danish sports, German relations with Danish cinema proprietors were marked by conflict and German interventions, while the Danish cinema public unlike sports enthusiasts were passive recipients of cultural messages and not active competitors and fans.

As discussed in the introduction, this study tries to demonstrate the validity of four theses: that throughout the 1930s a sports-political goodwill was established in Denmark towards Germany; that the Danish sports leadership began to work actively to enable collaborative sports with the occupying forces to function, and that only external factors prevented greater development; that Danish-German sporting relations were the most comprehensive form of cultural collaboration; and that DIF legitimised its actions through the slogan that sport was not political, which meant that at any point DIF could justify its initiatives and that Danish sport was subject to its strongest politicisation ever.

After the Nazi seizure of power in Germany in 1933, Danish sport developed a deep fascination for the Third Reich's expansive sports politics. At the 1936 Olympic Games in Berlin, Danish sports officialdom in its near entirety mustered and could report on the series of impressive German victories and their fantastic ability to create an atmosphere and sense of unity at the most grandiose Olympics up until that time. For the German organisers, the Olympics were arranged as one enormous occasion for giving the international scene an impression of Nazi attempts to create new cultural forms, based on the cult of the Führer, the exaltation of the body, mass displays and a dazzling, blinding aesthetic surface. Only among Communists, cultural radicals, workers' sports movements, Jewish sports and in the social-democratic press was there resistance to a racist, military regime being allowed to hold Games in the name of peace and understanding between peoples.

In the second half of the 1930s, the Nazi regime did much to attract Danish sportspeople into its fold – such as the internationally renowned Danish swimming star Jenny Kammersgaard. The situation, therefore, drew on a tradition of strong acquaintance between Danish and German competitors that continued during the Second World War. These well-functioning relations towards German sport meant that during the occupation Danish sport was willing and even enthusiastic about playing football with the occupying forces.

After Germany embarked upon the Second World War in September 1939, the Danish sports federation, in contrast to its corresponding organisations in Sweden and Norway, and with the support of the Danish foreign ministry, continued to meet German sportsmen and -women on the sporting field. The German Reichssportführer Tschammer placed great emphasis on these Danish-German sporting relations, marking them with a well-orchestrated handball match on 8 October 1939 in Leipzig to trumpet sounds, before the eyes of 12,000 thrilled spectators.

Shortly after 9 April 1940, the top leadership of the Danish sports federation (DIF) decided to abstain from competitions against foreign nations. The reason was anxiety that holding highly emotional football matches so shortly after Denmark had been occupied would bring Danish sporting tempers to boiling point and thereby ruin future opportunities for international sporting relations.

Nevertheless, at the beginning of the occupation, sport turned out to be *the* cultural activity that the German authorities showed greatest commitment to resuming. The German authorities were enthusiastic about re-establishing sporting relations because Denmark was defined as an Aryan-Germanic region and it would be beneficial to incorporate the country within the greater Fatherland. Other countries – especially those in Eastern Europe – were never given the same opportunity for large-scale sporting relations but were instead brutally treated as nations of inferior people. In addition, there was the propaganda effect of providing sports entertainment for the German people, demonstrating German surplus capacity for competitive sports at a time of War.

At the same time that Germany could show off a humane occupation policy to the world, Danish-German sports also meant that Danish workers in Germany had an opportunity to support their home country at matches held in Germany.

Hitler and Goebbels wanted to use open-air concerts, military parades and sporting events in Denmark to encourage a chain of Danish mental associations to friendly German relations. Therefore, the first German plenipotentiary (former ambassador to Denmark) Renthe-Fink put pressure on the Danish sporting authorities, which was eventually seconded by the Danish foreign ministry, on 8 July 1940, that regarded sport as a suitable instrument for achieving German goodwill, thereby enabling their collaborative policy to run smoothly. The situation produced a shift in May 1940 towards sport authorities accepting local competitions against Germans and German membership to Danish sports associations and clubs – only that these events should take place without the loud ceremony of official games.

At the end of April 1940, despite a ban on international matches, Leo Frederiksen entered a covert agreement with the German football leadership designed to kick-start sporting relations with an international football match against Germany in the autumn of that year. After Germany achieved the capitulation of Belgium, Holland, and invincible France through its *Blitzkrieg* of May and June 1940, the leadership of Danish sports adapted itself to getting international sporting relations up and running again. It seemed that Europe was about to experience a generation of German dominance, and for DIF the aim became to survive with as much autonomy as possible in Europe under the New Order.

These opening moves led to an agreement reached with Renthe-Fink on 5 August that sporting relations should be resumed and that a group of international football matches be held involving German and Swedish teams; allowing the Danish public

*By March 1943, Swedish commentators noted that Danish-Swedish sporting relations had built a bridge over the Øresund separating the two countries, during the occupation.*

to realise there was no question of a one-sided collaboration with the occupying power. Sport became one of the most important avenues of communication over the Danish-Swedish Sound, during the occupation, and Danish sport was very early (and remained very late) in contact with its Swedish sister nation, ending with a tennis match against Sweden in January 1944.

The collaboration by Danish sporting organisations with the occupying powers was far more widespread than until now has been publicly known. In the relatively short period from the first games on 22 August 1940 until the last match against a German team – an international handball match on 22 November 1942 – a wealth of international matches, inter-city matches, tournaments, games and series were held, where especially the boxing and wrestling associations together with the athletics association were active as organisers. There were international matches against Germany in football, handball, boxing and wrestling – all at least twice – as well as in weight lifting, fencing and hockey. International matches were also held against other Axis alliance countries, such as against Italy in tennis, against Hungary in athletics and against Croatia in wrestling.

Banners of the Nazi swastika flew side by side with the Danish flag, Dannebrog, while German competitors gave the 'heil' salute and German spectators gave the 'heil' in return, and the Danish crowd sang Danish anthems such as *Kong Christian Stod ved Højen Mast* and the German crowd *Deutschland, Deutschland über Alles*, followed in Germany by the Nazi *Horst Wessel* anthem. Collaboration in sports provided the most comprehensive example of cultural collaboration with the occupying powers. The first years of the occupation became a golden age of Danish-German collaborative sports that was far more intense than any period before or since. The Danish national football team played against Germany both in 1940 and 1941, aside from a match at Idrætsparken in Copenhagen in 1940 being cancelled, and besides other matches arranged in 1941 at Idrætsparken involving two of the European Continent's strongest city teams that both came from Austria under German annexation.

Since the DIF leadership did not wish to take responsibility for what went on at club and member-association level, the planned resumption of collaborative sports was not brought about by an international match against Sweden: because Nazi circles within the leadership of Danish athletics were quicker off the mark and organised a large athletics games on 22 August 1940. The desertion of Danish athletics in these crucial years is partly due to athletics being one of the most popular sports of the day, where achieving records was of great importance for the athletics sports public.

Around 4,000 spectators watched the competitions at Østerbro stadium in Copenhagen against German athletes from the Berlin Luftwaffe under the musical direction of a German military orchestra. The German military commander-in-chief, Lüdke, and Renthe-Fink both took part as a gesture of German interest for collaborative sports, along with much of the top leadership of the occupying forces in Denmark.

Professional sport, too, was quick to re-emerge after the ban on international competition was lifted. Inasmuch as professional sportspeople made a living from their sporting disciplines, their efforts were part of an economic collaboration with Germany. When the market for professional European boxers became severely reduced because of the war, it gave Danish adventurers – perhaps coming to the end of their careers – a chance of quick gains in the famished German market.

German enthusiasm for sporting relations to flourish again was seen at the first competitions: when top-level German athletes were speedily flown into Denmark; where German authorities approved matches that in sporting terms were worthless games against poor opponents; and at German acceptance of being cheated of victory in the boxing ring apparently because the propaganda effect outweighed the sporting value.

For German propaganda served to the occupying forces' own service people, the role of German soldiers playing sports in Denmark and in collaborative sports with Danes was important. Representatives from the Wehrmacht turned up in large numbers at several Danish-German events, which for German propaganda was a sign of sports' ability to unite the two nations. Collaborative sports gave the German colony in Denmark a perfect opportunity to involve themselves in friendly relations with a people under occupation.

A typical image was of the German soldier called home from the front, pulling on his sportswear and lining up to compete. The German authorities made sure that elite sport was one of the few civil activities that continued to receive significant resources and the opportunity to function almost at pre-war levels, as a sign of German mastery of the war situation. Danish sportspeople, therefore, competed against soldiers in sportswear, which was never concealed by the Danish press.

But German national-team sportspeople who competed in Denmark were far from a homogenous group. Among them might be absolutely top-level Nazis and war criminals, such as the director of the Reich Security Main Office, Reinhard Heydrich, who was one of the chief architects of the holocaust. He took part in an international fencing match against Denmark on 1 December 1940, where incidentally he met the national-team fencer for Denmark, the Italian Raimondo Carnera. Heydrich's political ambition with sport was to become leader of a newly-organised European fencing association, which in all probability he considered to be a springboard for a larger political career within sports, which, however, never occurred.

A German competitor who was often in Denmark was the champion wrestler Werner Seelenbinder. Seelenbinder was a Communist and had been given by his Communist cell the task of establishing contact with anti-fascist groups whilst travelling for competitions. Seelenbinder's cell was eventually exposed, and in February 1942 he was arrested and two years later executed.

For Goebbels, German minister of propaganda, the sporting victories of German soldiers was a sign to the German people of their invincibility – and win they did. Only *extremely* rarely did Danish sportsmen and -women manage to steal a victory from Germany and thereby demonstrate that Denmark could also bite back. If only Denmark had won occasionally as Sweden had, especially in football. But in this regard, too, Denmark was a model nation, confirming German convictions of being the master race.

Sporting relations with Germany involved the entire Danish elite-sports world, both amateur and professional. On a personal level, all of the top leadership of DIF and decision makers among the associations entered into these collaborative relations, although only a few – such as the leaders of the athletics association – were influenced by Nazi ideology and an infatuation with the occupying power. On an organisational level, too, collaboration also took hold. Danish trainers, coaches and heads of sport led Danish teams on trips to Germany; Danish sports physicians contributed at Danish-German competitions; Danish referees adjudicated at matches held internally within Germany and at German matches against other countries; and German referees and trainers were regularly in Denmark.

There is much to suggest that the highest levels of the DIF leadership, the ordinary heads of the various associations, and the ordinary Danish sports competitors were by far ideologically indifferent, and therefore not susceptible to Nazi ideology in its generality and to anti-Semitism in particular. This attitude comes to the fore on occasions as when DIF prevented sports orienteering with its military potential to fall under the Nazi influence of the Danish athletics association and instead had it officially placed under the direction of the skiing association in September 1942. The resistance by the DIF leadership to Nazi ideology means that their cooperation with the occupying powers cannot be characterised as abject pro-German collaboration. On the other hand, they opened the flood gates so that many young sports competitors and spectators perhaps less well-armoured could have their 'mental and spiritual immune system' weakened through too close contact with the enemy and his propaganda.

Denmark's most well-known sports competitors such as 'little captivating' Inge Sørensen, the athletic phenomenon Svend Aage Thomsen, and the multi-discipline ball player Knud Lundberg all took part in competitions against Germany. The war was a great misfortune for those Danish elite sportsmen and -women whose opportunities for culminating sporting achievements lay within the period of occupation, bringing with it a break in their careers and lost opportunities to compete at the Olympics in Tokyo, 1940, and in London, 1944. Both these Olympics were cancelled because of the war. It might therefore be a dreadful human temptation for a young person to enjoy excellent opportunities for meeting sportspeople from Axis power countries, now that the rest of the world with the exception of neutral Sweden and to a very limited extent occupied Holland were closed off.

The occupation provided a unique opportunity for Danish sportspeople to compete far more than before against German teams that were often so superior that they should have been playing against better opponents. Danish sportspeople could compete against sporting stars such as Werner Seelenbinder, the wrestler, Rudolf Harbig, athletics star and world-record holder, and Gustav Eder, the professional German ex-European champion boxer. The best German sportspeople – and a well-known football referee, Alfred Birlem – were popular as never before. In the Danish sporting press, they were described with only a lightly disguised admiration for their male aesthetic qualities, as being beautiful, elegant, technically equilibristic, with a superior tactical sense. On the whole, German elite sports from 1936 and well into the occupation provide an exemplary image for Danish sports.

Therefore, it might be difficult for young people such as Jenny Kammersgaard, who in addition had received telegrams of congratulation from Hitler in 1937 and 1938, to keep a cool head and avoid the appreciation from becoming mutual. The

German authorities tried to present Jenny Kammersgaard's phenomenal long-distance swimming as being in harmony with Nazi conceptions of sport and Nordic-Germanic unity. It is a remarkable testament to the fascination exerted by Nazi sports policies and politics that two of Denmark's greatest women swimmers maintained their collaborative work with German circles for so long.

Shortly after 9 April 1940, Danish world record swimmer Ragnhild Hveger allowed herself to be interviewed for a piece of German propaganda in which she was photographed together with Wehrmacht soldiers that she welcomed to Denmark. Together with other Danish girls, Ragnhild Hveger competed in Denmark against Dutch swimming stars and also swam at several Danish-German events in Germany. In contrast to Jenny Kammersgaard, who studied sports and physical education in Berlin, making a living as a swimming instructor there in the first two occupation years before returning to Denmark, Hveger took a job in 1943 as a swimming coach in Kiel.

A painful sense of emptiness was left in the Danish self image when the country's outstanding swimmer with the elegant glide, darling of the media, Hveger, together with the phenomenon of duration swimming Jenny Kammersgaard, who had both done so much for Danish national pride, no longer could make a splash either in water or the columns of the Danish sporting press. In terms of gender studies, it completes something of a paradox that the two women athletes who more than any other symbolised a new dynamic forward-looking female ideal also became chief examples of prostration to the sporting political allure of the Third Reich.

During the war, Jenny Kammersgaard was taken on for a period at a German airbase in Aalborg, in northern Denmark, and had contact to persons within the Nazi orbit, such as the man who was her manager both before and after the war. She attempted to plead on his behalf in court and pay bail, but he was nevertheless judged and sentenced to five years' imprisonment for his collaboration with the occupying power. After the war, in 1947, she was convicted of sailing persons who were refgugees from the ruins of Germany, to Sweden. Among the refugees could be German and Baltic war criminals, which seems not to have concerned Kammersgaard overly.

The Danish sports world – as well as the Swedish – often made a great deal out of its relatively increased sporting progress during the occupation, but the achievements resulted largely from the ability in a cosseted country like Denmark to still be able to train, eat sufficiently, and avoid military service on the battlefield. Denmark made rapid advances, not least in athletics, and in football where the country's matches against Germany went from losing 8-0 to Germany in 1937, 2-0 in Copenhagen in 1939, to losing 1-0 in Hamburg in 1940, and finally drawing 1-1 in Dresden in 1941.

From autumn 1940, Danish Nazis caught the scent of victory and began preparing for the Nazification of social life that German authorities had set in motion in all other occupied countries. National-socialist sports groups wanted to take control of Danish sport, which would henceforth be divided into departments under the single command of a national leader, linked to the ministry of health. According to their plans, several well-reputed heads of sport had agreed to participate in the change of power, a list that included Jørgen Beyerholm, head of Dansk Bicycle Club. Fortunately, a puppet government was never set up in Denmark. The internationally renowned gymnastics pedagogue Niels Bukh, however, had already been marked out in a German ministerial list as a Danish youth minister. There was clearly a potential in terms of organisational leadership within the world of Danish sports – along with a measure of goodwill that had accumulated from the Danish public – that could be expected to step forward under German colours.

Much of the very limited resistance to sporting relations with Germany came from individuals with British roots, within typically English sports such as hockey and cricket. The chairman of the Danish hockey association, English-born George Peel Harvey, refused to vote for a resumption of sporting relations at a DIF board meeting in 1940. In the legal press, the only voice of opposition was heard with the publication of a magazine, *Fodbold*, which with its clear pro-British editorial line came out in the first quarter of 1941. The editor, Harold Philipson, was one of the grand old men of Danish cricket. But there were other examples of resistance. On the occasion of an athletics games in Oslo, in September 1941, and an international football match in Dresden, in November 1941, both the BBC and the London-based magazine *Frit Danmark* launched a sharp attack on Danish-German collaborative sports that obviously had not gone down well in a country thrown out into a war for its own existence against Germany.

Sports competitors in the Hakoah Jewish club movement, not to mention Denmark's best wrestler, Abraham Kurland, who won a silver medal at the Olympics in 1932, were highly succesful in Danish wrestling during the early days of the occupation. In November 1941, the Hakoah won the Copenhagen team tournament in front of a sold-out house against mighty teams such as Sparta and Dan, which were the main suppliers of wrestlers for the national team. But for the elite wrestlers of the Hakoah, the occupation was a period of drought with little opportunity for competing in the many matches against Germany, which may have resulted both from the organisers' resignation to German racial policy, the impossibility, especially where games in Germany and Sweden were concerned, of obtaining travel visas for Jewish athletes and from their own reluctance to having sporting relations with an anti-semitic regime.

Abraham Kurland first withdrew from the 1936 Berlin Olympics because of Nazi racial policies, then missed out on the Olympics of 1940 and 1944 because of the war, and had to escape Denmark along with his sports companions in October 1943. It was of course not normal under Nazi conditions that Jewish sportspeople should line up for matches against Germany, and not even one of Denmark's strongest sporting figures, Ivan Osiier, the fencer, could be part of the Danish national team against Germany in December 1940, whose participation would probably be hindered alone through the presence of Heydrich. Both Osiier and Kurland continued their careers after the occupation; Osiier competing at the 1948 Olympics in London. In practice, DIF accepted the consequences of German racial policy within its own ranks in resigning itself to the exclusion of Jewish sportspeople from international sporting relations.

It seems that team sports like football made it easier for individual players to disappear into the background. Such was the way Alex Friedmann, a Danish Jewish footballer, managed to play for Denmark against Germany at Hamburg in November 1940, although not at the second match in Dresden in 1941. It is possible that the German organisers of the first game, which would recommence Danish-German sporting relations, were so intent on getting the event off on a good footing that they chose to ignore the exception made for Friedmann. On the second occasion the roles were reversed and it was the Danish football association (DBU) that desperately wanted footballing collaboration, which perhaps encouraged DBU not to provoke the occupying powers.

Among DIF board members, it was only Ernst Petersen from Odense Terrænsportsforening, an orienteering club practising semi-military exercises (Petersen would later feature in the Danish resistance), who from the very first consistently spoke out against collaborative relations with the Third Reich. The Terrænsportsforening, based at Odense on Funen, together with the South Jutlandic Idrætsforening, became representatives of an opposition line taken against the policies of DIF and the rural shooting and gymnastics organisation DDSGI. In one Danish sports association and club, Tønder Sportsforening, resistance became truly a member-only affair, when the young football players of the club's first team nearly all entered into illegal operations in the last years of the war. In this hard-pressed border region of South Jutland, it was more Danish national pride, however, rather than sporting values that were the catalyst for their orientation towards resistance. In contrast, the main organisation, DDSGI, were against this form of politicisation of sports within its associations.

During the occupation, German sports authorities continued their charm offensive toward the Danish sporting world. At ceremonial reception banquets and gatherings in Denmark and Germany, with exchanges of gifts, fine food and wines at a time of scarcity, Danes and Germans were urged together on the initiative of the German hosts. Vice-Admiral Mewis, commander in chief of the German Naval forces in Denmark, introduced an Admiral's cup to the Danish Furesø regatta in the autumn of 1940. At sports events in Germany, there was military music, and Danish competitors could be invited to see the impressive Alpine facilities at Garmisch Partenkirchen.

Intense collaborative sporting relations continued until the summer of 1941 when, to the outrage of Renthe-Fink, a Danish crowd sang vulgar rhymes at the German 'war-time' champion Willy Schertle during a professional cycle track race at Ordrup. A month later, at the beginning of June 1941, there were spectator disturbances at Idrætsparken in Copenhagen, at a football match against an Austrian city team, FK Austria Wien, which culminated in whistling during the team's final 'heil' salutes, much to the irritation of the German military authorities. The same thing happened at a match against another Viennese team, SK Admira Wien, on the very day commemorating the Danish Constitution, Grundlovsdag – when Admira (who were also wearing red and white, the Danish national colours) demonstrated German superiority by beating a select team from Copenhagen 4-1. The Danish supporters quite simply dropped the business of sporting relations – pouring scorn on the political gestures of the guests and humiliating off-duty but uniformed German soldiers among the crowd with verbal and physical assaults. Their tactics worked so well that the German supporters drew bayonets; and both Germans and Danes needed hospital treatment.

It was resistance to occupation at the football stadium, therefore, that caused Danish-German sporting relations to shake. The disturbances became the first notable example of open collective aggression against the occupying forces in Denmark, taking place before the student street demonstrations against the Government's agreement to the Anti-Comintern Pact at the end of November 1941. But whereas the student demonstrations were conscious political protests against the policy of collaboration, the Admira unrest was rather a spontaneous reaction against politicised collaboration within the field of sports. It cannot be discounted, however, that some supporters may have turned up with the express intention of challenging the occupying forces in the sure knowledge that the Viennese players would present their 'heil' salutes, as the FK Austria team had done. The football disturbances demonstrate that a form of resistance to Germany was clearly displayed – earlier, and borne by other and more broadly ranging social groups than has previously been thought by studies of the Danish occupation. It continues to be an open question, though, as to how or whether the 'success story' of an open confrontation with Germans at the stadium later encouraged young men to enter into armed resistance. Renthe-Fink did not regard the disturbance as simply frustration at a sporting defeat, but ascribed to it serious political signals. To calm Renthe-Fink's anger, the chairman of DBU Leo Frederiksen assured him that it was morally defect elements among the crowd who threatened to ruin their excellent relations. Renthe-Fink would not be pacified and to Frederiksen's great regret reacted by toning down relations and cancelling the remaining Admira matches, as well as the coming international match against Sweden to be held at Idrætsparken in Copenhagen. The last international football match against Germany thereby took place in Germany. It was German interests, therefore, that diminished the sporting relations while the top leadership of DIF wished them to continue at the highest levels. In contrast, at the beginning of the occupation the DIF leadership had been fearful of unrest, while Renthe-Fink had pushed for collaborative relations: the roles were now swapped over.

An end was put to the immediate continuation of collaborative sports: developments that included the planned international football match against Germany, set for 29 June 1941, at Idrætsparken, that in any case would have been withdrawn after the German invasion of the Soviet Union on 22 June, all of which resulted in a break in sporting relations until 8 October 1941.

Taking his cue from the football disturbances, Renthe-Fink applied pressure onto Prime Minister Stauning and the Minister for Foreign Affairs, Scavenius, whereby he was able to dump the Danish Minister of Justice, Harald Pedersen, who had long been a thorn in the side of the occupying body.

At the end of 1940, the DIF leadership was willing to allow sporting relations with newly organised Norwegian Nazi sports groups, in contradiction to the wishes of the democratic Norwegian sports leadership that had stepped down and to those of the majority of Norwegian sportspeople who had embarked on a sports boycott. This led to DIF breaking the sports boycott, when a Norwegian women's handball team with the sporting phenomenon Laila Schou at their head played against a select Danish team in Copenhagen on 2 December 1940.

That Swedish organisations consistently said no to relations with Norwegian collaborator sports, though, put the Danish sports leadership into another frame of mind. But subsequent DIF attempts to avoid participating with Norway were hardly effective, as DIF would not challenge the German authorities by issuing an outright ban on Norwegian games. The Danish athletics association, therefore, in September 1941, travelled to Bislett stadium in Oslo for a competition, and it later enabled Turid Hellan-Bjørnstad, the Norwegian 'skating princess' to present displays in Denmark.

As a measure of the great plasticity in the slogan that sport should be free of politics, the DIF leadership first wished to participate in occupied Norwegian sporting life, because a boycott would be a political action. Shortly afterwards, DIF then decided not to play against Norway for the reason now that it would be a political action to collaborate with a sports federation that had been put in place by an occupying force. Put briefly, the slogan could be used to legitimise diametrically opposed positions.

Since DIF would not risk assuming responsibility for concrete acts of collaborative sport by governing events centrally, their strategy also meant that DIF could not prevent any collaboration with Norwegian sport under the *Führer* principle. By all indications, it was a combination of the weak condition of Norwegian Nazi sports that were hit hard by the strike, together with a fading German enthusiasm for sports between occupied countries, that prevented Danish sports from becoming involved in greater collaboration with the Norwegians.

After the enforced break, overall Danish-German sporting relations got under way again even with national team matches going on in Germany. The Danish and German authorities were so concerned about the events of the Admira game being repeated that around 50 security officers were brought in for a boxing tournament in Copenhagen on 8 October 1941, which was the first competition in resumed collaborative sports to be held on Danish ground.

Gradually, as Germany began running into military difficulties, there was less and less interest, in the words of propaganda minister Goebbels, of seeing Germans losing to weaker nations. It was therefore German and not Danish authorities who began reducing collaborative sports levels from the beginning of 1942, which for a second time led to the cancellation of a planned international football match on Danish ground. Despite dwindling German interest, DBU (as late as March 1942) tried to place a call for attendance to Sweden, Finland and Germany to a conference that would settle the forthcoming season's international matches, and in May 1942 the DIF vice-chairman, the same Leo Frederiksen, travelled to Germany to negotiate yet another international match.

There are definite indications that German uniformed soldiers – often eager spectators, in part because of their training in Nazi doctrines about sport – felt increasingly less welcome at Danish sporting events. The newspaper of the Danish Nazi Party, *Fædrelandet*, complained in the summer of 1942 that Danish troublemakers were making life difficult for German spectators, who would now rather remain in their barracks than risk the consequences of attending. Sport, with its ability to gather large swathes of emotionally-charged young men, was the perfect place to provoke representatives of the occupying power, who for once were in a clear minority, and where Danish *provocateurs* could easily hide in the crowd.

DIF found itself in a dilemma when Tschammer, the Reichssportführer, in the late summer of 1942 applied himself fully to his vision of creating a new single European sports federation under German (and Italian) domination. For DIF, the plan meant the palpable threat of being excluded from the sporting community in a new German-dominated Europe, and thereby the loss of further vital, profitable matches not least against Sweden. DIF was therefore willing, if not partially forced, to sign up to the federation. However, in the final moments, when it became apparent that Sweden would not join, DIF decided to follow the Swedish lead. Once again, as in the case of competition with Norwegian collaborator sports, it was the Swedish position that saved DIF from walking the plank to its full extent.

In October 1943, the occupation force announced that Jewish people would be removed from public life in Denmark. A coalition of Danish youth organisations and associations, Dansk Ungdomssamvirke, reacted by setting up a petition against the persecution of Jews. Besides the many associations affiliated to the organisation, other signees included the Danish-Nordic youth association and the hikers' and ramblers' association Dansk Vandrelaug. DIF, who had given Dansk Ungdomssamvirke a cold shoulder earlier in November 1940, together with the rural gymnastics and shooting union refused to sign the protest against Jewish persecution on the grounds that it would be a political gesture. It seemingly did not effect the position of DIF that a member organisation, the Jewish Hakoah organisation, had been dissolved and its members had fled to Sweden as a consequence of the political persecution.

In the closing years of the war, Niels Holst-Sørensen, a young talented Danish athlete, took over the status of sports star from Ragnhild Hveger, although not quite so remarkably. An international athletics games in August 1943 in Stockholm took place in the middle of the Danish August revolt, a period of increased resistance activities and widespread strikes, which gave the games a special community-singing atmosphere at the Stockholm stadium, where Holst-Sørensen achieved his great triumphs. Holst-Sørensen did not have roots in the German-Danish traditions of the 1930s and, unlike many other competitors, he had not taken part in the impressive Nazi Olympics of 1936. He did not compete against Germans, but did, however, compete against Hungary in July 1941. On his homecoming from Stockholm, Holst-Sørensen was arrested by the Gestapo and sent to a camp at Sandholm. By the end of October 1943, he was released, after which he went into the courier service and to the Danish military in waiting, both of which provided Danish sports with a much-needed resistance appeal after the liberation. In 1977, he was named as the International Olympics Committee representative in Denmark.

Could DIF have said no to collaborative sporting relations with Germany? The leadership of DIF was exposed to terrific pressure from both German sources and from the Danish foreign ministry. But there was also a strong interest in resuming relations among many of DIF's member associations, who negotiated with Germans about joint sporting events long before the ban had been lifted. At the same time, Leo Frederiksen, the strong man of Danish sport, actively worked for the re-establishment of collaborative sports, which made it difficult for General Castenschiold, the DIF chairman, to pursue a policy of procrastination, and for both Castenschiold and his successor to establish working relations with Dansk Ungdomssamvirke during the occupation.

Were the decisions made at the top of DIF an expression of nervousness that German forces would intervene in Danish sports, should their refusal to collaborate continue? When asked directly, Renthe-Fink denied to Castenschiold that he would use force in the matter of Danish sports. The brief period in which Danish Nazis were able to rattle their sabres and talk of taking over power, and a new order for Danish sport, only came to the fore after autumn 1940, when the decision to resume sporting relations had long since been taken. It was rather the massive German victories in Western Europe that created a mental background for DIF's change of course. To survive as well as possible in Europe under the German Führer allowed the apolitical organisation DIF to carry out a politicisation of Danish sport that was without precedent. Moving from a position of waiting, DIF organisations became highly active in their attempts to take advantage of an historically beneficial situation for Danish-German relations.

Any anxieties on the part of the DIF leadership about threats of Nazi power with regard to Danish sports turned out to be ungrounded, since the occupying authorities decided to respect the relative autonomy of Danish institutions. It is rather improbable that force would have been used to implement Danish-German sporting events under duress, for fear that Danish unwillingness would develop into boycotts and demonstrations. In occupied Holland, the ruling authorities in general chose not to establish international sporting relations for fear of public reactions, but allowed Dutch sports to continue within the national framework. The reason for this was that sport had the capacity to channel the potentially dangerous energies of young Dutch men. The same rationale would without doubt have applied to Denmark – particularly since DIF guaranteed the neutral character of Danish sports.

From a current perspective, it is easy to be incensed that DIF chose to play football with the occupying powers but, before judging too hard, it is worth asking what today's people would have done, if they were convinced that for the rest of their lives Germany would rule Continental Europe and thereby decide which nations would be allowed to compete in the arena of sport. Would we, modern as we are, also choose to bow to historical inevitability just to have the possibility of fielding a national team or pursuing an elite sports career? Would we too concede to play against Germany and other axis powers?

Were the dispositions within Danish sport an expression of failure or of powerlessness? Denmark was a small nation oppressed by superior power, and in Danish sports actions were taken that are absolutely understandably human, but which later were deeply embarrassing when the scene had changed completely, because they illustrated the Danes' helplessness, unimportance, lack of independence and opportunism.

The greatest phantom antagonist of the Danish sporting authorities – the rebellious crowd – ironically on Constitution day 1941 saved DIF from continuing to take part in international matches on Danish ground; and when the most pressing matches began to drift from the records in the amnesia of liberation euphoria, they could slide almost completely from discussion when the time came for a national judicial purge. Afterwards, DIF's veiling of collaborative sporting relations could begin. Just as in the August revolt in 1943, where broad sections of the population set down sharp clear lines between the occupiers and the occupied, against the wishes of the politicians, so was it that during the unrest at the football stadium it was the Danish public who caused collaborational sports to shudder and who prevented future international football matches on Danish ground.

After 9 April 1940, sport acquired a forceful symbolic value in the attempt to demonstrate unity between the occupiers and the occupied during Danish-German games. In the euphoria of liberation, sport then became a means to demonstrate solidarity between the liberators and the liberated, in football matches between saboteurs and English paratroopers on 16 May 1945, with an opening speech by Leo Frederiksen. Overall, sport was used as an important arena in which to demonstrate Denmark's membership of the Allied club, culminating in a sold-out game at Idrætsparken on 10 July 1945 between a professional English and a select Danish team. It was no longer a German but an English military orchestra that played the fanfare. First Danish sport played against soldiers from Luftwaffe, then from Royal Air Force.

After the liberation, there were voices that demanded a judgement on sporting collaboration with Germany. At the same time, the DIF leadership managed to turn the spotlight away from its own ranks and instead itself focus a spotlight on those individual competitors who had been either members of the Nazi party or who had held private positions of trust with Nazis. Despite its declared apolitical stance, then, DIF chose to base its own 'purge' on clear political criteria, which was even stricter than the judicial system or the courts to judge private conduct and honour set up by various associations and unions, since neither membership of the Nazi party nor having Nazi sympathies was deemed to be punishable in itself.

With his unbelievable ability for political reorientation, Leo Frederiksen is reminiscent of the German grand-old-man of sport and great organiser of the Berlin Olympics, Carl Diem. Diem did not belong to the Nazi party but to conservative elite circles, and German sporting organisations were more or less able to continue with the same leaders after the war. In this way, Diem managed to become a leading figure within post-war West German sports, in the same manner as Frederiksen in Denmark, who in 1946 became vice-president of the international footballing federation FIFA and a year later chairman of DIF.

Although it might be expected after the liberation that DIF would fall under a critical light because of its collaborative relations, the opposite occurred. Occupation brought with it a breakthrough for sport as a popular movement as well as a royalist, national focus of unity, and the voices of inter-war sporting comment increasingly fell silent. DIF were favoured by the shifts in interpretation that took place throughout the changing conditions of the occupation. Initially, DIF had showed little interest in promoting itself as a national project, but under the influence of the Danish community-singing atmosphere and its royalism it could increasingly make capital out of national opinions. Towards the end of the occupation, national manifestations were to a higher degree associated with declarations of democracy and a clear expression of full Danish sovereignty; all very useful for DIF given that the federation had waved the Danish flag at sports matches with a dictatorship.

The ideology of DIF to not mix sport and politics was deployed to legitimise the most comprehensive politicisation of Danish sport ever and resulted in the most notable example of cultural collaboration with the occupying power. It is an irony of fate that DIF was in fact far too apolitical to prevent the German power's cynical use of Danish sport for the purposes of its propaganda.

# Endnotes

## Introduction
1. Merleau-Ponty, 1962.
2. Bourdieu, 1984.
3. Elias and Dunning, 1966.
4. For masculinity and sport in the Danish context, see Bonde, 1991.
5. Cf. Mangan, 1995, p. 1.
6. For economic collaboration, see Andersen, 2005.
7. Rünitz & Kirchhoff, 2007.
8. Cf. Gads Leksikon, 2002, pp. 336ff.
9. Cf. Andersen, 2003.
10. Frei, 2004. Frei's masters-degree thesis is 104 pages long.
11. Holmäng, 1988, pp. 201ff.

## Sporting relations in the 1930s
1. Cf. Hansen, 1993, p. 135.
2. Teichler, 1991 p. 108.
3. Havemann, 2005 p. 337.
4. Teichler, 1991 pp. 368ff.
5. Huggins & Williams, 2006, pp. 129ff.
6. Beck, 1999, pp. 238ff.
7. Trangbæk, 1995, I, pp. 117 and 147ff.
8. Teichler, 1991, pp. 113ff.
9. Op. cit., p. 118.
10. Bonde, 2006A, passim.
11. *Fyns Venstreblad* 27/03, 1935.
12. Ibid.
13. *Idrætsbladet* 04/08 1936, no. 32, p. 4.
14. Cf. Hansen, 1993, pp. 121ff.
15. Thelmark, 1999.
16. Hansen, 1993, pp. 122ff.
17. *Jydsk Idræts Blad* 09/12 1935.
18. For the Swedish sports associations' sporting relations, generally, see Holmäng, 1988. For Swedish protests, see Welander, 2000 p. 282.
19. Andersen, 1936, pp. 159ff.
20. Cf. *Berlingske Aftenavis* 3/8 1936 and Dansk Sport, 1946.
21. *Berlingske Tidende* 6/8.

22 Thamer, 1986, pp. 56ff.
23 Idorn, 1976, p. 106.
24 "Die Olympischen Spiele von 1936 im Spiegel der ausländischen Presse", source material from J. Bellers, Münster, 1986.
25 See D.K.G. – Medlemsblad for Dansk Kvinde-Gymnastikforening, no. 2, January 1936. See also Ellen Paul Petersen, "En samtale med Medau", D.K.G. – Medlemsblad for Dansk Kvinde-Gymnastikforening, no. 1, November 1937, pp. 1ff.
26 Kammersgaard, 1937, chapter 9, pp. 84ff.
27 Meidell, 2005, p. 160.
28 Bellers, 1996, passim.
29 *Nordisk Familjeboks Sportlexikon*, 1946, pp. 1096ff.
30 *Idrætsbladet* 23/02, 1939 no. 8, p. 12.
31 Beyerholm, 1941, pp. 383ff.
32 Op. cit., pp. 234ff.
33 *Idrætsbladet* 27/06, 1939.
34 *Dansk Sportsleksikon*, I, p. 115, *Idrætsbladet* 25/07, 1939. See also Beyerholm, 1941, p. 249.
35 *Idrætsbladet* 27/6, 1939.
36 *Dansk Sportsleksikon*, I, p. 269, and II, p. 109.
37 *Idrætsbladet* 03/03 1938, no.9, p. 22.
38 *Dansk Sportsleksikon*, 1945, II, p. 522. The war-time name Holland is used here instead of the Netherlands.
39 *Idrætsbladet* 27/06, 1939.
40 DIF pakke 14 – bestyrelsesmøde 23/10 1939, Rigsarkivet.
41 Teichler, 1991, pp. 118 and 276.
42 Op. cit., pp. 277ff.
43 *Idrætsbladet* 10/10, 1939.
44 Teichler, 1991, p. 278.
45 Op. cit., p. 279.
46 *Idrætsbladet* 10/10, 1939.
47 *Idrætsbladet* 15/2 1940, p. 17.

## Danish sport under siege, 1940-41

1 *Idrætsbladet* 08/05 1941, p. 4.
2 *Idrætsbladet* 17/10 1941, p. 27, cf. http://www.ishof.org/66rhveger.html
3 Schoug, 1997, pp. 19ff.
4 Bovrup-Kartoteket, 1946, cf. the entry for Helsingør, p. 23.
5 *Idrætsbladet* 09/12 1940, pp. 3ff.
6 "Ragnhild Hveger erzählt – Soldatenbesuch bei dem erfolgreichsten Sportmädel der Welt. Ein Kind erschwamm 32 Weltrekorde für Dänemark," *Kopenhagener Soldatenzeitschrift* 07/07 1940.
7 E.g. op. cit., no. 3, 21/07, 1940, pp. 8ff; no. 5, 04/08, 1940, p. 2 and p. 13; no. 6, 11/08, 1940, pp. 3 and 14; and no. 49, 15/06, 1941, p. 17.
8 Thomsen, 1971, p. 40, Havemann, 2005 p. 270.
9 *Kopenhagener Soldatenzeitschrift*, no. 34, 02/03, 1941, p. 15.
10 Op. cit., no. 30, 02/02, 1941, pp. 8ff.
11 *Kopenhagener Soldatenzeitschrift*, no. 48, 08/06, 1941, p. 5.

12 Op. cit., no. 48, 08/06, 1941, p. 19 and no. 37, 23/03, 1941, p. 15.
13 Rasmussen, 1981 p. 20.
14 DIF pakke 17 – Forretningsudvalgsmøde 13/04 1940.
15 DIF pakke 16 – letter from Ernst Petersen to Castenschiold 12/04 1940.
16 DIF pakke 196 – 'Castenschiolds beretning'.
17 Andersen, 2003, p. 251.
18 Cf. Gads leksikon 2002 p. 483.
19 Op. cit., p. 392.
20 DIF – pakke 196 "Referat af mødet i Udenrigsministeriet mandag den 29. april 1940". The minutes were written by Leo Frederiksen, dated 01/05 1940 and signed by Leo Frederiksen and Castenschiold. No minutes of the meeting are to be found in the archives of the Danish foreign ministry.
21 Addendum to Castenschiold's report.
22 Kuper, 2003, pp. 93 and 97.
23 Teichler, 1991 p. 285.
24 *Dansk Sportsleksikon*, 1945, vol. I, p. 535.
25 *Gads Leksikon* – "Hvem var hvem" 2005 pp. 371ff.
26 *Gads leksikon* on "dansk besættelsestid", 2002, p. 57. Furthermore see Lauridsen, 2002, pp. 149, 495, 500 and 504.
27 DIF – pakke 14 – bestyrelsesmøde 07/06 1940, together with Castenschiold's report. Furthermore see DIF – pakke 16 – beretninger fra provinsrepræsentanterne til bestyrelsesmøde 07/06 1940.
28 Hæstrup, 1979/1993 p. 148.
29 Nissen & Poulsen, 1963 p. 182.
30 Wøllekær, 2001 pp. 154-156.
31 Referred to is a complex question about the Danish-German border, the regions of North Schleswig and South Jutland, and conflicts between Germani and Danish speaking people in those regions: the fear being that Germany would annex the (Danish) South Jutlandic region. The question, however, was academic since Hitler did not intend to retain Denmark as a sovereign State.
32 Castenschiold's report. Detailed minutes from the meeting were provided by Leo Frederiksen and Castenschiold, dated 3 July 1940. 'Bilag' in Castenschiold's report. A short account by Nils Svenningsen is likewise held in Udenrigsministeriets pakke 84. C.15. These minutes confirm the minutes taken by Castenschiold and Leo Frederiksen.
33 Cycling, however, was not a DIF activity at that time.
34 Holmäng, 1988, p. 187.
35 DIF – pakke 14 – 'Dagsorden' dated 13 July 1940.
36 Bonde, 2006, p. 117.
37 DIF – pakke 14 – Bestyrelsesmøde 05/08, 1940.
38 DIF – pakke 196 – "Castenschiolds beretning" as well as Udenrigsministeriet – pakke 84.C.15 – "Breve til Udenrigsministeriet" 07/08 and 09/08 1940.
39 Havemann, 2005 p. 272.
40 *Socialdemokraten* 07/08 1940.
41 *Idrætsbladet* 08/08 1940.
42 Bovrup-Kartoteket, Kbh., 1946, Storkøbenhavn, p. 64, as well as Rasmussen, 1981, p. 54.
43 *Fædrelandet* 28/06 1940.

## The struggle for Denmark's youth

1. Lauridsen, 2002, pp. 56ff.
2. Rasmussen, 1981, p. 68.
3. Hæstrup, 1979, p. 99 and DIF – pakke 14 – bestyrelsesmøde 05/08 1940.
4. *Fædrelandet* 25/10, 16/11 and 10/12 1940, 03/01, 11/06 and 16/03 1941. Cf. too, ibid. 16/08 and 17/08 1940 (anonymous).
5. DIF – pakke 196 – "plan for nyordning af den danske idræt", as well as Lauridsen, 2002, pp. 189 and 191.
6. Three of the drafts are dated.
7. *Dansk Sportsleksikon*, II, 1945, p. 60 together with vol. I, p. 115.
8. Beyerholm, 1941 pp. 243 and 251.
9. Jørgensen, 1997 pp. 226-227.
10. Lauridsen, 2002, pp. 187 and 194.
11. DIF – pakke 18 – Forretningsudvalgsmøde 04/12 1946.
12. Cf. Munck, V., "Nationalsocialismens opdragelsesprogram" in *Vor ungdom*, Det pædagogiske selskab, Copenhagen, 1933/34. Cf. also Munck's introductory article to the Berlin Olympics in: Ungdom og Idræt, no. 22, 1936, pp. 238ff.
13. *Fædrelandet* 16/03 1941.
14. DIF – pakke 14 – bestyrelsesmøde 03/03 1941.
15. Lauridsen, 2002 pp. 190ff.
16. Op. cit., p. 486.
17. DIF – pakke 196 – Arbejdernes Idræts Klubs Medlemsblad 23. Årgang, nr. 4, Juli 1945 – written by Vagn Hansen, who was a member of the athletics association committee.
18. DIF – pakke 72 – Ansøgning fra NSU, 20/05 1943. See also DIF – pakke 18 – Forretningsudvalgsmøde 10/01 1944.
19. Hertel, 1998 p. 73.
20. Bonde, 2006A, passim.

## English opposition to collaboration

1. *Socialdemokraten, Politiken, Berlingske Tidende* on selected dates.
2. *Arbejderbladet* 18/08, 21/08 and 22/08 1940; 05/05, 25/05, 27/05, 30/05 and 31/05 1941.
3. *Fodbold – Hele landets magasin*, January 1941.
4. Op. cit., February 1941.
5. *Idrætsbladet* 06/05 1941, p. 15.
6. Bergstrøm, 2005, p. 677.
7. Kuper, 2003, p. 93.
8. *Fodbold – Hele landets magasin*, February 1941.

## Professional sport

1. Andersen, 2005.
2. *Idrætsbladet* 06/05 1941, pp. 11ff. Cf. also *Fædrelandet* 03/06 1941.
3. *Idrætsbladet* 28/10 1940 and Sports-Bladet no. 44, 01/11 1940, p. 5.
4. *Idrætsbladet* 03/02 1940, p. 3 as well as p. 15, 1941. Cf. also *Fædrelandet* 10/12 1940.

5 *De olympiske*, 1996, p. 181.
6 *Idrætsbladet* 13/06 1941, p. 7.
7 *Sports-Bladet* 31/01 1941 p. 7. Cf. also *Fædrelandet* 14/12 1940.
8 *Idrætsbladet* 3/2 1940, p. 3, as well as 05/08, 1941, front page.
9 Bovrup-Kartoteket, 1946, Storkøbenhavn, p. 55.
10 *Idrætsbladet* 06/05 1941.
11 *Idrætsbladet* 06/01 1940, p. 11.
12 *Idrætsbladet* 27/01 1941, p. 14.
13 *Idrætsbladet* 02/12 1940, p. 3.
14 *Idrætsbladet* 20/01 1940, p. 15.
15 *Idrætsbladet* 13/02 1941, p. 15, and also 17/02, p. 15.
16 *Idrætsbladet* 13/02 1941, p. 6.
17 *Box-Sport* cited by *Idrætsbladet* 16/05 1941, p. 2.

## Amateur sports

1 DIF – pakke 196 – Sander-periodens beretning. The 13 associations and unions that had contact with the Germans were the associations for athletes, athletics, boxing, ball games, fencing, gymnastics, hockey, handball, rowing, skiing, shooting, swimming and tennis. The following associations declared no joint activities: workers' sports, badminton, archery, golf, kayak and riding, along with the Danish military sports association and the association for winter sports.
2 Rasmussen, 1981, p. 63.
3 DBU – pakke 113 – Officielle Meddelelser 30/11 1940, Rigsarkivet.
4 The skiing coach is named in *Idrætsbladet* 23/12 1940. For German trainers and Ragnhild Hveger cf. *Berlingske Tidende* 08/10, 1940, cited in Rasmussen, 1981, p. 64.
5 *Kopenhagener Soldatenzeitschrift*, no. 10, 1940, p. 15.

## Athletics take the lead

1 *Idrætsbladet* 22/08 1940.
2 *Politiken, Socialdemokraten* and *Berlingske Tidende* 23/08 1940.
3 *Idrætsbladet* 22/08 1940.
4 *Fædrelandet* 24/08 1940.
5 Centralkartoteket, Pkr. Nr. 1., Anholdelsesprotokol løbenr. 10376, Rigsarkivet.
6 *Idrætsbladet* 26/08 and 19/12 1940.
7 Polfoto.
8 *Idrætsbladet* 26/08, 1940. Also Teichler 1991 p. 285 and Rasmussen, 1981 p. 53.
9 Answärtiges Amt (AA) – pakke 311 – which is a 77-page dissertation on the function of radio and the German plans for it 25/11 1940, Rigsarkivet. Cf. also *Kopenhagener Soldatenzeitschrift* 08/09, 1940.
10 *Idrætsbladet* 19/12 1940, p. 2, as well as 06/02 10/02 1941.
11 *Idrætsbladet* 06/02 1941.
12 *Idrætsbladet* 28/03 1941, p. 15.
13 *Idrætsbladet* 20/06 1941.
14 *Idrætsbladet* 08/04 1941.
15 *Idrætsbladet* 13/03 1941.

16 *Idrætsbladet* 03/03 1941, p. 5.
17 *Idrætsbladet* 17/03 1941. Cf. also *Fædrelandet* 18/03.
18 *Idrætsbladet* 08/05 1941.
19 *Idrætsbladet* 04/07 1941.
20 *Fædrelandet* 15/03, 25/04 and 24/06 1941.
21 *Idrætsbladet* 29/04 1941, p. 11.
22 *Idrætsbladet* 16/05 1941.

## Boxing
1 *Dansk Sportsleksikon*, II, pp. 96ff.
2 Cited in *Fædrelandet* 17/08 1940. See also *Spartaneren*, no. 9, September 1940, p. 10. In regard to the size of Sparta in general, in 1945 the club had 1,100 members, cf. *Nordisk Familjeboks Sportlexikon*, p. 490.
3 *Idrætsbladet* 19/08 1940.
4 *Fædrelandet* 13/09 1940. Presumably, a Danish Dannebrog would also have been displayed as well.
5 *Idrætsbladet* 12/09, 1940. *Spartaneren*, no. 10, October 1940, p. 4. Cf. also *Fædrelandet* 17/10 1940.
6 *Spartaneren*, no. 10, October 1940, p. 4. Entirely without ideological hidden motives, it was stated "let's admit, honestly, that we tolerate far too much unclean boxing at home." The Søborg tournament is mentioned in *Idrætsbladet* 07/11 1940.
7 *Idrætsbladet* 20/01 1941.
8 *Idrætsbladet* 16/01 1941.
9 *Idrætsbladet* 20/01 1941. *Sports-Bladet* 17/01, 1941, p. 5.
10 *Idrætsbladet* 20/01 1941.
11 *Idrætsbladet* 09/01 1941.
12 *Idrætsbladet* 23/01 1941.

## Swimming with the tide
1 *Idrætsbladet* 28/03 1941.
2 Report from Dansk Svømme-Forbund 1941, p. 66, cf. also 1942, p. 7.
3 Op. cit. 1941, p. 66.
4 Op. cit. 1941, p. 100.
5 Report from Dansk Svømme-Forbund, January 1942, p. 6.
6 Report from Dansk Svømme-Forbund December 1942, p. 78.
7 *Idrætsbladet* 03/03 1941, p. 2.
8 In the period from 27/09 until 04/10, 1940, Ragnhild Hveger and Lykke Larsen took part in competitions in Mönchengladbach on 29/09, in Duisburg on 01/10, and in Oberhausen on 02/10. From 14/03 to 25/03, 1941, she competed at Krefeld on 16/03, at Düsseldorf on 19/03 and again at Mönchengladbach on 23/03. From 28/06 to 03/07 she took part in contests in Leipzig, on 29/06. And finally in December 1941, Ragnhild Hveger swam in Vienna on 06/12, Linz on 07/12 and 11/12, and in Munich on 13 and 14/12. Sources: Report from Dansk Svømmeforbund 1941, p. 37, as well as *Idrætsbladet* 19/12 1941.

9  Rasmussen, 1981, p. 63. *Fædrelandet* 17/10 1940, 14/11 1940 and Lauridsen 1999 p. 451 and p. 656, together with *Dansk Sportsleksikon*.
10  *Idrætsbladet* 11/11 1940.
11  *Fædrelandet* 28/08 1941.
12  *Idrætsbladet* 30/09 1940.
13  A type of early swimming goggle.
14  *Fædrelandet* 07/10 1940.
15  *Fædrelandet* 14/03 1941.
16  *Idrætsbladet* 17/03 1941, *Sports-Bladet* 14/03 1941, p. 3.
17  *Idrætsbladet* 24/03 1941.
18  *Fædrelandet* 26/03 1941.
19  Undated interview with Jenny Kammersgaard, Security Police, Intelligence Department, Helsingør Politi Straffeakt 148-1947, Landsarkivet for Sjælland.

## Other sporting disciplines

1  *Idrætsbladet* 11/09 1940.
2  DIF – pakke 196 – report from D.H.F. after the occupation.
3  *Sportsbladet* 17/01 1941, p. 5 and *Fædrelandet* 07/11 1940. Cf. also *Idrætsbladet* 03/01 1942, p. 15.
4  Thelmark, 1999, p. 45 and p. 1 about the placing of the Star of David. Information about the homecoming is gathered from a website page "Noget af Hakoahs historiske fortid", by Simon Kurland, Abraham's brother, at http://www.hakoah.dk/brydning.htm
5  *Idrætsbladet* 03/11 1940 and *Fædrelandet* of the same date.
6  *Spartaneren*, no. 12, December, 1940, p. 6.
7  *Dansk Sportsleksikon*, II, p. 107. Four international competitions were staged between 1931 and 1937.
8  *Idrætsbladet* 18/11 1940.
9  Dansk Kvindebiografisk Leksikon, 2000-2001.
10  *Idrætsbladet* 18/11 1940.
11  Teichler, 1991, pp. 354ff.
12  Kristensen, 1996, pp. 271ff.
13  Letter to Museum Director Henrik Lundbak of The Museum of Danish Resistance, from Dina Carnera 11/05 2006.
14  DIF – pakke 196 – D.S.O.F.'s report to DIF June 1945.
15  Teichler, 1991 p. 309.
16  Teichler, 1991 p. 312.

## Football with the foe

1  Meidell, 2005, p. 177.
2  *Idrætsbladet* 14/11 1940, p. 15.
3  Hansen, 1945, pp. 44ff. Cf. also *Idrætsbladet* 18/11 1940.
4  Andersen, 1964, pp. 166ff.
5  This section is based on DBU – pakke 17 – DBU journaler 26/10 1940, and Andersen 1964, p. 129. Cf. also Meidell, 2005, p. 177; DBU – pakke 113 – DBU Officielle Meddelelser 30/11 1940; *Fædrelandet* 18/11 1940; and finally *Idrætsbladet* 18/11 1940.

6 *Idrætsbladet* 18/11 1940.
7 Brøndsted 1941 I, p. 246.
8 Larsen H., *Boldklubben 1903 gennem 50 år*, Copenhagen, 1953, p. 76. Cf. also Rasmussen, 1981, p. 64.
9 *Sports-Bladet* 23/05 1941, p. 3.
10 *Idrætsbladet* 17/03 1941.
11 *Idrætsbladet* 27/05 1941.
12 *Idrætsbladet* 30/05 1941.
13 A.A. – pakke 201 dated 07/06, by Renthe-Fink to an enquiry from von Grundherr, and Auswärtiges Amt – pakke 201 dated d. 14/06 by Renthe-Fink to "Auswärtiges Berlin", Rigsarkivet.
14 *Kopenhagener Soldatenzeitschrift*, no. 48, 08/06, 1941, p. 19.
15 *Nordisk Familjeboks Sportlexikon*, I, p. 30.
16 *Fædrelandet* 05/06 1941.
17 *Idrætsbladet* 06/06 1941.
18 Brøndsted, 1946 I, pp. 246ff.
19 Udenrigsministeriet (U.M.) – pakke 84.g.5/82 – "Tysk-dansk fodboldkamp 05/06 1941 – tyskfjendtl. Demonstr. og Slagsmaal" – police report A. dated 05/06, 1941, Rigsarkivet.
20 A.A. – pakke 201 dated 14/06 by Renthe-Fink to "Auswärtiges Berlin", Rigsarkivet.
21 U.M. – pakke 84.g.5/82 – police report C.
22 U.M. – pakke 84.g.5/82 – police report A.
23 *Fædrelandet* 11/06 1941.
24 A.A. – pakke 201 dated 07/06 by Renthe-Fink to an inquiry from von Grundherr, and Auswärtiges Amt – pakke 201 dated 14/06 by Renthe-Fink to "Auswärtiges Berlin".
25 U.M. – pakke 84.g.5/82 – police report A.
26 U.M. – 84.C.15 – transcript in Danish sent to the Ministry for Foreign Affairs.
27 A.A. – pakke 201 dated 07/06 written by Renthe-Fink to an inquiry from von Grundherr. To various German authorities.
28 Koch, 1994.
29 A.A. – pakke 201 dated 10/06 1941. To various German authorities.
30 A.A. – pakke 201 dated 12/06 1941.
31 Brøndsted, 1946, p. 248.
32 DIF – pakke 14 – bestyrelsesmødereferater.
33 *Statsadvokatens Daglige Rapporter om Sammenstød mellem Danske og Tyske*. U.M. – pakke 84.C.16 – from 08/11, 1941 until 05/10, 1943.
34 Kirchhoff 2001, pp. 103-106.
35 U.M. 84.C.2a – Notits fra U.M., dated 02/04 1942.
36 *Fædrelandet* 01/07 1942.
37 Teichler, 1991 p. 325.
38 *Idrætsbladet* 18/07 1941, p. 10. Cf. also 19/08 1941, p. 3, together with 06/01 1942, front cover. In addition, see *Fædrelandet* 24/07 1941.

## Collaboration with Norway
1 *Fædrelandet* 17/10 1940.
2 Cf. Olstad and Tønnesson, 1987, pp. 50-59.

3 Ibid.
4 SR, p. 75.
5 Olstad and Tønnesson, 1987 p. 46, Goksøyr, 2002, p. 54.
6 *Fædrelandet* 12/11 and 04/12 1940. See also *Idrætsbladet* 28/11 1940.
7 *Idrætsbladet* 02/12 1940, p. 15.
8 DIF – pakke 17 – forretningsudvalgsmøde 30/01 1941.
9 DIF – pakke 78 16/3-41 – Transcript of a private letter to Major E. Raaberg from Svenska Gymnastik- och Idrottsföreningars Riksförbund, from Castenschiold.
10 DIF – pakke 14 – bestyrelsesmøde 03/03 1941.
11 DIF – pakke 17 – Forretningsudvalgsmøde 12/06 1941 and pakke 52.
12 *Fædrelandet* 29 Marts 1941.
13 DIF – pakke 18 – Forretningsudvalgsmøde 22/06 1942.
14 *Idrætsbladet* 28/03 1941, p. 13.
15 *Fædrelandet* 29/03 1941.
16 Centralkartoteket løbe no. 38912, Rigsarkivet.
17 *Fædrelandet* 02/08 1941 and 20/09 1941.
18 UM – 84C15, 'Udenlandsk radio og ikke offentliggjort nyhedsstof', 18 November 1941.
19 *Frit Danmark* 13/11 1941 London.
20 *Fædrelandet* 29/09 and 30/10 1941.
21 *Idrætsbladet* 30/09 1941, *Politiken* and *Berlingske Tidende* 28/09 1941.
22 *Idrætsbladet* 13/01 1942, p. 3.
23 *Dansk Sportsleksikon* vol. I, p. 192 and vol. II, p. 215.
24 DIF – pakke 18 – Forretningsudvalgsmøde dated 13/01 1942.
25 *Socialdemokraten* 21/11 1941 and *Berlingske Tidende* 22/01 1942.
26 *Fædrelandet* 13/02 and 03/07 1942.
27 Officielle Efterretninger – Dansk Athletik-Forbund, 1 April 1941, passim.
28 DIF – pakke 18 – Forretningsudvalgsmøde 12/08 1942.
29 DIF – pakke 18 – Forretningsudvalgsmøde 02/02 1942.
30 *Fædrelandet* 14/01, 19/01 and 04/02 1942.
31 UM – 84.C.15, memo.
32 Olstad and Tønnesson, 1987, p. 40 and pp. 56ff.
33 Bonde, 2006B, 273ff.

## Renewed German contact
1 Holmäng, 1988 p. 211 as well as Teichler 1991, p. 326.
2 *Idrætsbladet* 19/08 1941, front cover, together with 10/10 1941.
3 *Idrætsbladet* 26/09 1941, p. 10.
4 *Spartaneren* no. 11, Nov. 1941, p. 4. Cf, also *Idrætsbladet* 14/10 1941.
5 *Idrætsbladet* 10/10 1941.
6 *Spartaneren* no. 10/10 1941, *Idrætsbladet* 24/10 1941.

## Games in Germany
1 *Idrætsbladet* 07/11 1941.
2 *Fædrelandet* 03/11 1941.

3 DBU – pakke 17.
4 B 1903 official website http://www.b1903.dk
5 *Idrætsbladet* 14/11 and 18/11 1941.
6 Around 100 Danish workers had travelled from Leipzig, Berlin and several other German cities. Many Danes missed out on tickets to the sold-out match, and during the buildup to the game, contact was taken up between players and Danish guest workers in Germany trying to buy tickets. *Idrætsbladet* 18/11 1941.
7 *Fædrelandet* 17/11 1941.
8 *Idrætsbladet* 11/11, 14/11 and 18/11 1941.
9 UM 84.C.15 – *Udenlandsk radio og ikke-offentliggjort nyhedsstof* – resumé – 18/11 1941.
10 *Idrætsbladet* 20/01 1942, p. 3.
11 *Idrætsbladet* 17/03 1942, p. 12.
12 DBU – pakke 113 – DBUs Officielle Meddelelser 31/05 1942 – referat af forretningsudvalgsmøde 09/05 1942.
13 *Idrætsbladet* 24/10, p. 15 and 04/11 1941, front page.
14 *Idrætsbladet* 25/11 1941.
15 *Fædrelandet* 15/01 1942 and *Berlingske Tidende* 23/01 1942. The evidence suggests there were around 5.000 spectators present.
16 Holmäng, 1988 pp. 223ff.
17 *Idrætsbladet* 20/01 1942, p. 8.
18 *Idrætsbladet* 18/04 1941, *Fædrelandet* 26/01 1942.
19 *Sports-Bladet* 30/01 1942, pp. 4ff.
20 *Idrætsbladet* 24/02 1942, p. 2, which mentions *Der Kicker* that had cited *Westfälische Landeszeitung* after the fight.
21 *Berlingske Tidende* 23/01 1943.
22 Rasmussen, 1981, p. 59.
23 *Idrætsbladet* 30/12 1941, p. 2.
24 Mattausch, 1988, pp. 72-85.
25 Kulavig, 2004.
26 Bergstrøm, I, 2005, p. 401.
27 *Sports-Bladet* 18/01 1940, p. 8 and 11/12 1942, p. 6 and p. 11. *Idrætsbladet* 30/01 1940, front page, together with 14/12 1942, p. 11.
28 *Sports-Bladet* 21/11 1941, p. 7, and 29/01 1943, p. 7. Furthermore, see *Idrætsbladet* 09/12 1941, p. 16.

## The last collaboration

1 *Fædrelandet* 02/12 1941.
2 *Idrætsbladet* 24/03 1942, p. 7. HIK had 907 active members.
3 *Fædrelandet* 22-23/04 1942.
4 DIF's 'Aarsberetning' 1941 and 1942.
5 *Idrætsbladet* 23/06 1942, p. 14.
6 *Dansk Sportsleksikon*, II, 1945, p. 492 and *Fædrelandet*.
7 DIF – pakke 91 – memo to the Federation from Sander, dated 04/05 1942.
8 *Idrætsbladet* 22/05 1942, front page.
9 *Idrætsbladet* 22/05 1942, p. 14.

10  Rasmussen, 1981, p. 64.
11  *Fædrelandet* 07/01 1942.
12  *Fædrelandet* 19/01 1942.
13  *Idrætsbladet* 30/12 1941.
14  *Fædrelandet* 19/01 1942.
15  Krüger 1998 pp. 90-91.
16  DIF – Pakke 74 – Skrivelse til Special-Forbundene 24/01 1942.
17  DIF – Pakke 17 – Forretningsudvalgsmøde 13/02 1942.
18  DIF – Pakke 17 – Forretningsudvalgsmøde 05/03 1942.
19  *Idrætsbladet* 13/2 1942, p. 14. See also *Sports-Bladet* 30/12 1942 and *Fædrelandet* 08/12 1942.
20  *Fædrelandet* 20/8 1942 and DIF – pakke 196 D.Sky.U. 'indberetning' 16/06 1945.
21  *De Frie Danske*, April 1942, Rigsarkivet.
22  DIF – pakke 196 – 'Indberetning' to DIF from D.Sky.U. 16/06 1945.
23  *Sports-Bladet* 30/12 1941, p. 3, and *Idrætsbladet* 16/01 1942, p. 4.
24  *Fædrelandet*, 07/01 1942. See also *Idrætsbladet* 08/05, and 10/07 1942, p. 15.
25  *Idrætsbladet* 15/5 1942, p. 15.
26  *Fædrelandet* 13/06 1942.
27  *Idrætsbladet* 03/07 1942, p. 15.
28  *Idrætsbladet* 14/09 1942, front cover.
29  *Idrætsbladet* 12/05 1942, p. 2.
30  *Idrætsbladet* 12/06 1942, p. 15.
31  *Idrætsbladet* 12/05 1942, p. 16, and 25/08 1942, p. 13.
32  *Idrætsbladet* 18/11 1941, p. 2.
33  *Idrætsbladet* 2/12 1941, p. 3, and 23/06 1942, p. 15.
34  *Idrætsbladet* 28/07 1942, p. 15.
35  *Sports-Bladet* 04/12 1942, p. 6.
36  Teichler 1991 p. 366.
37  *Sports-Bladet* 30/12 1942, front page.
38  Holmäng 1988 p. 287, as well as *Sports-Bladet* 29/12 1943, front page and p. 2.
39  *Sports-Bladet* 16/6 1943, front page.
40  *Sports-Bladet* 29/12 1944, front page.
41  Andersen 1964, p. 122.

## Other cultural collaboration
1  Nordlien 1998 passim.
2  Ibid.
3  Bay Petersen, 2004, passim.
4  Dinesen and Kau 1983, pp. 170ff.
5  Hertel, 1998 p. 78.
6  Thomsen, 1971, pp. 40f.

## Sport in 'Neuropa'
1  Teichler, 1991 p. 356.
2  Cf. Teichler, op. cit., pp. 294ff.

3 Teichler op. cit., 1991, p. 292.
4 *Idrætsbladet* 28/04 1942, p. 13.
5 Teichler, op. cit., p. 362.
6 Holmäng, 1988 pp. 254-255 together with p. 350.
7 Teichler, 1991 p. 363 and p. 366.
8 Ibid.
9 Op. cit., pp. 328-330 and p. 364.
10 DIF – pakke 196 – 'Forløbsbeskrivelse' referring to negotiations about "*Det Europæiske Sportsforbund*", written by Sander. Sander had noted down the process and in Rosearkivet pakke 196 can be found a large appendix to this description which provides the basis for this chapter. At the top, Sander had written that the documents were confidential and he asked readers "not to refer to this matter outside of these four walls". Sander's description is coloured by a defensive tone, in the event of his actions being criticised in Denmark in relation to the new European sports federation.
11 Andersen, 2003 pp. 250ff.
12 In diplomatic circles, an unsigned memoranda or note is called a verbal note. These are sent in protracted exchanges when a relevant reply has not been forthcoming. The unsigned note is supposed to avoid the appearance of urgency but also indicate that the matter will continue to be pursued [Translator's note].
13 UM 84.C.15 – *note* dated 20/07 1942. Furthermore, letter to Udenrigsministeriet from Tschammer, dated 24/07 1942.
14 DIF – pakke 196 – Sander's description of the Europæiske Sportsforbund. Cf., too, UM 84.C.15 – "anmodning om telegrafisk besked til rigssportsføreren" and UM 84.C.15.
15 DIF – pakke 18 – forretningsudvalgsmøde dated 12/08 1942.
16 Fælleskomitéen was established in 1916. It was tradition that principal issues were discussed in this forum between the Nordic sports federations.
17 DIF – pakke 196 – communication to Tschammer 19/08.
18 DIF – pakke 196 – Sander's résumé for the Europæiske Sportsforbund.
19 DIF – pakke 196 – letter from Bo Ekelund to Sander, dated 24/08 1942.
20 DIF – pakke 18 – forretningsudvalgsmøde 04/09 1942.
21 DIF – pakke 196 – Leo Frederiksen and Sander's minutes of the meeting dated 16/09 – marked 'confidential'.
22 Teichler, 1991 p. 238.
23 Confirmed in Holmäng, 1988 p. 252.
24 Holmäng, 1988 p. 252.
25 Bergstrøm, 2005, I, p. 595.
26 *Idrætsbladet* 29/5 1942, s. 2.
27 *Idrætsbladet* 7/7 1942, s. 15.
28 *Fædrelandet* 13/6 1942.
29 *Idrætsbladet* 16/6 1942, s. 3.
30 *Fædrelandet* 13/6 1942.
31 *Sports-Bladet* 30/12 1942 og *Fædrelandet* 1/9 1942.
32 DIF – pakke 196 – answer to Tschammer from Sander in both a Danish and a German version.
33 DIF – pakke 18 – forretningsudvalgsmøde 29/10 1942.
34 DIF – pakke 6 – repræsentantskabsmødereferat 22/11 1943.
35 *Fædrelandet* 11/09 1942.
36 Teichler, 1991, pp. 362-366.

37 Steinhöfer, 1973, p. 77ff. Cf. also *Idrætsbladet* 29/03 1943, p. 15.
38 U.M. – 84C15, notits.
39 Holmäng, 1988, p. 255.
40 Bergstrøm, 2005, I, p. 595. Cf. also *Idrætsbladet* 29/05 1942, p. 2.
41 *Idrætsbladet* 07/07 1942, p. 15. Cf. also Holmäng, 1988, p. 225.
42 Holmäng, 1988, pp. 225ff. *Fædrelandet* 13/06 1942.
43 *Idrætsbladet* 16/06 1942, p. 3.
44 *Fædrelandet* 27/04 1943, p. 15.
45 *Sports-Bladet* 30/12 1942 and *Fædrelandet* 01/09 1942.
46 The sections covering labour service are based on Bonde 2006B pp. 551ff.
47 Bonde, 2006A, pp. 522ff.

## Turn of the tides

1 *Terrænsport* is an extension of orienteering, in which teams rather than individuals compete, and involves additional military activities such as shooting.
2 *Idrætsbladet* 07/11 1941 p. 9 and 02/12 1941. The orienteering race in Grib Forest was well attended. Taking part were 57 men and a good number of women competitors.
3 Sander, 1946 p. 247. See also *Idrætsbladet* 17/09 1942, p. 15.
4 *Idrætsbladet* 01/10 1942, pp. 9ff.
5 *Idrætsbladet* 05/10, 1942, p. 6, and 19/10 1942, p. 11.
6 *Idrætsbladet* 16/11 1942, p. 15. See also *Dansk Sportsleksikon*, 1945, I, p. 288. In 1941 there were 40-50 competitors in each race, in 1942, between 90 and 100, and in 1944 200 competitors took part in the so-called Stifinderløbet.
7 *Fædrelandet* 27/10 1942.
8 *Idrætsbladet* 05/11 1942, p. 5, and 25/02 1943.
9 *Frit Danmark*, July 1943.
10 KAF – pakke 20 – from 'atletikforbundets Officielle Efterretninger' no. 383, 1 May 1942. When Svend Jensen's fate as chairman was decided 29 voted for and 41 voted against, while 27 ballot papers were left blank.
11 KAF – pakke 8 – Dansk Atletik Forbunds O.M. 1 April 1943.
12 Udenrigsministerium 84.C.2a, dated 13 and 14 July 1943.
13 DIF – pakke 7 – Repræsentantskabsmøde, November 1943.
14 DIF – pakke 196 – 'Indberetninger' to DIF 26/6 1945.
15 Meidell, 2005, pp. 169ff.
16 Centralkartoteket. Pk. Nr. 8, Anholdelsesprotokol løbenr. 9830.
17 *Hermes*, no. 5, May 1944, as well as no. 4, April 1945, front page. See also Buch 1949 p. 74 and p. 77.
18 *Idrætsbladet* 27/4 1943, p. 11.
19 *Idrætsbladet* 19/12 1941.
20 Interview with Georg Poulsen 28/06 2006.
21 *Idrætsbladet* 10/4 1942, p. 15. See also 02/11 1942, p. 16.
22 *Sports-Bladet* 24/04 1942, p. 6.
23 *Orientering fra Dansk Svømme-Forbund* 1942, p. 6, *Idrætsbladet* 06/06 1941 and 21/01 1943, *Sports-Bladet* 18/02 1942, p. 6 as well as *Fædrelandet* 30/10 1942.
24 *Idrætsbladet* 15/02 1942, front page.
25 *Sports-Bladet* 19/03 1943, p. 5.
26 *Idrætsbladet* 01/04 1943, p. 6.

27 *Informationsdienst Pressedienst Nord* 30/06 1943.
28 *Dansk Sportsleksikon*, 1945, I, p. 551. *Frit Danmark* 04/06 1943.
29 *Idrætsbladet* 12/04 1943, p. 15 and 24/05 1943, p. 2.
30 According to a lead article in *Idrætsbladet* 06/05 1943, p. 2.
31 *Sports-Bladet* 16/04 1943, p. 6 and 18/05 1943, p. 6. Cf. also *Idrætsbladet* 12/04 1943, p. 5.
32 *Sports-Bladet* 20/08, 1943, p. 6.
33 *Sports-Bladet* 29/12 1943, 04/08 1944, p. 7, as well as 26/01 1945, p. 5.
34 "Rapport, Sikkerhedspolitiet, Efterretningsafdelingen", 07/07, 1947, Helsingør Politi Straffeakt 148, 1947.
35 Johansen, 1999, passim.
36 This section is based on: Generalierapport, Rigspolitiet, politikreds nr. 6, 21/8 1947; Helsingør Politi Straffeakt 148-1947; and an undated interview with Kammersgaard recorded in Sikkerhedspolitiet, Efterretningsafdelingen, Helsingør Politi Straffeakt 148-1947. There is also an undated report by Helsingør Politi, Straffeakt 148-1947. For information about Kammersgaard's swimming, cf. Dansk Kvindebiografisk Leksikon, 2000-2001.
37 *Horsens Avis* 29 and 30 June 1944. See also Rapport, Sikkerhedspolitiet, Efterretningsafdelingen, 07/07, 1947, Helsingør Politi Straffeakt 148-1947.
38 Cf. *Gads leksikon* on "Dansk besættelsestid", 2002, p. 11.
39 Kirchhoff, 2001 pp. 194-206.
40 Brøndsted, 1946 II, p. 512.
41 Hansen, 1944.
42 Hansen, 1944.
43 Hansen, 1944.
44 Interview with Niels Holst-Sørensen 19/07 2006.
45 Teichler, 1991 p. 358.

## Jewish persecution

1 Kirchhoff, 2001, p. 219 and p. 224.
2 The delay was caused when Dansk Ungdomssamvirke sought recommendation and were advised by the informally leading Danish politician Vilhelm Buhl not to send the petition for fear of angering the Germans further and thereby inciting an increase in the persecution.
3 Nissen & Poulsen, 1963 pp. 278-280.
4 Sander, 1946, p. 236.
5 Lundberg, K., *Idræt på godt og ondt*, Copenhagen, 1951, p. 63.
6 DIF – pakke 74 – Sander had written the proceedings by hand.
7 DIF – pakke 74 – Letter to DIF's secretariat, secretary C. Vincent 09/10 1943.
8 DIF – pakke 74 – Letter from K.E. Enrum to Sander, dated 12/10 1943.
9 DIF – pakke 74 – Letter to Leo Frederiksen from Sander, dated 13/10 1943.
10 DIF – pakke 74 – Letter to Sander from Leo Frederiksen, dated 14/10 1943.
11 DIF – pakke 74 – Letter to Enrum from Sander, dated 21/10 1943.
12 DIF – pakke 74 – Letter to Sander from Enrum, dated 26/10 1943.
13 DIF – pakke 18 – Forretningsudvalgsmøde 21/10 1943.
14 Thelmark, 1999 p. 45.

15 Communication from the Hakoah sports association in *Hakoahneren* no. 15, September 1943.
16 Extracts from Hakoah's historic past: by Simon Kurland, Abraham's brother, cf. http://www.hakoah.dk/brydning.htm
17 Andersen, 1964, p. 121.
18 *Sports-Bladet* 24/09 1943, p. 6.
19 DIF – pakke 195 – Aarsberetning 1944.
20 [Translator's note] *Schalburgtage* refers to acts of counter sabotage. The name derives from the Schalburg Corps, a Danish pro-Nazi group that took action against popular Danish venues to bring anti-German sabotage into disfavour. The group was named after the Danish Nazi SS officer C.F. von Schalburg.
21 Aarhus Politi – Besættelsestiden 1940-1945, http://www.politi.dk/Aarhus/da/omos/om_politikredsen/historie/1940_1945.htm
22 [Translator's note] 'Ration-quality-priced wear' refers to Danish wartime *maksimalpriser*, a regulation on the maximum daily price rise that retailers could impose on certain goods, leading to reductions in quality to offset the manufacturer's losses. In the language of the time, *maksimal* clothing, and *maksimal* underwear, could be said as ironic comments on minimum quality and maximum profiteering.
23 Hertel, 1998, pp. 74, 86 and 78.
24 Dansk Sportsleksikon, 1945, I, pp. 255ff.
25 Sander, 1946, p. 236.
26 Secker, 1992 passim.
27 Hansen, 2003, pp. 137ff.
28 Thelmark, 1999 p. 46.

## New alliances
1 Sander, 1946, p. 269.
2 Andersson, 2002, p. 585.
3 *Dansk sport i billeder og ord*, 1946, p. 631. See also Hansen, 2003, pp. 137ff.
4 *Sports-Bladet* 17/05 1945, p. 6.
5 *Sports-Bladet* 17/05 1945, p. 7.
6 *Sports-Bladet* 06/07 1945, p. 3.
7 *Sports-Bladet* 07/09 1945, p. 5.
8 Hansen, K.Å. and Jensen I., *På rejse med landsholdet*, 1948, pp. 17ff. Cf. also *Sports-Bladet* 23/11 1945, p. 7.
9 *Sports-Bladet* 28/09 1945, p. 6.
10 *Sports-Bladet* 26/10 1945, p. 6.
11 Hansen, K.Å. and Jensen I., *På rejse med landsholdet*, 1948, p. 21.
12 Op. cit., pp. 45 and 49.
13 *Sports-Bladet* 09/11 1945, p. 5.
14 *Sports-Bladet* 09/11, 16/11 together with 23/11 1945, p. 5.
15 *Sports-Bladet* 24/8 1945, front page and 31/08 1945, p. 4.
16 *Sports-Bladet* 31/08 1945, p. 4.
17 *Sports-Bladet* 28/12 1945, p. 2.
18 *Sports-Bladet* 08/06 1945, p. 6.

## A 'juridical purge'?

1 Bonde, 2006, pp. 379ff.
2 Bonde, 2006, pp. 384ff.
3 Lauridsen, 2002 p. 656 n. 8.
4 A note in *seddelregistret* of Rigsadvokatens P-journalsager on "Ragnhild Nordfalk, Hveger" shows that no case was brought against her, Rigsarkivet.
5 Centralkartoteket p. V. Hveger, Pkr, nr. 7, anholdelsesprotokol løbe nr. 12864 and Hveger V.A., Pkr.nr. 6, not numbered.
6 Undated interview with Jenny Kammersgaard, Sikkerhedspolitiet, Efterretningsafdelingen, Helsingør Politi Straffeakt 148-1947.
7 *Kontrakt*, appendix in Helsingør Politi Straffeakt 148-1947 stamped 09/10, 1947.
8 *Ekstra Bladet* 08/04, 1946, appendix from Helsingør Politi Straffeakt 148-1947.
9 Kryger & Foged, 1985, pp. 41ff.
10 *Rapport* 21/08 1947, 6' politikreds Espergærde, Helsingør Politi Straffeakt 148-1947.
11 Interrogation of Jenny Kammersgaard 25/08 1947, Helsingør Politi Straffeakt 148-1947.
12 *Rapport*, Sikkerhedspolitiet, Efterretningsafdelingen, 07/07, 1947, Helsingør Politi Straffeakt 148-1947.
13 Extract from *Dombogen* (records) for retskreds no. 6, Helsingør Købstad m.v., 25/09, 1947, Helsingør Politi Straffeakt 148-1947.
14 Dansk Kvindebiografisk Leksikon, 2000-2001.

# LITERATURE

**Abe, I. et al. (April, 1992)** Fascism, Sport and Society in Japan, The International Journal of the History of Sport, London, pp. 1-28.
**Alkil, N. (ed.) (1945)** Besættelsestidens Fakta – Dokumentarisk Haandbog med henblik paa Lovene af 1945 om landsskadelig Virksomhed, vol.s I & II, published by Sagførerraadet, Copenhagen.
**Aly, G. (2005)** Hitlers Volksstaat, Frankfurt a.M.
**Andersen E. (1936)** Olympiaden i Berlin, Copenhagen & Oslo.
**Andersen, E. (ed.) (1964)** Dansk Boldspil-Union 1889-1964, Copenhagen.
**Andersen, S. (2003)** Danmark i det tyske storrum, Copenhagen.
**Andersen, S. (2005)** De gjorde Danmark større, Copenhagen.
**Andersson, T. (2002)** Kung Fotboll, Stockholm.
**Bay Petersen, H. (2004)** En selskabelig invitation – Det Kongelige Teaters gæstespil i Nazi-Tyskland i 1930'rne, Copenhagen.
**Beck, P.J. (1999)** Scoring for Britain – International Football and International Politics, London.
**Bellers J. (1986)** Die Olympischen Spiele von 1936 im Spiegel der ausländischen Presse, Münster.
**Bergstrøm, V. (2005)** En borger i Danmark under krigen I-II, Copenhagen.
**Best W. (1978)** Dr. Werner Bests kalendernotater, vol. 2, Copenhagen.
**Beyerholm, J. (1941)** Dansk Bicycle Clubs Historie – Strejflys over dansk Cyklesport – 1881-1941, Copenhagen.
**Birkelund, P. (2000)** De loyale oprørere. Den nationalt-borgerlige modstandsbevægelses opståen og udvikling 1940-1945. En undersøgelse af de illegale organisationer De Frie Danske, Studenternes Efterretningstjeneste og Hjemmefronten, Odense.
**Bonde, H. (1991)** Mandighed og sport, Odense.
**Bonde, H. (2001)** Niels Bukh – En politisk-ideologisk biografi, (vol.s I & II), Copenhagen.
**Bonde, H. (2006)** Fodbold med fjenden, Odense.
**Bonde, H. (2006A)** Gymnastics and Politics, Museum Tusculanum Press, Copenhagen University (including a DVD with 131 film clips in English, Danish and Japanese).
**Bonde, H. (2006B)** Niels Bukh – En politisk-ideologisk biografi, Copenhagen University (CD-ROM 900 pages text including 131 film clips in English, Danish and Japanese), Copenhagen.
**Bosworth, R.J.B. (2002)** Mussolini, London.
**Bourdieu, P. (1984)** Distinction – A Social Critique of the Judgement of Taste, Massachusetts.
**Bovrup-kartoteket (1946)**, Copenhagen.
**Bruhn, V. (1997)** Det skæve træ – Træk af ungdomsforeningernes og gymnastikforeningernes historie efter 1945, Vejle.

Bruhn, V. (2005) Idræt i Esbjerg, Esbjerg.
Bryld, C. (1982) Samarbejde eller modstand 1940-45, Copenhagen.
Bryld, C. (et al.) (1999) At formidle historie – vilkår, kendetegn, formål, Roskilde.
Bryld, C. & Warring A. (1998) Besættelsestiden som kollektiv erindring, Roskilde.
Brøndsted, J. & Gjedde, K. (1946) De fem lange år, Copenhagen.
Buch, R. (1949) Sådan har vi det i Hermes, Copenhagen.
Buschardt, L. (ed.) (1965) Den illegale Presse 1940-45 – En antologi, Copenhagen.
Christensen, C. (et al.) (2005) Danmark besat – Krig og hverdag 1940 – 45, Copenhagen.
Christmas Møller, W. (1993) Christmas Møller og Det Konservative Folkeparti, bd. 1 & 2, Copenhagen.
Dansk sport i billeder og ord gennem 50 år (1946), Odense.
Dansk Kvindebiografisk Leksikon, Larsen J. (2000-2001) Copenhagen.
Dansk Sportsleksikon (1945), Lundqvist Andersen, A. & Budtz-Jørgensen, J., (eds.), Copenhagen.
De olympiske – Biografi af danske OL-deltagere 1896-1996 (1996) Copenhagen.
Dethlefsen, H. (1998) Arven fra Hæstrup, fra: Fra mellemkrigstid til efterkrigstid – Festskrift til Hans Kirchhoff og Henrik S. Nissen, in: H. Dethlefsen & H. Lundbak (eds.).
Dethlefsen, H. & Lundbak, H. (eds.) (1998) Fra mellemkrigstid til efterkrigstid, Copenhagen.
Dinesen, N.J. & Kau, E., (1983) Filmen i Danmark, Copenhagen.
Downing, D., (2000) Passovotchka: Moscow Dynamo in Britain, 1945, London.
Ehn, B. (et al.) (1993) Försvenskningen af Sverige, Stockholm.
Elias, N. & Dunning E. (1966) Zur Dynamik von Sportgruppen. Unter besonderer Berücksichtigung von Fußballgruppen, in Kölner Zeitschrift für Soziologie und Sozialpsychologie, 118 – 134, Köln.
Encyklopædi, Den Store Danske (1994-2001), Danmarks Nationalleksikon, Copenhagen.
Fanø, K. (1983) Det unge Grænseværn, Sønderborg.
Fischer, G., Lindner U., Skrentny W. (eds.) (1999) Stürmer für Hitler. Vom Zusammenspiel zwischen Fußball und Nationalsozialismus, Göttingen.
Fischer-Jørgensen, E. & Ege, J. (2005) Interneringskartoteket – Om Carsten Høeg og hans gruppe under besættelsen, Copenhagen.
Frandsen, S.B., (1991) Det tredje Rom, Copenhagen.
Frederiksen, L. Bindsløv, (1960) Pressen under besættelsen – Hovedtræk af den danske dagspresses vilkår og virke i perioden 1940-45, Copenhagen.
Frei, M. (2004) Idræt og politik under besættelsen (unpublished thesis), Roskilde University Center.
Gads leksikon om dansk besættelsestid 1940-45 (2002) Kirchhoff, H.; Lauridsen, J.T. & Trommer, Aa. (eds.), Copenhagen.
Gads Leksikon – Hvem var hvem 1940-1945 (2005) Kirchhoff, H.; Lauridsen, J.T. & Trommer, Aa. (eds.), Copenhagen.
Gerhmann, S. (1996) Symbol of National Resurrection, Max Schmeling, German Sports Idol, in: Holt R. & Mangan, J.A. (eds.), European Heroes – Myth, Identity, Sport, London.
Goksøyr, M. & Olstad, F. (2002) Fotball!, Olso.
Grass, Günter (2002) Im Krebsgang, Gerhard Steidl Verlag, Göttingen.
Hansen, G. (1944) Med mennesker og mikrofon, Copenhagen.

Hansen, G. (1945) Danmarks kamp for frihed og ret, Copenhagen.
Hansen, J. (1991) Fagenes Fest – Arbejderkultur og idræt, in: Idrætshistorisk Årbog 1991, pp. 113-134.
Hansen, J. (2003) Ikke at syne, men at være, Odense.
Havemann, N. (2005) Fussball unterm Hakenkreuz – Der FdB zwischen Sport, Politik und Kommerz, Frankfurt/Main.
Heimerzheim, P. (1999) Karl Ritter von Halt, Leben zwischen Sport und Politik, Sankt Augustin.
Hertel, H. (1998) Det belejrede og det besatte åndsliv, in: Dethlefsen & Lundbak, 1998, pp. 25-92.
Hitler, A. (1925/1966) Min Kamp – Vol. 2: Den nationalsocialistiske bevægelse, Copenhagen.
Holmäng, P. O. (1988) Idrott och Utrikespolitik, Den svenska Idrottsrörelsens internationella förbindelser 1919-45, Göteborg.
Huggins, M. & Williams J. (2006) Sport and the English 1918 – 1939, New York.
Hæstrup, J. (ed.) (1979/1993) Besættelsen og Frihedskampen 1940-45 – Hvem – Hvad – Hvor, Copenhagen.
Hæstrup, J. (1979) Krig og besættelse i Odense, 1940 – 45, Odense.
Johansen, A.C. (1999) Flugplatz Aalborg West, Den tyske udbygning af Aalborg Flyveplads, 1940-45, Aalborg.
Jørgensen, P. (1997) Ro, Renlighed, Regelmæssighed – Dansk Idræts-Forbund og sportens gennembrud ca. 1896-1918, Odense,
Jørgensen Winther, M. & Philips L. (1999) Diskursanalyse som teori og metode, Roskilde.
Kaarsted, T. (1991) Gyldendal og Politikens Danmarkshistorie, vol. 13, Gyldendals Boghandel, Nordisk Forlag A/S, Copenhagen.
Kammersgaard, J. (1937) Svømmeturen, Copenhagen.
Karlsson, I. & Ruth, A. (1984) Samhället som teater – Estetik och politik i Tredje riket, Uddevalla.
Kirchhoff, H. (1978) Review of Viggo Sjøquist: Erik Scavenius –en biografi, vol. II, in: Historisk Tidsskrift, vol. 78, hæfte 1, Copenhagen, pp. 323-334.
Kirchhoff, H. (2001) Samarbejde og modstand under besættelsen – en politisk historie, Copenhagen.
Koch, H. (1994) Demokrati slå til! Statslig nødret, ordenspoliti og frihedsrettigheder 1932-1945, Copenhagen.
Korsgaard, O. (1982) Kampen om kroppen, Copenhagen.
Krarup H. & Møller L. (1989) Da sporten var ung – en billedkavalkade fra 1920 – 1945, Copenhagen.
Krüger, A. (1998) The role of sport in German international politics 1918-1945, in: Sport and International Politics, Arnaud, P. & Riordan, J. (eds.), London.
Krüger, A. (1999) Strength through joy – The culture of consent under Fascism, Nazism and Francoism, in: The International Politics of Sport in the Twentieth Century, Riordan, J. & Krüger (eds.), London.
Krüger, A. & Murray W. (eds.) (2003) The Nazi Olympics: Sport, Politics, and Appeasement in the 1930s, Illinois.
Kryger, H. & Foged, H. (1985) Flugtrute Nord, Copenhagen.
Kulavig, E. (2004) Stalins hjemmefront – 1941-1945, Odense.
Kuper, S. (2003) Ajax, the Dutch, the War, London.

**Lammers, K.C. (2004)** Da DBU var på nippet til at anerkende DDR, in: Den kolde krig på hjemmefronten, Petersen, K. & Sørensen, N.A. (eds.), Copenhagen, pp. 183-190.
**Lauridsen, J.T. (1995)** De danske nazister, Copenhagen.
**Lauridsen, J. T. (2002)** Dansk Nazisme – 1930-45 – og derefter, Copenhagen.
**Lidegaard, B. (2005)** Kampen om Danmark, Copenhagen.
**Lundbak, H. (2001)** Staten stærk og folket frit – Dansk Samling mellem fascisme og modstandskamp 1936-1947, Copenhagen.
**Mangan, J.A. (ed.) (1995)** Tribal Identities, Nationalism, Europe and Sport, London.
**Mattausch, W.D. (1988)** Werner Seelenbinder, Sozial- und Zeitgeschichte des Sports, II, 1988, pp. 72-85.
**Meidell, B. (2005)** Slået med beundring, Copenhagen.
**Merleau-Ponty M. (1962)** Phenomenology of perception, New York.
**Mosse, G.L. (1966)** The Crisis of German Ideology, London.
**Nielsen, N. Kayser, (1996)** Idræt ved fronten – Fra uorganiseret til organiseret idræt i Finland under og efter 2. verdenskrig, in: Idrætshistorisk Årbog, 1996, Odense, pp. 71-82.
**Nissen, H.S. & Poulsen, H. (1963)** På dansk friheds grund – Dansk Ungdomssamvirke og De ældres Råd 1940-1945, Copenhagen.
**Nordby, I. (1995)** Sablen og den bløde hat – De danske skytte-, gymnastik- og idrætsforeningers forhold 1940-45 med et indledende historisk tilbageblik, Odense.
**Nordisk Familjeboks Sportlexikon (1938 – 1949),** Stockholm.
**Nordlien, N.H. (1998)** Træk af den tyske propaganda og kulturpolitik i Danmark 1940-43, unpublished thesis, Copenhagen University.
**Nøkleby, B. (ed.) (1982)** Norge i krig, Oslo, 1982.
**Ohlsson, A. (2003)** Berättelser om idrottshjältar: exemplet Gunder Hägg, HumaNetten, Växjö Universitet, nr. 12, pp. 1-9.
**Olstad, F. & Tønnesson, S. (1987)** Norsk Idretts historie – Folkehelse, trim, stjerner 1939-1986, vol. 2, Oslo.
**Poulsen, H., (1970)** Besættelsesmagten og de danske nazister, Copenhagen.
**Pfeiffer, L. (2004)** Sport im Nationalsozialismus – Zum aktuellen Stand der sporthistorischen Forschung – Eine kommentierte Bibliographie, Göttingen.
**Pfister, G. (1997)** Conflicting Feminities – The Discourse on the Female Body and the Physical Education of Girls in National Socialism, in: Sport History Review 28, 89-107.
**Pfister, G. & Niewerth T. (1999)** Jewish Women in Gymnastics and Sport in Germany, in: Journal of Sport History 9 (1999), 287-326.
**Popolow, U. (1988)** Rudolf Harbig – Vom unbekannten Sportsmann zum Weltrekordläufer, Sozial- und Zeitgeschichte des Sports, II, 1988, pp. 8-30.
**Poulsen, H. (1989/1995)** Hitlers krig – den 2. verdenskrig 1939-41 (vol. I) Copenhagen.
**Rasmussen, E. (1982)** Christmas Møller og P. Munch – Betragtninger over politikeres råderum in: Larsen, H. & Skovmand, R. (eds.), Festskrift til Troels Fink, Odense, pp. 161-183.
**Rasmussen, S. (1981)** Dansk Idræts Forbund 1940-45 – Med specielt henblik på forholdet til Tyskland, unpublished thesis, Copenhagen University.
**Rasmussen, S. (1985)** Dansk Idræts Forbund og forholdet til Tyskland 1940-45, Idrætshistorisk Årbog, vol. 1, 1985, Odense, pp. 109-124.
**Riemann Hansen, L. (1996)** Tyskernes forgæves forsøg på førergreb, published by DIF, Copenhagen.
**Riefenstahl, L. (2000)** Fünf Leben, Köln
**Rünitz, L. & Kirchhoff, H. (2007)** Udsendt til Tyskland, Odense.

**Sander, H., Andersen, E. & Hansen, G. (1946)** Dansk Idræt gennem 50 Aar, vol.s I & II, Copenhagen.
**Schoug, F. (1997)** Intima samhällsvisioner, Stockholm.
**Secher, O. (1992)** Hvis et folk vil leve, Copenhagen
**Statistiske efterretninger**, Idrætsstatik I & II, nr. 60 1943 & nr. 24 1944.
**Steinhöfer, D. (1973)** Hans von Tschammer und Osten, Berlin.
**Tamm, Ditlev (1984)** Retsopgøret efter besættelsen, Copenhagen.
**Teichler, H.J. (1991)** Internationale Sportpolitik im Dritten Reich, Schorndorf.
**Thamer, H.U. (1986)** Verführung und Gewalt, Berlin.
**Thelmark, S. (1999)** Jødisk Idrætsforening Hakoah København, unpublished thesis, Syddansk Universitet, Institut for Idræt og Biomekanik, Odense.
**Thomsen, E. (1971)** Deutsche Besatzungspolitik in Dänemark 1940-45, Düsseldorf.
**Thorborg, K., (1977)** Arbejdspapirer til historisk metode, (unpublished), Institut for Historie, Copenhagen.
**Thostrup Jacobsen, E. (1995)** Kaj Munk – Mellem fascisme og konservatisme i 30'rnes og 40'rnes Danmark, in: Auchet, M. (ed.), Kaj Munk – Dansk rebel og international inspirator, Copenhagen.
**Trommer, Aa. (1973)** Modstandsarbejde i nærbillede, Odense.
**Trangbæk, E. (ed.) (1995)** Dansk Idrætsliv, vol. I & II, Copenhagen.
**Vilhjálmsson, V.Ö. (2005)** Medaljens bagside – Jødiske flygtningeskæbner i Danmark, 1933-1945, Copenhagen.
**Welander, L. (2000)** Sverige och olympiaden 1936, in Nordberg, J.R., Studier i Idrott, Historia och samhälle, Stockholm, pp. 280-292.
**Wijk, J. (2000)** Idrott, krig och svenska löparstärnor, in Nordberg, J.R., Studier i Idrott, Historia och samhälle, Stockholm, pp. 293-325.
**Wijk J. (2005)** Idrott, krig och nationell gemenskap, Stockholm.
**Winther, H. (1994)** Et portræt af Mary Whigmann – de mørke kræfters danserinde, Idrætshistorisk Årbog, 1994, pp. 49-66.
**Wøllekær, J. (2001)** Odense i bevægelse – strejftog i byens idrætshistorie, Odense.

# ILLUSTRATIONS

26: Polfoto
28: Dansk Sport i Billeder og Ord, 1946
29: Idorn, J., Dansk Idrætsforbunds Jubilæumsskrift 1971, s.96
31: German Press photo Atlantic
32: Dansk Sport i Billeder og Ord, 1946
33: German Press photo Atlantic
55: Idorn, J. Dansk Idrætsforbunds Jubilæumsskrift 1971, s.104
36: Berliner Illustrierte Zeitung. Olympia Sonderheft, 1936
37: Polfoto
38: Polfoto
40: Kammersgaard, 1937
41: Kammersgaard 1937.
42: Berliner Illustrierte Zeitung, august 1937.
44: Riefenstahl, 2000
47: Beyerholm 1941
49: Polfoto
55: Polfoto
56: Polfoto
58: Kopenhagener Soldatenzeitschrift 7/7 1940
65: Det Kgl. Bibliotek
67: Besættelsens Hvem Hvad Hvor (1979)
84: Idrætsbladet, 2/12 1940
85: Idrætsbladet, 18/7 1941
86: Fodbold. Hele Landets Magasin, 1941
96: Kopenhagener Soldatenzeitschrift, 15/7, 1940.
100: Kopenhagener Soldatenzeitschrift, 8/9 1940
101: Polfoto
102: Polfoto
105: Polfoto
122: Frihedsmuseet
123: Frihedsmuseet
125: Polfoto
129: Lundberg, K., Idræt på godt og ondt, Copenhagen, 1951.
131: Idrætsbladet 11/7 1941
133: Idrætsbladet 6/6 1941
147: Idrætsbladet 13/1 1942
156: Det Kgl. Bibliotek
157: Det Kgl. Bibliotek
161: Det Kgl. Bibliotek

162: DIFs billedarkiv
188: Det Kgl. Bibliotek
212: DIFs billedarkiv
217: Hansen, 1945
219: Dansk Idræts gennem 50 år, 1946
228: Krarup, 1989
229: Sander, 1946